Effective Study Skills

James K. Semones
San Jacinto College

WADSWORTH

™

THOMSON LEARNING

Wadsworth/Thomson Learning
10 Davis Drive
Belmont, CA 94002-3098
USA

For information about our products, contact us:
Thomson Learning Academic Resource Center
1-800-423-0563
http://www.wadsworth.com

International Headquarters
Thomson Learning
International Division
290 Harbor Drive, 2nd Floor
Stamford, CT 06902-7477
USA

UK/Europe/Middle East/South Africa

Thomson Learning
Berkshire House
168-173 High Holborn
London WCIV 7AA

Asia
Thomson Learning
60 Albert Street, #15-01
Albert Complex
Singapore 189969

Canada
Nelson Thomson Learning
1120 Birchmount Road
Toronto, Ontario MIK 5G4
Canada
United Kingdom

ISBN 0-03-053793-2

The Adaptable Courseware Program consists of products and additions to existing Wadsworth Group products that are produced from camera-ready copy. Peer review, class testing, and accuracy are primarily the responsibility of the author(s).

BRIEF CONTENTS

C O N T E N T S

To the thousands of students who over the years have assisted me in trying, testing, refining, validating, and benefiting from the principles, steps, skills, and tasks explained in this book.

ABOUT ESS:
An Open Letter to the Student

Over two decades ago, I entered college with all the hopes and dreams and fears and uncertainties that characterize many beginning students. Psychologists refer to this as approach–avoidance conflict. I wanted to go to college and was excited about the prospects, but I was also somewhat unsure of myself regarding the unknown challenges that lay ahead. Fortunately, however, I was able to take the risks and sustain the efforts necessary to reach my educational objectives. You will have to do the same to meet the educational challenges you will face.

My First Semester at College: What I Did Wrong

When I began my first semester, I was like many entering freshmen in that I had poor study habits and few study skills. In all honesty, my study habits were terrible. My primary study technique was procrastination or cramming. My credo was "Never do today what you can put off until tomorrow." Study aids consisted mainly of a large coffeepot, with an ample supply of No-Doz tablets as a back-up system. I quickly found that staying up into the wee hours of the morning immediately before a major test sometimes worked. In some instances I was able to regurgitate enough information onto the exam paper to get a passing grade.

What I Learned from the Experience

However, I also discovered my first semester that the cramming approach to study is doomed to failure for several reasons. In addition to producing exhaustion and high anxiety, cramming—which is little more than the rote memorization of concepts and lists of facts—results in course content being stored mainly in short-term memory. Unfortunately, this information is quickly lost after the exam is over. Consequently, the student gets cheated by perhaps passing the test or course but leaving with little or nothing in terms of real education. Also, if the teacher tests for understanding and critical thinking (the ability to apply clearly understood concepts and facts to a new situation) as some do, the student almost invariably fails. In this sense then, cramming is actually a passive form of learning that results mainly in recognition and identification rather than understanding and critical analysis. It didn't take me long to realize that this is inappropriate in a highly education setting.

As a college freshman, this was vividly impressed on me during my first exposure to hell week. *Hell week* is the term many students use in reference to what professors and other college officials call final exam week. However, for students who (as I did) make the mistake of using the cramming approach to study, "hell week" reflects a more accurate description of what actually is experienced. Staying up all night to cram for a midterm exam in history, biology, or sociology is one thing. To accomplish this five nights in a row for fifteen to eighteen semester hours' worth of comprehensive finals is quite another.

A semester's inattention to study simply cannot be overcome in a week; many students learn this lesson the hard way. Some, figuring they have an iron constitution, stock up on coffee and other stimulants and give it the good fight, but then fizzle out after the second or third night and do poorly on their last few exams. Others try to strategize by cramming for what they think are their hardest exams and then attempt to "fake it" through the others, but often find that the others are much more difficult than they had anticipated. Then too, it simply is amazing when, coincidental with final exam week, so many relatives of college students become hospitalized or die, particularly grandparents. Such illnesses or deaths, real or imagined, more than occasionally become the excuse for why a student either did poorly on the exams or misses one or two tests that need to be rescheduled.

So, regardless of the approaches, strategies, or excuses crammers use in an attempt to survive the final exam period, the results are usually the same. Many of those who don't flunk out or end up on academic probation vow to find something better, to never go through hell week in this manner again. The reason I know this is because I was one of those students. My experience as a college educator the past several years has taught me that, during the time since I was an undergraduate, not much has changed.

My Second Semester: Learning to Be a Serious Student

During my second semester at college I took a political science course, and the professor, a caring and conscientious teacher, offering to teach the rudiments of effective study to those students who cared enough to come to his office on Friday afternoons—the only time he had available. There, in these afternoon sessions, I learned some of the fundamentals of scholarship. With these tools I was able to begin substituting effective study habits for the unsuccessful approaches I had used before.

As I recall, there were only three of these meetings, involving eight or ten students who met with the professor for about an hour each time on consecutive Friday afternoons. He was an inspirational fellow and was quite fond of quoting famous people to illustrate certain points. At the end of our last meeting, he left us with the following quote from the late NFL coach Vince Lombardi: "The quality that people get from life is in direct proportion to their commitment to excellence, regardless of their chosen field of endeavor." He then challenged us to take what we had learned in the meetings and make a commitment to pursue excellence in our studies. He reminded us that the difference between ordinary and extraordinary is that little extra effort, the willingness to make a habit of always doing more than the minimum requirement.

A Needed Student Resource: A Skill-Based Study System

Years later in graduate school, as I pursued studies in sociology with a special interest in the sociology of education, I remembered my experiences with my former teacher, not so much for the content of the study tips he gave me (which were very general and largely conceptual), but because he was willing to spend time with students in helping them to become more effective learners. As I studied the literature in both the sociology and the psychology of learning and teaching, it became clear that a concise, skill-based study system for high school and college students that really worked was greatly needed.

There have been, of course, such approaches as the SQ3R method of Francis P. Robinson (1946) and the more recent book by Gordon W. Green (1985), *Getting Straight A's*. While these approaches and others like them can be of some value to students and do identify some of the skills needed for academic success, regrettably they are largely conceptual and tend to lack the comprehensive and systematic nature of a truly effective study system that focuses on the building of skills in a coherent step-by-step manner.

ESS: A Skill-Based System for Student Success

To meet the need for a concise yet comprehensive study system that is skill-based rather than largely conceptual, Effective Study Skills (ESS) was developed:

1. ESS meets the needs of students for a clear, concise system with which to learn and master all essential principles and skills needed for success in most areas of academic study. Although designed specifically for the readings courses that constitute the majority of subjects in the high school or college curriculum, it can be applied to such areas of study as chemistry, physics, mathematics, and technical career courses with some slight fine-tuning.

2. ESS consists of Principles, Steps, Skills, and Tasks that may be implemented as a total study system by students pursuing studies at various levels. This includes those attending high schools, private career schools, colleges and universities, and graduate/professional schools.

3. ESS is applicable to individuals who must continually upgrade their knowledge and job skills. For this reason, it is recommended that corporate human resource and training professionals expose their companies' employees to ESS either as a prerequisite for or first course in various training programs.

4. ESS provides students with step-by-step procedures for using each of its components. The numerous elements in the ESS curriculum include such topics as how to use the library, how to take effective class notes, how to choose the best professors, how to develop critical thinking skills, how to deal with textbooks for maximum comprehension and retention, and how to prepare for various types of tests.

5. ESS shows students how to diagnose their level of skill usage after each exam so that, ultimately, mastery of all skill elements can be achieved and A grades obtained.

To repeat, ESS is special in that it is a *skill-based* learning system. This means that, if the student has the appropriate reading, writing, math, and other requisite skills for the academic or technical courses in which he or she is enrolled, diligent application of the entire ESS system for six months to a year should result in mastery of essential study skills and superior academic performance.

ESS was developed in basic form during the 1970s. After extensive field-testing, refinement, and follow-up research was completed on over two-thousand college and university students, it was subsequently revised, expanded, and first published in 1988. As a skill-based system, ESS incorporates some of the latest research in both cognitive psychology and clinical sociology. For example, cognitive mapping and memory-retention principles are integral elements of this system.

Unfortunately, about 30 percent of all beginning students nationwide fail to complete their first college term successfully and almost one-half fail to complete a four-year degree. Although the college experience is not for everyone and many people lead happy and productive lives without it, those who are challenged by the special opportunities offered by higher education can benefit greatly in a variety of ways. In addition to providing the individual the preparation and credentials necessary to enter many desirable occupations, a college or university education may have a particularly humanizing and liberating impact in that it often provides a person insights and alternatives that might not have been obtained otherwise.

Consequently, ESS is invaluable to a person who wishes to succeed academically because it clearly explains what study skills to use, when to use them, and how to develop them to mastery. Follow-up research on ESS users has demonstrated that those who implement the entire ESS system report a grade-point average their first semester about one letter grade higher than those who don't. Continued use of this system results in both the mastery of all essential study skills and superior academic performance.

ESS is nevertheless not designed to show marginal students a series of short-cuts to enable them to "survive" in school. Being successful at school is a serious responsibility. It requires a great deal of commitment and hard work and there are no such shortcuts. The successful student will spend a minimum of one to two hours of study each week outside class for every hour spent in class. The purpose of ESS is to show students how to make the most effective and efficient use of that study time for maximum learning and peak performance on exams.

Therefore the serious student must put in the time and "pay the dues" necessary for academic success. If this is done, there are no limits to how far the principles and skills learned in ESS can take the practitioner. Some ESS users have not only earned four-year degrees but have gone on to successfully complete studies in graduate and professional schools as well.

It normally takes typical first-year college students six months to a year to master all the elements covered in ESS fully. After that time, most of those who diligently apply this system perform on a level that qualifies them for the dean's list. However, most ESS users report significant if not dramatic improvements in their study skills within a few weeks. In other words, improved grade performance occurs almost immediately in most cases. But more important, course content is more readily retained in long-term memory, and ESS practitioners are on their way toward becoming much more effective learners and better-educated people.

ESS is fully explained in the pages that follow. Take advantage of it and use it, because it works. I used this system myself in 1983 to complete a doctorate at the University of North Texas with a 4.0 average. You can do the same with your high school, undergraduate, career-school, graduate, or professional studies and make straight A's—just as I did. All it requires is work and some patience on your part as you develop the skills. I like to think of ESS as a key that can open the door to academic success. It certainly has benefited me and thousands of students across the country. It can do the same for you.

To explain this scientific system, this book is organized into four parts. Part 1, ESS—AN INTRODUCTION, is designed to show you how to transform essential life skills into the characteristics and skills you will need to exhibit for success as a student. Part 2, ESS—THE BASIC COURSE, explains twenty action principles for student success. Even if your intent is only to pass your schoolwork and earn average grades, these principles can be referred to as key elements for student success when needed. Part 3, ESS—THE ADVANCED COURSE, is intended mainly for students who are serious about earning straight A's. It sets forth a four-step skill-based system for achieving unlimited academic success. The last section, Part 4, is called MASTERING ESS. It explains what you will experience after you complete this book and begin to make progress through the four stages of skill-based learning. In addition it includes a 90-Day ESS Assessment to measure your acquisition of the ESS skills and the use of successful student behaviors.

As you begin to read about and apply this system to your studies, remember these words of Winston Churchill: "The price of greatness is responsibility." If you will take the responsibility for using all the Principles, Steps, Skills, and Tasks in ESS, academic success can be yours.

I am always interested in students and how they are getting along. Therefore, as you implement ESS, feel free to write me and let me know how you are doing. I'll make every effort to respond to your letter personally as soon as possible.

Acknowledgments

Many people furnished me with their expertise, encouragement, and support during the time devoted to the development of ESS and the completion of this book. Space is inadequate to properly name them all. However, I would like to acknowledge some of those who have helped me the most.

First, several colleagues from across the country and abroad served as sounding boards or reviewers for material that went into this book. They include Mary Bixby, University of Missouri; David Dunn, Sales and Business Development Consultant; John Eddy and Bill Martin, University of North Texas; Patricia Faulkner, Bristol, Virginia Public Schools; George Marchelos, DOD Schools, Germany; Ronald Mertz, St. Louis Public Schools; Kathryn Moore, St. Louis Community College; and Delores Wheatley, Tennessee Technological University.

Appreciation is also extended to the many people at Holt, Rinehart and Winston who worked with me from project idea to finished book. Joe Morse, Manager of Professional Sales, attended the live ESS seminar and championed this project from the outset. Christopher Klein, Acquisitions Editor, and Michael Hinshaw, Project Editor, assisted me in numerous ways throughout the writing and production process.

In addition, several colleagues at San Jacinto College offered their expertise and support. Jan Crenshaw, Jan Corbin, and Mary Elizabeth Wilbanks read and critiqued portions of the manuscript. James Hall, Chairperson of the Division of Social and Behavior Sciences must be given special thanks. His flexibility and encouragement made this book project possible. Colleagues in the social sciences who have supported ESS include Sandra Hawley, MaryLou Robins, Lonnie Sinclair, and Dennis Toombs. Special thanks are also due Granville Sydnor. He, perhaps more than anyone else, has strongly supported the ESS concept because of the benefits this system of study has furnished to his students. Then there is Lilian Kirkham, a new colleague, whose interest in the teaching/learning process and support at the end of this project is greatly appreciated.

Those most deserving of thanks, however, are the thousands of high school, college, and university students who, during the past several years, have served as research subjects in the development and testing of various ESS components. Without their participation, the development of this system and book would not have occurred.

Dr. James K. Semones
San Jacinto College
Department of Sociology
5800 Uvalde
Houston, Texas 77049

PART 1

ESS—AN INTRODUCTION:

How to Transform Life Skills into Student Skills

There is at bottom only one problem in the world and this is its name. How does one break through? . . . How does one burst the cocoon and become a butterfly?
—Thomas Mann
Dr. Faustus

Use the force, Luke. Let go, Luke.
—Ben Kenobi to Luke Skywalker
Star Wars

The first step is the hardest.

—Marie DeVichy-Chamrond
Great Quotations

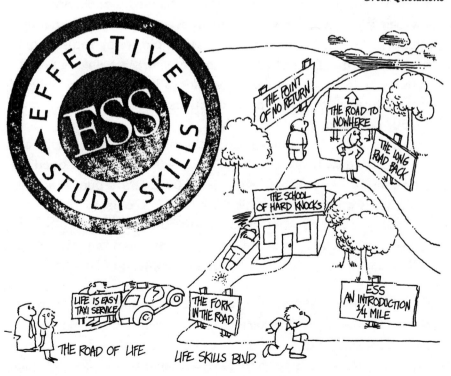

Congratulations! You have just taken two small but necessary steps toward releasing the superior student that lies within you. First, you have wisely acquired this book, which will explain the ESS (Effective Study Skills) system for academic success. Second, you have read far enough for me to make you this promise: The continued use of the entire ESS system will provide you with the tools needed to make superior grades, whether you attend a high school, business or technical school, · college, graduate school, or professional school. All you have to do is use it as a total learning system and stick with it.

But, perhaps more important, this system also includes many valuable life principles. If put into practice, they can help empower you to become a no-limit person. ESS can serve to help you develop the self-discipline, self-confidence, and intensity of focus you need to be successful in life.

The basic shortcoming of many so-called study-skills books and seminars is their failure to address the student as a total person—a multidimensional human being. They ignore the big picture by focusing only on the student role. Each of us, first and foremost, is a unique person. The basic way in which we carry out various life scripts—as student, teacher, spouse, parent, employee, or others—flows out of our inner being, our personhood.

Behavioral and educational research both show that life skills are closely associated with student skills. Those with their lives in good order also tend to perform better in school. By contrast, poor academic performance is often symptomatic of larger life problems. Those who find it hard to manage school responsibilities often have difficulty handling the larger challenges of life. Any study approach that fails to address these larger life issues and problems is doomed to failure from the start.

With this in mind, ESS—AN INTRODUCTION is designed first to address the life challenges that face us all and briefly to explain what is required from each of us to meet them. Then we discuss the importance of education and how master students are able to transfer life skills into student skills. Next we briefly examine five success stories: how ESS has affected the lives of five typical students. These students are representative of the thousands of people of different ages and backgrounds who have used ESS during the last several years.

Finally, this section of the book includes an instrument called the ESS PRETEST. By taking it early on, you can later assess your student behavior and grades both before and after exposure to the system (see the 90-Day ESS Assessment at the end of the book). The plain fact is that ESS works. If you are at the appropriate ability for your grade level—reading, writing, math, and so on—use of the entire ESS system can give you the tools to become a superior student. If you have deficiencies in these areas, ESS can help you overcome them.

1 TEN LESSONS FROM LIFE 101

The most important course any of us will ever take is what some people call Life 101. As with other, more formal learning experiences, some of us succeed at life, some of us fail, and many of us just muddle through. Those who do succeed make progress toward becoming self-actualized, fulfilled, and happy human beings. In essence, then, success is **self-actualization**—the development of one's potential on the journey toward excellence—and the fulfillment and happiness that usually follow. Success, therefore, is not a thing, an achievement, a material possession. It represents the process of becoming a better person.

To succeed in school as well as in life requires that you learn the lessons of Life 101 and practice them each day. If you rise to this challenge, you will learn to recognize and use the force that lies within each of us, the power to make success happen. This force can be awesome if you learn to tap into it and go with it. To do so you must learn and implement the basic lessons of Life 101. Ten of the most fundamental of these universal principles for living are discussed briefly in this chapter.

LESSON NO. 1: There Are No Secrets to Success

A good way to begin on the road to self-fulfillment is realizing that there are no secrets to success. That's right: THERE ARE NO SECRETS TO SUCCESS. The principles that lead to success are well established. They are known by those who are successful and have been taught and retaught by great teachers since before the times of Confucius and Socrates.

These principles are clear in the lives of great achievers, who practice them on a daily basis. So if you really want to enter the ranks of the truly successful, listen carefully to what these people say and watch closely what they do. To assist you in your efforts, I have incorporated throughout this book some key quotes from wise and accomplished people. All these great achievers, past and present—authors, politicians, philosophers, scientists, corporate and business leaders, sports figures—have learned much of the wisdom of the ages and used it to excel in their respective fields. You can use their words as powerful beacons to light the way toward finding meaningful success in your life.

The ingredients for success—and failure—are, however, most evident in the actions and interactions of people all around us. Success is a way of living, not merely a list of accomplishments. It is an attitude manifested in how we live our lives. Accomplishments are little more than visible benchmarks of our progress along the way. Therefore, you do not have to become a great achiever in the eyes of society to be a success in life. Because of the accidents of birth and circumstance, few of us start out in the same place. Far more important is what we do with the lives we have been given. Heroes and heroines with a passion for striving and doing are everywhere: the sacrificing parent, the dedicated worker, the caring teacher, the struggling student. How these people live their lives can serve as an inspiration to us all.

LESSON NO. 2: Success Is Difficult: It Requires Hard Work

Significant achievement in anything—athletics, the arts, business, career, politics, personal relationships, school, even hobbies—takes a great deal of ongoing commitment, self-discipline, and hard work. There are no easy shortcuts, no panaceas, no magic potions that can make you successful. Success by definition is difficult. If it weren't, high achievers such as professional athletes, millionaires, corporate executives, PhDs, and even straight-A students would be commonplace. One thing that *is* commonplace is mediocrity. It is quite common precisely because it is so easy.

The flip side of success is failure—which, if it becomes a life pattern, occurs mainly because of worry, self-doubt, inattention to detail, and (most important) lack of adequate commitment and action. People who are consistently unhappy and unfulfilled often pay little attention to the workings of the world around them. They are distracted from the world of action mainly because they are consumed by worry and self-doubt. Focusing inward on themselves and what they are not accomplishing, they become self-absorbed and let the world pass them by. Time passes and nothing gets done. Then, as a result of having done little or nothing to make success happen, they fail by default in making specific accomplishments. If this pattern persists, they fail in life as well.

Ongoing achievement in any of life's endeavors can only be attained through action. World-class athletes, artists, and musicians reach high levels of achievement only as a result of almost fanatical practice and refinement of technique. Successful authors are those who write and rewrite and rewrite. Likewise, the best students put in many long hours developing and refining their study methods.

Of course, hard work alone will not bring success. You also must have a certain level of native ability, talent, or aptitude. Finally, you must acquire and use the best tools and techniques. The virtuoso violinist will use an instrument made by Stradivarius if he or she can find and afford one. The successful writer today has exchanged the typewriter for a word processor or computer. A person who desires to become the best student now has ESS.

LESSON NO. 3: Your Success Is Your Responsibility

Success—your own happiness and sense of fulfillment—begins and ends with you and what *you* do to make it happen. It cannot be bestowed or even imposed by others. Each of us in our own way must "pay our dues" to achieve anything of significant value. You have to give in order to get; successful people give a great deal of their time and energy and, in some cases, make great personal sacrifice to achieve their goals.

In the end, success is a journey marked by milestones of accomplishment along the way. To reach it, you must first sign up for the trip. Then you must take the journey and overcome the inevitable obstacles that crop up along the way. No one can do this for you.

Defense Mechanisms: The Enemies of Responsibility   If we're not careful, we can act as our own worst enemy by preventing ourselves from taking the responsibility necessary for success. People who have difficulty adjusting to the realities of life often exhibit what behavioral scientists call **defense mechanisms.** These are mental reactions to stress and frustration that, if carried to an extreme, result in maladjustment and self-delusion.

Although defense mechanisms come in many forms, three of the most common are denial, rationalization, and projection. These three are especially important to understand because they often occur together and act in an insidious way to mutually reinforce one another. When this happens, a person can become trapped in a vicious cycle of self-delusion, inaction, and—ultimately—failure.

Denial is the "screening out" of unpleasant life events or situations by ignoring them or refusing to acknowledge their existence. Those who continually expect that an effortless way to success will be revealed to them are living in a constant state of denial. Through this mechanism they avoid taking responsibility for doing the work necessary to succeed. Extreme cases of this can become delusion.

Denial comes in many forms: The writer who waits for inspiration rather than face the empty page; the athlete who expects to be competitive on native talent rather than develop that talent; the procrastinating student who expects to make good grades through cramming rather than through daily study. When those who use denial come to a fork in the road to success, they take what they perceive to be the easiest and thus "smartest" path. In most cases, this is the road to nowhere.

Then, when they get nowhere, they often engage in **rationalization,** perhaps the most common of all defense mechanisms. Rationalization occurs when a person uses what appear to be plausible reasons for engaging in or not engaging in a particular behavior rather than face the real reasons. Some sales representatives may attribute not making their yearly sales quota to a poor economy. Likewise, some students develop a variety of excuses for having failed tests or courses: "The test was too hard"; "I didn't need that course anyway"; "School is such a drag." Rationalizations like these can help to temporarily take the edge off of disappointment. In the final analysis, however, those who habitually use them are only fooling themselves.

Another commonly used defense mechanism is **projection,** the process of displacing unconscious attitudes about oneself onto another person, group, or even an object. A baseball player who strikes out may blame it on a faulty bat. People who have poor self-esteem may feel that most people dislike them. The unmotivated and disorganized student may project his or her shortcomings onto a "lousy" or "uncaring" instructor.

While each of these situations may sometimes involve more than a grain of truth (there are indeed a few mediocre or incompetent teachers) this in no way excuses us from taking responsibility for our own success. After all, the baseball player chooses the bat, there will always be a few people in life who don't like us, and straight-A students earn their A's in spite of an occasional lousy teacher.

It is true that each of us occasionally resorts to these and other defense mechanisms as necessary coping devices. They can sometimes help to soften the blow of unexpected problems, adversities, and the tragic losses that go with life. However, to continually use such devices as a life pattern is to be immature, irresponsible, and maladjusted. The destiny for those who keep avoiding responsibility by hiding behind defense mechanisms is misery and discontent.

In the final analysis, both success and failure are measured by the choices we make and the actions we take based on those choices. As therapist Shad Helmstetter has said, "Those who choose to succeed always do better than those who never choose at all." Their life is a testament to having taken responsibility for their lives and, in doing so, having conquered the temptations that often consume those who fail.

When confronted with the choice to succeed or fail, both winners and losers exhibit a predictable pattern of behavior. Winners muster the courage to size up each situation, meet its realities head-on, and then carry through with the work necessary to get the job done. Losers do just the opposite. They underestimate the task at hand, look for the easy way to wish it done, and then try to rationalize or blame their failure away when it inevitably comes (see Table 1–1). If ever you find that you are losing in school or in life, it usually is because of the choices *you* have made. Change them. It's the only strategy that will turn things around.

Table 1–1—Characteristics and Attitudes of Those Who Succeed and Those Who Fail

Those Who Succeed	Those Who Fail
Courage/strength *My life is what I make it.*	Cowardice/weakness *My life depends on what others do.*
Optimistic *It can be done.*	Pessimistic *It can't be done.*
Committed/focused *I'll do it.*	Uncommitted/no focus *I'll think about it.*
Responsible *I did it.*	Irresponsible *Something came up.*
Mature *I did it to myself.*	Immature *He/She/They/It did it to me.*
Persevering *I'll do better next time.*	Defeatist *It wasn't worth doing anyway.*

LESSON NO. 4: To Succeed You Must Sometimes Fail

We all fail from time to time. We test ourselves against the task at hand and come up short because we were not well prepared. Indeed, we can never appreciate the sweet taste of victory until we have experienced the bitter disappointment that follows losing.

Have you ever watched a small baby learn to walk? Therein lies a universal principle of life. Think of how many times the infant must fall before he or she can stand, how often the child must stumble before he or she can master walking. Life itself is the continuing pursuit of the next step, the next goal, the next meaningful accomplishment. To get there, we must risk and sometimes experience failure.

Examples are all around us. We observe a man with a sledgehammer break through a brick wall. Yet most of us haven't seen the dozen blows it took to finally succeed. We watch the Olympic figure skater perform both her short and long programs flawlessly in the finals and win the gold medal. It looks so easy. What we don't see are the years of sacrifice, the thousands of falls, the bruises, the injuries, and the lost competitions it took to get her there.

Periodic failure is a fact of life. It's part of the dues we must all pay to reach any meaningful goal. You cannot achieve success without it.

LESSON NO. 5: Some People Will Try to Prevent Your Success

Even if you don't try to short-circuit your own achievement through the trap of defense mechanisms, there are those who are more than willing to do it for you. Don't allow yourself to be victimized by such people. They may try to (1) waste as much of your time as you will give them, (2) discourage you with their negative energy, or (3) take advantage of you for selfish gain.

There are three main categories of people who may try to discourage or side-track you or block your success: fools, liars, and exploiters. A fourth type, composites, exhibits some combination of two or all three of these characteristics.

Fools   Fools are normally just misguided people who, although they usually mean you no harm, can distract or discourage you from achieving your own success. They are often easily identified because they tend to be long on talk and short on action. They tend to talk about two things in particular to get sympathy and rationalize their own failings: (1) how they have been prevented by external forces—family, friends, teachers, employers, and a variety of circumstances—from being successful and (2) how success really isn't important because successful people really aren't happy. Somehow the contradictions in these statements escape them as they get trapped in a loop of circular reasoning.

While anyone may experience obstacles, life tragedies, and unforeseen setbacks that can inhibit success, fools often wear these negative experiences proudly as victim badges to rationalize their dismal existence. Mainly they use past experiences that no one can change as excuses for not taking the responsibility now to obtain success and happiness in the future.

Observe fools closely and learn from them, particularly older fools. They tend to become more bitter with the passage of time. They represent what you could become if you don't take responsibility for your own success.

Liars   While fools lie mainly to themselves and try to use you as a crying towel because they lack the willingness to do anything more meaningful, liars are another matter. Liars can be dangerous because often their aim is to exploit you, usually for immediate personal gain.

They will look you straight in the eye, know full well they are lying, and then tell you (1) they possess the "secrets" of success and (2) once you know what they know or do what they do, you too will have an easy, effortless way to achieve whatever you desire. And so, regardless of whether your goal is to reach heaven, find love, get rich, lose weight, or make straight A's, enough of us fall for their "hype" each year to keep them in business. They are masters of the feel-good message and the half-truth.

Everyone, of course, can benefit from encouragement if it is based on truth and substance. However, liars simply do not and cannot deliver the goods. The sizzle sounds great but the steak you want to sink your teeth into never comes. So watch out for these con artists and charlatans who survive and prosper only because of the laziness and gullibility of others. Remember that those who continually wait for a mythical easy path to success to be revealed to them have but one sure destiny. Fools all.

Exploiters   The most dangerous enemies of success are the exploiters, those who wish to consume and possess much or all of our lives through a variety of means, including lying. Exploiters will try to take some of our best and most admirable traits—love, responsibility, duty—and twist them in a perverse way into shackles to steal control of our lives from us.

Like sharks continually nipping away at a sick or injured whale, they will attempt to strip away the flesh of your life a bite at a time until nothing is left but a skeleton. Old fools are often little more than the skeletal remains of what could have been vital, fulfilled people had they not allowed liars to beguile them and exploiters to rob them of their life's blood.

For most of us, our loved ones and close associates would rarely if ever try to exploit us on an ongoing basis. Yours, for example, probably love and respect you and want only the best for you. However, what makes exploiters so dangerous is that sometimes they can come from the ranks of those closest to you—parents and other close relatives, spouses or fiancés, best friends, or employers. What makes them even more difficult to deal with is that, in their own selfish and misguided way, they often don't realize the damage they are doing to the lives of others.

While they often mean no harm, their preoccupation with themselves and their selfish need to control people represents an evil that can create a blight on the lives of others. This can make you very vulnerable because you may love and/or feel a sense of obligation toward some of these people.

The primary weapon of exploiters is the guilt trip. They will try to use your love, feelings of responsibility, and sense of duty to benefit them at your expense. Exploiters are masters of avoiding their own life responsibilities. They avoid coming to grips with the truth of Lesson No. 3 above—Your Success Is Your Responsibility—at all costs. From their perspective, why should they take responsibility for their lives when they have willing victims who will fight their battles for them with little or nothing asked in return?

The tragic flip side of this situation is that their victims end up living their lives on someone else's terms. People who allow themselves to be placed in such emotional and psychological bondage risk losing their best friend and ally, the only one who will ever truly understand them: themselves. If this persists, they first become slaves, next lose their human spirit, and then die as functional human beings. Finally, years or decades later when their hearts finally cease beating, they are buried.

How to Tell if You Are Being Exploited   Here is a sure-fire way to tell if you are being victimized: If you get little or no satisfaction from caving in to the demands of a particular individual or group other than not feeling guilty, you are probably allowing yourself to be exploited. You are doing something you really don't want to do. The only one who can prevent you from being exploited is yourself. Likewise, the only one who can liberate you from being a victim is you. As author David Seabury has said, "When people won't let you alone, it's because you haven't learned how to make them do it." If this applies to you and you don't know how to say no to exploiters and mean it, learn quickly or the life you live won't be your own.

Composites   Most people are too complex to be pigeonholed into neat categories—although you may meet individuals who represent almost textbook examples of the fool, the liar, or the exploiter. Or you may have experiences with those who are living a maladaptive life and also exhibit a combination of the fool, the liar, or the exploiter. Thus the fool-liar will sometimes lie to others as well as to himself or herself by overtly denying reality, finding excuses for irresponsible behavior, and otherwise trying to explain away foolish behavior.

The liar typically is a mercenary individual who intentionally beguiles people quickly and superficially. This person usually wants to make a fast buck or otherwise succeed at a quick seduction and then move on to the next group of sheep to fleece. Sometimes this person will lie simply to avoid taking responsibility by saying "I didn't do it." However, the liar can sometimes become an ongoing exploiter if the stakes are high enough. When this happens, the liar-exploiter can and will latch on to a single or perhaps several victims and take from them everything they have to give by using the guilt trip or any other technique that will work effectively.

Composites, therefore, can be highly complex and versatile individuals. Like chameleons, who can take on many colors, they may shift from one destructive role to another as easily as most of us change our clothes. Since composites, in extreme cases, are sociopaths with no sense of conscience, they can be extremely ruthless and devious. Dealing with such individuals is often like trying to bottle smoke. Avoid them at all costs.

LESSON NO. 6: Ongoing Victimization Requires Your Permission and Cooperation

To be continually victimized by anyone or anything, past or present, requires both your permission and your cooperation. Many of those who are unsuccessful and unhappy in life are in this predicament mainly because of destructive relationships with other individuals, groups, and organizations. First, they allow fools to discourage them, liars to deceive them, and exploiters to use them. Second, they fail to realize that they themselves are largely responsible for their plight. Through their weakness, indecision, and lack of assertiveness they enable others to distract or deter them from achieving success.

There is an old proverb that warns "When you go to dance, take heed whom you take by the hand." Don't participate in a victim dance with those who have another agenda, even if it results in their own self-destruction. Many of them will take you down with them if you let them.

To prevent yourself from being victimized (or stop it if you are currently being exploited), internalize these principles as important guides to live by and act upon them immediately:

You are Not Responsible for the Happiness and Success of Others: They Are The most fundamental form of guilt trip emerges when others try to convince you that their happiness or success is dependent on what you do or do not do. They are just as much responsible for their happiness as you are for yours. In fact, the worst thing you can do for them is to continually prop them up, fight their battles, and help them avoid taking responsibility for their own lives. As the sociologist Herbert Spencer once said, "The ultimate result of shielding men from the effects of folly is to fill the world with fools."

Every adult, to be an adult, must learn to face life's responsibilities. Each of us must learn that, in order not to sink in life, we must swim. We must find our own way. No one else, no matter how long or how hard they might try, can ever do it for us. If you continue to shackle yourself to the insecurities, the negativism, and the failings of those who believe otherwise, you simply will sink along with them.

When It Comes to Your Own Happiness and Fulfillment, Selfishness is a Virtue, Not a Vice Another variation of the guilt trip is the "You are so selfish and insensitive" routine. Those who call you selfish for living your life on your terms rather than theirs are just trying to control and manipulate you through guilt. The best way to neutralize this ploy is to (1) not feel guilty (because you know why they are doing this) and (2) calmly but firmly let them know that you are asserting your right to live your own life, you are enjoying it immensely, and you will continue to do so. Although you may have to assert yourself in this manner several times, once would-be exploiters get the message, they usually will move on to easier victims.

Tell Others What You Want   It is important that you communicate clearly to other people in words as well as in deeds your agenda for your life. Inform them about your basic needs and your important goals. Of course, you should not go around telling everyone you meet what your business is, for your own self-protection. However, those with whom you have close relationships and associations need and deserve to be told your basic plan. Your loved ones and close associates often want to help you in your pursuit for happiness. However, they are not mindreaders. In fact, they may work very hard in trying to meet needs you don't have but they think you have simply because you haven't told them otherwise.

Effective communication is essential in all meaningful relationships if the people in them are to be successful. Therefore, understand this: If you don't speak up about what you need, what you want, and what you expect, you most likely will *not* get it.

Rely on Yourself   In the final analysis, *you* are all you have. No matter how empathetic others might be or how much they may try, no one else can climb inside your skin and know exactly how you feel or what you want. Only you can truly know what you need and want in order to be happy.

Each one of us is born into the world alone and naked and each one of us must face death alone. In between is our life experience and what we alone decide to do with it. You can be your own best friend or your own worst enemy. As William Shakespeare wrote, "This above all: to thine own self be true." So get in touch with yourself, talk to yourself, and be good to yourself. You deserve it. If you don't feel this way about yourself and practice self-reliance, you probably will never know happiness and fulfillment.

LESSON NO. 7: Life Is Not Fair

Each of us must play the game of life in a certain way in order to win. Often, however, we don't get to choose the playing field or, for that matter, even the conditions of play. None of us "deserves" to be born into royalty or the upper class and, likewise, none of us "deserves" to be born into poverty or with an inherited disability. None of us really "deserves" to win $25 million in a lottery and, likewise, none of us "deserves" to be the victim of an incapacitating accident or terminal illness. These things sometimes just happen because of the serendipities of life. When they do, there's often little or nothing we can do about it. Nothing, that is, except make the most of the circumstances we face.

FRANK AND ERNEST   Reprinted by permission of NEA, INC.

While many of us feel that life should be fair to everyone, in truth it isn't. LIFE IS NOT FAIR. It never has been; it probably never will be. Those who succeed in life develop the courage and maturity to face this truth head-on. They take responsibility for their own happiness and strive to do their best, regardless of the circumstances life has dealt them. By contrast, those who fail at life allow themselves to be overwhelmed by adversity and setback. They often use negative circumstances and misfortune as excuses for giving up their dreams and goals.

The Real Heroes   I recently saw a young Hispanic man on television playing a beautiful song on a guitar accompanying Crystal Gayle, the country-western singer. It was evident in the quality of his performance that he loved playing the guitar and had been practicing his craft for many years. What was surprising was the fact that the young man had no arms, the result of a birth defect. He was demonstrating amazing dexterity by playing the guitar with his feet. This is but one of many heroic testaments to the power of the human spirit to overcome any adversity. What one has to do is allow that spirit to run free. Other examples like this are around us everywhere if we just take the time to see.

The Poker Game Analogy   Life in many respects is like a poker game. You never know when you wake up each morning what hand will be dealt to you that day. From time to time, life deals each of us some excellent cards in the form of opportunities or good fortune. Likewise, each of us sometimes draws bad cards in the form of adversity or loss. We may get a string of good hands or several bad hands in a row. Such is the game of poker and such is the game of life. Life, like poker, contains elements of circumstance over which we have little control.

However, both poker and life are primarily games of skill, not chance. While we often cannot control or predict the cards or circumstances we are dealt, we alone bear the responsibility for deciding how to handle each situation. Taking that responsibility and playing each hand to the best of our ability is what separates the winners from the losers.

In poker, the best cards in the world won't make you a winner if you don't know how to play them. By contrast, the player with only two deuces can beat an opponent with three kings if that opponent is convinced that the other player has three aces. It's this ability to turn deuces into aces, whether to beat an opponent or to overcome adversity, that separates winners from losers in the game of poker and in the game of life.

Being successful requires that we face life as it comes rather than how we would like it to be. Life is not the way it is portrayed in movies and fairy tales, where everyone lives happily ever after. In real life there are winners and losers; the good guys don't always win; and being fulfilled or miserable is determined largely by what we do or don't do.

None of us can control the cards of both opportunity and misfortune we draw. However, each of us has the power to play each hand the way we choose. We either can decide to play and try to do the best with the circumstances we have drawn or we can fold so often that we lose the game of life by attrition because we finally run out of chips.

Using "Life Chips" Wisely   To carry the analogy one step further, the chips we amass in the game of life take several forms. They include time spent, money and material things acquired, psychic and emotional energy, creativity, personal relationships, education, and occupational position. Each of these is a precious resource that should be used wisely. Usually all most of us can do is amass enough life chips to stay in the game.

Although it is wonderful and magnanimous to have spare chips and to be able to give them or lend them to deserving people who need assistance, one must be careful. Most of us at some point in our lives have benefited from caring and selfless people who gave freely of their resources so that we might get ahead. However, be wary of those who would continually borrow or steal your life chips with no intention or ability to ever pay them back. These people will needlessly squander your precious resources over and over again because they only know how to fold in the game of life. If you continue to give your chips to them, you will be a fool. If you play the fool long enough, you too may lose the game of life.

LESSON NO. 8: Your Success Requires Positive Relationships with Others

In 1624 poet John Donne observed: "No man is an Island, entire of it self." By nature humans are social beings who need social and emotional support from others. Without it, happiness and fulfillment cannot exist.

Success in life consists of a dynamic dualism. It requires that each of us learn to be alone and self-reliant while simultaneously joined with others in a common effort. On the one hand, each of us ultimately must be alone in defining our own success and achieving it. On the other, our nature requires that our achievement of autonomy and self-determination be motivated and supported by the love and encouragement of others.

The major qualities that make for success—curiosity, self-confidence, decisiveness, motivation, optimism, passion—do not occur in a vacuum. They are not inborn, for the most part. Instead, they must be developed as a result of meaningful and positive interaction with others. Through our social contacts we tend either to be socialized for success or conditioned for failure. We all need the love, affection, recognition, encouragement, and support that only our positive relations with others can give us. Without it, we ultimately will be unhappy and unfulfilled.

As children we have no choice in determining the identities of our parents and teachers. Because of the accidents of birth and geography, we are placed in circumstances largely beyond our control. Consequently, these agents of socialization may serve mainly as benefactors and positive role models to encourage and empower us with the desire and self-confidence to achieve and become our own person or they may do just the opposite.

Many of us, because of our upbringing and previous social experiences, may have been discouraged into a state of insecurity, inaction, and stagnancy. We may have had parents who, although they may have meant well, had the effect of neglecting or harming us just the same.

As adults, conditions are different. We have choices. Even if we have low self-esteem and feel discouraged because of our previous relationships, we have choices. Remember Lesson No. 7: Life Is Not Fair. To be happy and fulfilled we must grow up, accept this principle, and get on with the rest of our lives. We must close the book of our past that we cannot change and face the present and future that we can affect. To accomplish this takes courage, hard work, and some risk.

Using Positive Relationships to Win at the Game of Life No wise person ever said life would be easy. To overcome any self-confidence deficit we might have, we must begin by seeking out positive people. They can serve as role models to emulate and learn from. In addition, they can help give us the encouragement and ego-support we need to become self-actualized, vital human beings.

The game of life is similar to a protracted tournament comprised of daily contests or "poker games." Therefore each of us must play a daily game with ourself and the circumstances and people that come into our life. Our future will be determined by a chain of these daily contests.

The strength of our life chain will depend on how well we forge each link. Our allies during this journey will be the loving, positive, and supportive people we meet and develop relationships with along the way. Likewise, we may become their allies in helping to encourage them as they search for success in their lives.

Our enemies will be the same fools, liars, exploiters, and composites mentioned before. If we pay attention to and implement the teachings of Life 101, we will be able to recognize them for what they are and deal with them effectively. If we don't, the game of life for us will be jeopardized and possibly lost.

LESSON NO. 9: Success Requires the Effective Use of Time

Those most successful in life are people skilled in time management. They are able to harness time as a valuable resource in making the greatest progress in the least amount of time. They see life as a precious gift and try to wring as much enjoyment and productivity as possible out of each year, each month, each day, each moment. When they work, they work hard. When they play, they play hard. When they relax, they attempt to savor the sweet calm of each moment of rest.

Even those who are only moderately time-conscious tend to be two to four times as productive as time-*un*conscious people. They get much more accomplished in any given day because they have the self-discipline to make task-related appointments with themselves and keep them.

Time-unconscious people typically are those who do not have clear-cut time-lines for achieving meaningful goals. Even though they may be very talented, have good ideas, and wish for success, they turn their backs on it by allowing time to slip through their fingers. In doing so, they ignore the inevitability of Lesson No. 2: Success Is Difficult. They find it more convenient to take the easy road and squander their time on meaningless distractions that add up to nothing. Such distractions are meaningless because they usually are forgotten within a few hours or days and produce nothing of consequence.

In habitually taking the easy path, time-unconscious people marshal dozens of rationalizations or excuses for doing so: "I'm too tired to do it now." "I need a rest." "It's late." "Something came up." "I had to do something else." "I wasn't feeling well." The continued compilation of squandered days leads inexorably to wasted weeks, months, and years. Enough squandered years can lead to a wasted life.

To become old, to look back at life, and realize that one has allowed time, and with it happiness, to escape like sand through an hourglass is the most bitter of destinies. Yet this same message has reverberated in the songs and writings of poets and philosophers throughout the centuries. Almost a thousand years ago the Persian poet Omar Khayyám first wrote these words:

> The Moving Finger writes; and, having writ,
> Moves on: nor all thy Piety nor Wit
>   Shall lure it back to cancel half a Line,
> Nor all thy Tears wash out a Word of it.

This warning is as true today as when first written. Indeed, most adult Americans have read this and other excerpts from Khayyám's *Rubáiyát* as a literature assignment either in high school or college. Nonetheless, many people don't pay attention to the wisdom of the ages that surrounds them everywhere. They look but don't see, hear but don't listen, read but don't comprehend. When this becomes a life habit, they lose the game of life. As far as time is concerned, they keep squandering it until one day, it's all gone.

Time waits for no one. It is one of the great levelers in life. We each get the same twenty-four hour day and 365-day year: corporate CEO or janitor, army general or private, nationally renowned chef or short-order cook, university president or high school junior. It's how that time is put to use that counts. One simply doesn't become a high achiever in any field of endeavor by working at it a few hours here and there.

Not only do high achievers wring every available minute out of each day in as efficient a manner as possible, but some of them consider sleep a waste of time. Inventor Thomas Edison, for example, conditioned himself to sleep only three hours a night during much of his adult life. While few of us will be as driven and efficient in our use of time as Edison, most of us could improve upon how we use it as a resource.

Today is all that any of us ever have for sure. It is our most precious resource. Within this twenty-four hour period lies the only playing field upon which the game of life can be played and won.

What is both frightening and exciting about life is that none of us really knows for sure how many more days we will be given. Today might be our last one, or tomorrow, or the day after that. However, we might have twenty thousand or more at our disposal. If we use each one to the best of our ability in our strivings for happiness and fulfillment, we most probably will have it.

LESSON NO. 10: To Succeed, You Must Give More Than Is Merely Required

The successful person loses himself or herself in the task at hand rather than just goes through the motions. Success is about doing and doing well. It is about finding joy in your work. Once you find joy in your work, you must tap into it and go wherever it takes you. This is the path to happiness and fulfillment, the road to success.

This path is not reserved only for presidents, kings, movie stars, Nobel laureates, and other luminaries. It is open to anyone who, in philosopher Joseph Campbell's words, will "follow their bliss." Winners, like losers, in the game of life surround us everywhere. Success in life, therefore, lies in the passion and quality attached to the process of doing, not so much with what is done. Martin Luther King, Jr. perhaps said it best:

> If a man is called to be a streetsweeper, he should sweep streets even as Michelangelo painted, or Beethoven composed music, or Shakespeare wrote poetry. He should sweep streets so well that all the hosts of heaven and earth will pause to say, here lived a great streetsweeper who did his job well.

Finding Joy in Your Work   How do I find joy in my work? How do I get the passion to do a job well? How do I find work that is meaningful in the first place?

It all starts when you make a contract with yourself to put a little more into each task than what is merely required. After a while you develop this as a habit, an ethic. With practice, the ethic gets stronger because you are noticed when you do things well. That is, the positive people will notice you, appreciate your efforts, and give you encouragement to continue. What negative people think really shouldn't matter to you; with their indifference and complaining, they rarely produce anything of value anyway. They mainly just consume their own and other's resources.

Successful people are those who come to take pride in their work. They realize that the quality of what they produce reflects on them as people. Their own positive sense of self-esteem and pride will not allow them to produce mediocre work.

When we learn to take pride in ourselves and the quality of the work we produce, we develop self-confidence. This in turn leads us to try new challenges, to extend what we can do into the realm of the unknown.

This journey into the unknown is what success at anything is all about. It's learning to let go of the familiar cocoon surrounding us to become a butterfly. It's learning to use the force lying dormant within each of us to break free and take the next step to who we will become. No one can tell us what that is to be. The answer is a mystery that dwells in the house of tomorrow.

Finding joy in one's work is the result of mastery. We enjoy what we do well. By striving to do better, we develop the value of excellence as a habit. When we do this, meaningful, joyful work is eventually revealed to us. We find our way to it as a reward for having signed on for the trip. Successful people are never in it just for the ride. They look at life as a great adventure. They approach it with passion and are always searching for something meaningful. This is not only necessary for growth; it is essential to be truly alive.

2 THE FORMULA FOR SUCCESS (CG + P + P = S)

Far better it is to dare mighty things, to win glorious triumphs, even though checkered by failure, than to take rank with those poor spirits who neither enjoy much nor suffer much, because they live in the grey twilight that knows not victory nor defeat.

—Theodore Roosevelt

For of all sad words of tongue or pen, The saddest are these: "It might have been!"

—John Greenleaf Whittier

While there are no secrets to success, there is a simple three-step formula that will take you there. Notice that I said simple, not easy. It goes like this: To succeed at anything significant, whether it takes a day, a month, a year, or longer, you must *do* these three things:

Step 1. **Commit** to a meaningful **goal**.

Step 2. Develop an effective **plan** for achieving the goal.

Step 3. **Persevere** by sticking to the plan.

In fact, the formula for success is so simple that it can be described in three words: commitment, planning, perseverance. Implementing this formula as a way of life, however, is the most difficult thing you will probably ever do.

Many if not most people, in fact, often waste a great deal of time and energy trying to avoid and even run away from these three principles. They stall. They ponder. They rationalize. And, most important, they keep looking for the mythical easy way out. When they do this, the results are almost always the same. They fail or, at the very least, do not succeed. And when they fail, they are following another three-step formula, the one for failure. Simply stated, those who habitually fail do so precisely because they (1) lack commitment, (2) are ill-equipped, and (3) give up easily.

STEP 1: Commit to a Meaningful Goal

A winner is someone who sets his goals, commits himself to those goals, and then pursues his goals with all the ability given him.

—Anonymous

The spirit, the will to win, and the will to excel are the things that endure. These qualities are so much more important than the events that occur.

—Vince Lombardi, NFL Coach

Commitment is the first requirement for becoming really good at anything. It matters not whether we want to become an astronaut, world-class tennis player, supersalesperson, effective parent, or straight-A student. We must first commit ourselves—our time, our energy, our being—to the task at hand. To make a commitment is to care deeply, passionately about the outcome. Tom Peters, co-author of *In Search of Excellence,* describes the commitment process as becoming "a fanatic with a mission."

To be committed, therefore, is to have a meaningful goal and to focus on achieving it with every fiber of our being. Success does not accrue to those who merely *wish* it. Winners are those who *will* it. With the imposition of their will, they make success happen by rising to life's challenges over and over again (see Figure 2–1).

How to Get Commitment   At this point, let us briefly examine two important questions. First, how do you get commitment if you don't already have it? The answers lies in finding a meaningful goal. If you want to obtain a goal badly enough, the commitment usually will come.

Have you ever watched a six- or seven-year-old child learn to ride a bicycle? That kid will suffer through falls, collisions, and even a skinned knee or two in order to master bike-riding. The child is able to muster the necessary commitment mainly because the goal is meaningful. This process is then repeated over and over again as the young person learns to achieve other goals on the journey to adulthood.

Unfortunately, there are millions of adult Americans wandering around aimlessly in life because they have no focus, no direction, no meaningful goals. In the

THE FORMULA FOR SUCCESS

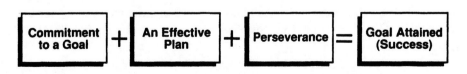

Figure 2-1

words of Henry David Thoreau, they are living "lives of quiet desperation." This happens basically because they accept and settle for what life has placed directly in front of them instead of actively, passionately seeking new experiences, relationships, and possibilities.

Those who lose in life are unhappy and unfulfilled because they get trapped by inertia. They somehow lose that vital spark and zest for living they had as children—the drive that sustained them through their struggles as they learned to walk, talk, ride a bicycle, swim, get as far as high school, drive a car, and establish relationships with new people.

How to Find a Meaningful Goal   A second important question is: How does a person find meaningful goals? This, of course, is one of life's most central questions and difficult challenges. Meaningful goals usually do not knock on our door or tap us on the shoulder. We have to take the responsibility to go seek them out. So one must seek in order to find, ask in order to receive.

To become an effective seeker requires the willingness and self-confidence to let go of the familiar and the comfortable and to test ourselves against the unknown. Each of us must do this to some extent when we enter a new school, begin a new job, or start a new business or personal relationship. Yet many of us do these things only because we feel forced to do so by necessity. Then, when we obtain the initial goal, it becomes so easy to settle into a habit, a routine, a take-it-for-granted attitude. When we do this, our lives often become stagnant and may deteriorate.

The most successful people look forward to new beginnings with eager anticipation. They see life as an exciting adventure and continually try to improve the quality of their life experience through seeking, setting, and attaining new goals.

Committing to the Goal of Making Good Grades   Hopefully, your goal as a student is to earn superior grades. You too must be committed in order to make good grades happen. Unfortunately, some students lack commitment because they have been pampered and petted all their lives by overindulgent parents who have not taught them the necessity of taking responsibility. They expect grades to be handed to them, with little or no effort on their part. Others have low self-esteem and don't believe they are capable of good grades. Still others suffer from both a lack of responsibility and low self-esteem. Sometimes they try to rationalize it all away by lying to themselves that grades and school really don't matter.

The only way out of such a failure syndrome is deciding on a goal, setting your course, and launching forth. While this is often not easy to do and takes a great deal of courage, there is really no other way.

STEP 2: Develop an Effective Plan for Achieving the Goal

> *The greatest thing in this world is not so much where we are, but in what direction we are moving.*
>
> —Oliver Wendell Holmes

> *The worst thing one can do is not to try, to be aware of what one wants and not give in to it, to spend years in silent hurt wondering if something could have materialized—and never knowing.*
>
> —David S. Viscott

Few goals of any consequence are ever achieved without a carefully crafted plan of action. This holds true at all levels. For example, the fates of nations have been determined by effective plans. The Allied invasion of Normandy that led to the end of World War II was carefully planned for over a year. Known as Operation Overlord, it involved thousands of details and hundreds of logistical problems that had to be solved. Except for problems with the weather, it went basically as planned and the rest is in the history books. In similar fashion, the United States landed men on the moon in July 1969 after almost a decade of meticulous planning.

This same principle also applies on an individual level. The successful painter uses a working sketch, the novelist an outline, the coach a game plan, and the college student a study plan. Therefore, whether the scale is large or small, with societal or only local or individual consequences, a good plan is essential.

The Elements of an Effective Plan   Effective plans typically have these characteristics:

Several Steps   To be successful, a plan must be divided into a sequence of clearly identified steps and tasks. Usually the more complex and important the goal, the more necessary it becomes to further divide each step into substeps. A baccalaureate degree, for instance, involves a long-term plan divided into freshman, sophomore, junior, and senior years, semesters within years, and courses within semesters. Even at the course level, *the most successful student will have a weekly study plan.*

Therefore several short-term plans may be needed to design a successful long-term plan. By organizing a plan into several steps, you will be able to (a) make a periodic assessment of progress and (b) obtain the positive reinforcement so necessary to sustain the motivation to continue toward your goal.

Established Timelines   For a plan to be successful, each of its steps should be referenced to a time frame for completion and a deadline to be used as a benchmark for measuring progress. Without established timelines as reference points for staying on schedule, plans lose momentum, stall, and sometimes are never completed.

Postponements and delays may also mean that the plan was flawed from the outset. By not keeping to a firm set of timelines, even a slight delay in completing each step can lead to a long delay in achieving the final goal. With each delay, the odds are increased that you will become discouraged, give up the plan and, with it, the goal. If that happens, you fail.

Contingencies for Unexpected Problems   As noted by the Scottish poet Robert Burns, "The best laid schemes o' mice an' men / Gang aft a-gley." No matter how well-crafted the plan, the unexpected can and often does happen in this imperfect world of ours.

Consequently, the effective planner always builds in contingencies that specify how to proceed if this or that situation should arise. By always expecting the unexpected and having a Plan B or back-door backup plan, you may have to take a slight detour at times, but you will reach the goal.

Computed Costs   Nothing of consequence is ever achieved without costs or trade-offs. Every goal has its price. Costs may be tangible (money, needed materials, and tools) or intangible (time, energy, and labor). An effective planner accurately estimates such costs, whatever they might be. In order to earn a profit, a building contractor must budget carefully the time, labor, and materials needed to construct an office building. The college student must do likewise by correctly estimating the time, energy, tools, and materials needed to earn straight A's or, for that matter, to get passing grades.

Use of Needed Resources and Tools   It is not enough to accurately estimate the costs of achieving a goal. You must also make continued use of these resources. A successful attorney, for example, must marshal all the resources and tools at his or her disposal to prepare a brief of sufficient quality to win the court case. A law student must do the same to first pass the courses required for the law degree and then ultimately pass the bar exams to become licensed to practice. For such a law student (and students in general), a powerful and effective plan with which to achieve academic success is explained in the next couple of hundred pages. If used as explained, it will help you to reach your academic goals.

Clearly Defined Responsibilities   Any plan that is to work must identify who is responsible for doing what, and when. In a corporate business environment, for instance, an organizational chart specifies the hierarchy of positions, reporting relationships, and lines of authority and responsibility within the company. Each individual is expected to perform his or her duties according to accepted standards of performance within an established time frame.

For the individual, whether a participant in a group effort or someone with a personal goal to achieve, a clear understanding of responsibilities is essential. It is also imperative that the individual rank-order priorities and keep them in proper perspective. What needs to be taken care of first? Which responsibilities are most important? Which are of secondary importance? Given the relative importance of various responsibilities, how should time, energy, tools, and other resources be allocated?

ESS: A Plan for Student Success   As a student, each of these planning elements also applies to you. How well you use them will greatly influence your degree of success in school.

On the first day of class each fall semester, my teaching colleagues and I look into the faces of our first-year college students. We know from experience that, on the average, 25 to 30 percent or more will not complete the term with a C grade or higher in each course attempted. Some lack the commitment and maturity to succeed for a variety of reasons. They may want mostly to socialize and party with their friends, an almost sure way to gain academic suspension. Others may be at college mainly because their parents wanted them to go or because no other viable options presented themselves. If these attitudes and characteristics continue, such students probably will not succeed at school.

However, many (if not most) students do have the necessary desire to succeed but lack an effective plan for study. Mainly they need the right tools for academic success, and this book is designed specifically for them.

If you are one of these students, ESS will help guide you through the courses, semesters, and years you will need in order to graduate. It will equip you not only with general principles for effective living but also with specific hands-on skills for academic success. With ESS you will have an effective plan for passing all your work successfully and, if you're willing to put forth the effort, for becoming a superior student (see Figure 2-2).

THE FORMULA FOR STUDENT SUCCESS

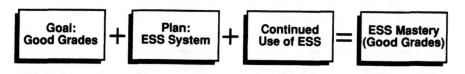

Figure 2-2

STEP 3: Persevere by Sticking to the Plan

Success in life is a matter not so much of talent and opportunity as of concentration and perseverance.

—C. W. Wendte

When you get into a tight place and everything goes against you, till it seems as though you could not hold on a minute longer, never give up then, for that is just the place and the time that the tide will turn.

—Harriet Beecher Stowe

Never, never, never quit.

—Winston Churchill

Regardless of the objective, the most effective plan in the world won't make you successful if you don't use it. Those who succeed at achieving any goal do so by being doers, not talkers; players, not spectators. If all you do is talk about success and watch others gain it, you will never acquire it for yourself. While you're watching, observe how others obtain their goals. How many become happy and fulfilled human beings by talking their way there?

Perseverance is absolutely essential for success. Those who ultimately fail are those who give up. There are dozens of clichés in the English language that speak to this. The familiar American versions include "When the going gets tough, the tough get going." "When you reach the end of your rope, tie a knot in it and hang on." "It's always darkest before the dawn." "When life gives you lemons, make lemonade." The message here is universal and clear. Don't give up. Don't allow anyone or anything to discourage you to the point that you quit trying.

This is so very important because when we give up, something inside us dies. When giving up becomes a life habit, we die as functional human beings.

Discouragement is the enemy of perseverance. It is also the enemy of growth, achievement, and life itself. If we allow it to gain a foothold in our psyche, it can shatter our dreams. Of course, it is easy to become discouraged when we meet with adversity and setback. We've all experienced this from time to time. When we are in the depths of initial despair and disappointment, all the inspiring words in the world don't seem to help much. They ring hollow in our ears. However, after we adjust to the first shock, those of us who ultimately win in life come to realize that we must go on. We must face the realities of life squarely in order to survive and prosper. Success cannot be acquired any other way.

I hope the preceding pages have encouraged you, perhaps even inspired you to read on, learn about ESS, and then use it as a total study system. Implementation of any effective plan, along with perseverance, is always the acid test that separates those who succeed from those who do not perform well. The solution to meeting the challenge of becoming an effective student lies within the covers of this book. If you will implement the entire ESS system and keep using it, you will succeed.

3 SCHOOL: WHY AM I HERE? WHERE AM I GOING?

THE FABLE OF THE LITTLE GREEN FROG AND OTHER STORIES

Scott Alexander, author of *Advanced Rhinocerology,* tells this story about a little green frog:

> It seems that a little green frog had fallen into a rut in a road and could not quite jump high enough to get himself out. His frog buddies were at the top of the ditch urging him on.
> "Come on! You can do it!" they would all yell at the top of their frog lungs. The little frog would jump as hard as he could, but he just could not jump high enough, despite everyone's encouragement and advice. After two hours, the frog was still in the rut and his buddies could wait for him no longer. They went hopping away without him.
> Later in the day, just as they were getting ready to swim in the lake and do some croaking, the frogs saw their little buddy who had been trapped in the rut. Figuring that he would never get out of there, they excitedly exclaimed, "What happened? How did you get out of the rut?" The frog turned to them and said, "A big truck came down the road and I HAD to get out!" (1982, pp. 62–63)

People from all walks of life, like the little green frog, are often motivated to get out of their respective ruts or crises by immediate negative incentives. Tom Peters, co-author of *A Passion for Excellence,* tells this story. It seems that a few years ago, Forrest Mars, founder and chairman of the board of the Mars Candy Company, was being given a tour at a Mars production facility by the local plant manager. When they reached the third floor where the vats of hot simmering chocolate were, Mr. Mars commented to the manager that the inside temperature of the building was unacceptably hot and that the facility needed to be air-conditioned. The plant manager replied that there was no way that he could fit air conditioning into his yearly budget. Mars went to the nearest phone, called maintenance, and ordered them to move the plant manager's desk and the rest of his office contents to the third floor right next to the simmering vats of chocolate. He then told the astonished manager that, as soon as the place was air-conditioned, he could return to his former office. A way to fit air conditioning into the budget was soon discovered.

Every semester I see a similar scenario involving negative incentive unfold among some of my first-year students. Some of them waste half or more of the semester, hardly opening a book. The result is almost always the same. These students perform poorly on the first exam or two.

Then, as the semester draws to a close and it dawns on them that they may fail the course, they suddenly become very interested in their grades and come to me seeking help. Some of them subsequently take my ESS seminar based on material presented in this book, make a dramatic turnaround, and end the semester with passing grades in all their courses. Unfortunately for some, however, the hole they've dug themselves into is so deep at that point that they cannot pass many of their courses.

Recently I had a situation develop with a student that underscores this point. This student, Joe, had taken Introductory Sociology with me twice before and had received an F grade both times. He was about twenty, a pleasant, courteous young man, but obviously with little or no motivation to study.

A couple more semesters passed and I had almost forgotten about Joe. Then, one fall semester, I entered my Intro Soc class—and there he was for the third time. However, this time he was sitting front-row center. Before, he had always sat at the very back of the classroom.

That semester Joe was a model student and worked as if possessed. He took the first available ESS seminar, implemented it as taught, and never missed a single class. He took detailed notes, asked incisive questions, and appeared very much interested in the course.

When only a few weeks remained in the semester, I just couldn't wait any longer. So I approached him and said, "Joe, I'm really impressed with your performance this semester. But I'm curious. What has brought about this change?" "Well," he said, looking a little sheepish, "part of it was ESS. It really works if you use it." He paused for a moment and then continued. "But a big part of it was my dad. He's a supervisor for the State Highway Department and paid my tuition for the first two semesters. Then, when I flunked out, he put me to work last year digging ditches. This semester is my last chance and I'm paying for my tuition this time. If I don't make all A's and B's, my parents are going to kick me out of the house."

He paused again and then a slight smile crept across his face. "You know what?" he exclaimed. "I didn't realize how tough it is for some people to make a living. I never want to see another ditch again." Joe received a 3.8 grade-point average that semester. He had found incentive.

Like Joe's initial behavior in the preceding story, many high school students and even some beginning college students view school with a mixture of indifference and hostility. Their assessments of school range from "Why am I here?" and "Where am I going?" to "School's a drag," "It's a bummer," "It's a waste of time," and even "I hate school."

Every fall semester I have some first-time students in my classes who are there because (1) "My parents wanted me to go," (2) "My friends were going to college so I thought I would go too," (3) "I'm going to college because I didn't have anything else better to do," or (4) a combination of these reasons. As often as not, these students get distracted from academics by campus social life and flunk out. I know because I ask them and they tell me.

In almost twenty years of college teaching, hundreds of these students have shared with me their confusion and indecision about school in one-on-one counseling sessions. Some of them then straighten up and get serious about their studies; some leave for a semester or two; some drop out for five to ten years or more; and some leave and never return. For the most part, however, those who leave, even if only for a short time, get jobs and enter the work force.

From those students who return after an absence of months or years and those who enter college for the first time several years after high school graduation, the messages are almost always the same: "I wish now that I had seen the importance of college right after high school. I would have been a lot better off." "I was foolish for not seeing the value of school when I was here several years ago." "I sure am glad to be back. I really love school now."

Why are *these* students so serious about the value of school and the importance of effective study? Why do they *now* have the motivation to do well in their studies that they lacked before?" Like the little green frog and Joe the student they have learned that, to succeed in American society today, there are few if any viable alternatives to a good education. Their attitudes about education are positive because they have learned from the "school of hard knocks" what I am about to tell you.

We Live in a Credential-Oriented Society

In the majority of careers today, credentials such as diplomas, technical certificates, degrees, and licenses are of crucial importance. It is becoming increasingly difficult to get any job whatsoever without at least a high school diploma or equivalent. The better jobs require postsecondary credentials such as technical certificates and licenses and/or college and graduate degrees. Experts agree that by the year 2000 the average worker will need at least thirteen to fourteen years of formal education. This is because our society has become increasingly complex and technology-oriented and this trend promises to continue into the foreseeable future. Consequently, those qualified only for unskilled and semiskilled jobs today receive the fewest rewards. In the near future, many of them are likely to be unemployable.

In today's society, intelligence and native talent alone won't take you very far.

You may be the brightest, hardest-working individual in your neighborhood, community, or company. Yet if you don't have the necessary recognized credentials, you won't even get your foot in the door for the better jobs, much less gain occupational advancement.

Students in their mid-to-late twenties and older have learned this lesson well. Many of them have returned to school because they have been unsuccessful in gaining career advancement without credentials. Others have been dislocated from their jobs and/or have no recognized credentials that would allow for transfer to other positions. Therefore they have returned to school to get them.

Those with the Best Education Get the Best Jobs

One myth prevalent among many young people today is that you can get a good job with advancement potential without technical certification or a college degree. Those most likely to believe this are working-class youth who are often bright, hard-working, and ambitious. Some of their parents have attained seniority and middle-class incomes without much if any postsecondary education. These young people think they will be able to do the same by getting a job, working hard, and ultimately moving up in the company or organization that has employed them. In most cases, they are dead wrong.

Many of these young adults get sidetracked from postsecondary education by the lure of a job and what seems to be a shortcut to the good life. However, few of them escape the demands of an ever-changing credential-oriented society. Although those who go into the work force after high school get a four- or five-year head start on college graduates, most technically certified or degreed people who entered their school programs immediately after high school have caught and passed them in yearly income by their mid- to late twenties.

A generation or two ago their parents and grandparents were often able to do fairly well without technical training or college because conditions were different. Yet many of these older people today are getting economically trapped by changes in their society and world that they didn't foresee and often don't understand. Fifty-year-old auto workers, steelworkers, millworkers, and others may lose union-scale jobs because of a shift in the world marketplace. Without transferable skills and credentials, these people may be forced to accept unskilled or semi-skilled jobs, making only a fraction of the money made before. For many of these dislocated workers, feelings of abandonment and bitterness are common. Their only alternative, in many cases, is to return to school and retrain for another occupation.

In their youth they went to work at the mill, the plant, or the company immediately after high school or even before, in some cases. So did many of their fathers before them. Once they got "hired on," their perception was that they had a job for life as long as they performed adequately. In those days after World War II, America was the dominant economic power and had a virtual monopoly on world markets. The future looked promising. Therefore, once a person had a job, the expectation was that the job and employer would always be there.

Today these conditions no longer hold true. Economic realities have changed dramatically. We now have to compete head-to-head with the Japanese, the Koreans, the Germans, and others. And in some cases, foreign competitors are beating us badly because they sometimes build better products than we do, with superior design and workmanship. It is unrealistic today to think that one can still get a job with advancement potential without postsecondary education. Likewise, the idea that the plant, the factory, the company, and the job will always be there is unrealistic.

The typical college graduate today will receive somewhere between half a million and one million dollars in increased lifetime earnings over the wages earned by the average high school graduate. The college graduate will also experience more job mobility, better working conditions, greater fringe benefits, and more social prestige and influence than a person with only the high school diploma. Those who go on to earn graduate and professional degrees typically will experience even greater rewards.

Education today represents the key to upward social and economic mobility in this country. To invest the time, energy, and money necessary to get a good education is the best investment most people can make. It represents an investment in yourself that will greatly influence the quality of your future.

Employers Prefer College Graduates Because of Their Learning Skills

College graduates are proved learners. College degrees often mean that their holders are specialists in certain such subject fields as accounting, computer science, or nursing. In some cases, however, it is not essential that the degree holder have a major closely aligned with the job function to be performed. In fact, some companies employ people with majors far removed from the job at hand. What is most important is that the person hired be able to think critically, find necessary information and resources with which to solve problems, weigh alternatives carefully, and then make decisions based on information and good judgment.

In this respect higher education serves as a competitive weeding-out process to separate the less capable and less disciplined from the best performers. It takes commitment, focus, determination, and flexibility to complete four years of college successfully. Those who do survive have developed the self-discipline coupled with the hard work necessary to do so. They have been able to pass courses they didn't want to take, listen to professors they sometimes didn't like, and take and pass exams often when they would have preferred to do something else.

Employers recognize that those with the capability to survive a college bureaucracy will most likely fare well in a corporate or business setting. Such employers often must invest several thousand dollars in training costs for each new employee to prepare them for work in their organization. It is therefore necessary to minimize risk and employ proved performers. This is a fundamental reason the college degree is held in such high esteem.

Career Advancement Today Requires Lifelong Learning

In the recent past a person could often obtain a high school diploma or college degree, get a job, and never have to worry about formal education again. Today, however, the reverse is true. Ours is a constantly changing, high-technology society. A continuing knowledge explosion that impacts the workplace is now a permanent fact of life.

Most of us today and in the future will be going to school for the rest of our lives as our culture adjusts to the concept of lifelong learning. Some of us will find it necessary to earn additional certificates, licenses, or degrees. In the business world, for example, the master of business administration degree (MBA) is becoming increasingly important for managerial career advancement.

Most people, however, will be required to take periodic short courses and seminars throughout their careers to upgrade job skills and acquire the latest job-related information. These formal learning experiences will range in length from half-day seminars to courses in technical areas lasting one or two weeks or more.

Those who expect to gain career advancement in their chosen fields will have to be fast and effective learners. It is now common for job-related seminars lasting two to five days to include as much information as that contained in a semester-long college course. In my capacity as a human resource consultant I have administered dozens of such seminars for organizations as diverse as Xerox Corporation, Gibraltar Savings, the American Heart Association, Phillips Petroleum, and Public Service Company of Oklahoma (an electric utility).

The pace is fast and intense because it has to be. Each day the employee is off the job in a training seminar is costing the employer significant amounts of money in training costs, salary, and lost productivity. Employing college graduates with the best grades drastically reduces the learning curve and minimizes costs. This is one of the main reasons the best college graduates are able to get the most desirable jobs with the greatest potential.

Therefore, whether you are a high school junior; college freshman; private career (that is, business or technical) school student; first-year medical, law, or graduate student; or a new employee faced with upcoming training seminars, ESS will provide you the tools you need to be successful.

Decisions You Make Today Will Shape Your Future

Often the really critical decisions that affect us for life are made between the junior and senior years in high school and the freshman and sophomore years in college—when most of us are very young and often unprepared. Nonetheless, we have to make these decisions. It is imperative that they be made conscientiously because, one way or another, we will have to live with the consequences.

However, students often don't realize that they are making crucial decisions at sixteen, eighteen, or twenty years of age that could influence the rest of their lives. And usually no one is there to tell them "Here's a big life decision. Make it carefully. Make it on the basis of good information." Instead, students often just fall into these decisions without much conscious thought at all.

The process begins in high school with decisions such as "Am I going to study for my courses?" "Am I going to do as well as I can or just do enough to get by?" Decisions regarding the type of student you will be often determine whether or not you will go to college immediately after high school. They also affect how you will do on college entrance exams, whether or not you will qualify for a scholarship, and which school you will be able to attend.

When you do go on to college, the decisions continue: "Am I going to seek out the easiest school, the easiest major, and the easiest teachers, or am I going to get the best education I can possibly obtain?" "What will be my college major?" "What type of student am I going to be?" "Are my grades going to be the most important thing to me, or am I going to place most of my priorities on my social life, hobbies, or part-time or full-time job?"

These decisions have monumental consequences. They determine, among other things, whether you will be eligible to go on successfully to college or graduate school or have a chance to get a job with one of the better companies that employ only the cream of the crop from the pool of college graduates.

Yet many students fall into these decisions almost unconsciously. In fact, very few students have the attitude "Wow! This is going to affect me for the rest of my life." Unlike the decision to marry someone, which is overt and conscious, the decision as to whether to make A's or just get by with C's or worse tends to be unconscious.

Students often don't understand the cumulative impact such a decision can have on their futures. Many don't seem to realize that their academic records are permanent and follow them for life. The fact is that how they perform in high school and college, the types of learners they become, and the other school-related choices they make may be just as important as whom they take for a spouse.

It Is Important to Make Informed Career Decisions

Often students make decisions about their majors and their career goals on the basis of impressions and hunches rather than solid information. Since these are critical decisions that may affect a person for the rest of his or her life, they should be made very carefully. Unfortunately, some students will spend more time comparing brands and store prices to save fifty or a hundred dollars on a stereo system or portable TV than they will expend to get information with which to make decisions about their major or career.

Five Techniques for Making an Informed Career Decision

1. *Learn from the mistakes of others.* Many of us in my generation did not approach the choice of major and career in a rational way when we were in college. I changed majors several times and ended up in sociology because I liked it and had an inspiring professor. Little did I know or even imagine at the time that I would become a college professor, author, and consultant. Today I consider myself very fortunate in that I enjoy what I do and make a good living doing it.

Dr. Dennis Toombs, a professor of political science at San Jacinto College, echoes my sentiments: "I picked political science because I liked it and I liked current events in high school. However, I really didn't know what political science majors do or what career opportunities were available. Likewise, I had no idea what kind of income I could expect. My decision, therefore, involved almost no thought about what was going to happen after I got the degree in political science. So I encourage students to put a lot more time and care into it than I did."

Unlike myself and Dr. Toombs, many students who drift into majors without much care and thought are not so fortunate or happy. It is very disappointing to invest four years of your life in a college education and then discover that there aren't any available jobs in that field. Likewise, it is unsettling to discover that you don't like the job your education prepared you for or the salary and growth opportunities are not what you expected. Unfortunately, this happens all the time. Then many people are faced with either remaining miserable in their career or returning to school to retrain at a tremendous cost in time and expense.

2. *Conduct library research.* What else can you do to keep from falling into such a trap other than observe the mistakes of others? The answer lies in information. When it comes to planning your future, you need to be well-informed. Conduct some library research to get specific information from academic sources about majors and careers.

3. *Use the services of counselors.* Seek information from school counselors and go to the private sector if you can. It might be wise to consult a professional career counselor, even if it costs you a few dollars. Although this may seem expensive, it can be money well spent because you're investing in something that could affect you for a lifetime, the choice of a career.

4. *Take aptitude tests.* Regardless of whether you use a school counselor, a career counselor, or both, it's important that you take some aptitude tests to find out your likes, dislikes, aptitudes, and so on. These tests are often useful in helping students to narrow down career possibilities.

5. *Consult practicing professionals.* Once you have identified some fields for career consideration, seek out practicing professionals in these areas and make an appointment to talk with them. These people can provide you invaluable information about the way things really are in a given profession or career. They often have the most current information concerning salaries, changes, and trends in the field, prospects for employment now and in the future, and the best type of academic preparation needed to qualify for entry-level positions. Practicing professionals are also in the best position to tell you about both the joys and the frustrations attached to their jobs.

Armed with such information, you will be in a much better position to make an informed decision regarding a possible major or career goal. By taking the time necessary to approach this task in a conscientious way you will be much more likely to make the right choices and be happy with them in the future. When you think that these choices might affect you for thirty or forty years or more, it is important that they be taken seriously.

Grades Are Important

What many students often don't realize is that grades count. They are the benchmarks against which learning ability, knowledge, and potential for achievement are measured and assessed. Grades begin to be critical in high school because they reflect how well students are prepared to take college board exams. Thus they affect how well students will score on the SAT or the ACT exams. They also affect eligibility for gaining entry into the most selective colleges and universities.

Yet there is a peculiar ethic among many high school students and some college students that grades really don't count for much. Neither does reading or studying. Particularly among high school students, those who excel in academics are sometimes branded bookworms or nerds. What is ironic is that twenty years later, those same "bookworms" and "nerds" are disproportionally represented in the professions and thus tend to earn the highest incomes and live in the most exclusive neighborhoods.

Good grades in both high school and college can help correct many social inequities. Even students from very humble origins can often get into the most prestigious colleges and graduate schools by studying their way there. The best colleges in the country actively seek National Merit Scholars and often award them full scholarships. Once at college, those who study hard and make good grades can qualify for graduate scholarships, assistantships, and fellowships at the best universities and professional schools in the country.

In reality, a C or two or even an occasional low grade on your transcript probably won't affect your future opportunities. But the impact of a thoroughly mediocre to poor academic record may haunt you for the rest of your life. Poor grades might cause you to cheat yourself out of obtaining a job at a leading corporation. They might ruin your chances of getting into a good college, graduate school, or professional school.

Many leading corporations—IBM and Xerox Corporation, among others—do look at grade-point-averages; they look at the class standings of job applicants. Many employers today are increasingly looking at grades as one variable to be considered. Therefore, don't allow yourself to unconsciously misperceive the importance of grades, to blindly fall into a pattern of mediocrity. Oftentimes, those who just get by at school will be as likely to just get by in life.

4 STUDENT SUCCESS

CHARACTERISTICS OF MASTER STUDENTS

In almost twenty years as an educator and behavioral scientist, I have had the opportunity to directly observe thousands of students from ages sixteen to eighty-four from various socioeconomic, ethnic, and occupational backgrounds. This, coupled with my research and reading of the educational literature on students, has allowed me to identify fifteen outstanding characteristics of master students. These characteristics are indicative of those who are able to transfer the general life skills discussed earlier into student skills.

1. *Curiosity.* The pathway to knowledge and wisdom begins with curiosity. Three-year-olds seem to burst with it as they explore their surroundings and ask Why? and How? about most everything. Master students at any age, indeed students of life, want to know. They ask questions. They are inquisitive. The child-like ability to experience wonder and excitement at discovering something new in our lives or to look at something familiar in a new way is part of what keeps us vital and growing.

Poor students tend to ask few questions aimed at mastering the material. Often they are disengaged and unfocused and appear oblivious of the fine details of information that surround them everywhere. Master students, by contrast, ask questions constantly. They have never lost that inquisitive desire to know that characterized their behavior as small children.

2. *Self-confidence.* To do well in school or in life, you must first believe that you can and do deserve to succeed. Success and failure both hinge on this central point. If you don't believe you are worth it, you probably will not invest the time and energy to strive for success. If you do believe in yourself, you will tend to make success happen.

This has been explained by sociologist Robert Merton as the **self-fulfilling prophecy**, a prediction by a person that something will occur which is then caused to come true because of his or her actions. Those who fail often make it happen because they don't believe they can succeed. Likewise, success in school and in other life pursuits is the end product created by those who believe in themselves and feel that they deserve the best, whether it be grades or anything else of significance. Master students exhibit this self-confidence in their ability to succeed in school.

3. *Goal orientation.* Master students are able to focus their energies outward toward the task at hand rather than inward toward themselves. They almost al-

ways have both short-term and long-term goals. Short-term goals are those focused on such specifics as an upcoming exam, a research paper to be completed, or getting good grades for a semester's work. Long-term goals include graduating from school, planning which school might be attended next if necessary, and career goals.

The more successful high school students, for example, begin to think seriously by their junior year about which college to attend. Mediocre to poor students just muddle through day by day. They apply little focus and direction either to long-term goals—such as life after high school—or short-term goals such as the current semester or upcoming test. By the time they realize that they need to focus some energy on the task at hand, it is often too late. The result many times is a failed exam or a failed semester. If this lack of focus and direction continues both in school and in life, one may fail at both.

4. *Commitment.* Partially because of their curiosity and self-confidence, master students tend to be highly motivated. They seem to burn inside with an energy that propels them onward. Mostly this energy is positive. They truly want to succeed for the positive rewards rather than to avoid the negative feelings that accompany failure.

Much of the source for this energy comes directly or indirectly from others. Most master students have been encouraged by others, such as parents and close friends, while growing up. Therefore they have developed the ego strength to persevere. Others less fortunate have wisely and responsibly sought out positive people who, through their strength and encouragement, have helped give them the desire to continue. At times, such students also may have found it necessary to rid themselves of negative and destructive relationships with those who would try to destroy their motivation to succeed.

5. *Tenacity.* One has to be tough both in mind and in body to survive several years of college, technical school, graduate school, or professional school. Master students are that. Call it determination, drive, grit, or whatever. They have it. They are tenacious in their efforts and never give up.

It is important to make the distinction between commitment and tenacity. Commitment is very important since it represents the impulse, the incentive, the desire to do something. However, you can lose incentive or commitment; you can become unmotivated. By contrast, tenacity tends to be a deep-seated character trait. Whether it is inborn, developed, or a combination of both, it is rarely lost. You might say that tenacity is commitment carried to the nth degree. It's what kicks in when motivation alone will no longer suffice. You could call it plain old stubbornness, a never-say-die attitude. This is what sustains master students and others faced with a challenge when all else fails.

6. *Enthusiasm.* Master students are enthusiastic about learning even if they

sometimes don't show it outwardly. They enjoy the journey to increased knowledge. They revel in the wonder of it all when they discover something new and intriguing. Sometimes they just bubble over with what they have learned or with what they have accomplished and have to share it with others. Other master students are much more private with their enthusiasm and just quietly smile to themselves. Regardless of the style in which they manifest their pleasure in broadening their horizons, they have a need to know that is evident in the quality of their performance.

7. *Sensitivity Toward Others.* Because they tend to have high self-esteem, master students are sensitive to the feelings and needs of others and try to be cooperative. First, they tend to be helpful and encouraging to fellow students. Sometimes they find that academic success is facilitated by working with other students in study groups. At many of the better colleges, law and medical schools, and graduate schools in the United States, study groups are very common and often necessary for maximum success.

Second, master students have respect for their teachers and demonstrate it by being cooperative. They work with their instructors in an attempt to create a positive learning environment both in and out of the classroom.

8. *Decisiveness.* The best students assess the learning situation in front of them, develop a plan, and then act. While one must certainly "look before one leaps," master students have learned that continued vacillation and procrastination are the characteristics of losers. They try to study some each day. They keep abreast of their reading assignments. They complete their research papers, book reviews, and other class projects well ahead of instructor-imposed deadlines. When faced with a problem or course content they find confusing, they often contact their instructor immediately. By being decisive and timely in their actions, master students avoid many of the problems and pitfalls that beset poor students. Most important, they avoid cramming for exams and other forms of procrastination that contribute to poor grades.

9. *Maturity.* Taking responsibility for their performance in school is one of the most important hallmarks of successful students. They rarely miss class or arrive late, take detailed notes, and cooperate with their instructors in trying to create a positive learning environment. Mature students take the initiative in finding out what is expected of them and go the extra mile in trying to perform to the best of their ability. They take school very seriously and readily sacrifice other interests to it. They realize that to succeed in life one needs a good education. When they don't perform as well as they had hoped they are often visibly disappointed. However, they take full responsibility for their actions and subsequently try to improve their performance.

10. *Friendliness.* Because they have high self-esteem and self-confidence,

master students tend to be friendly toward others. They like people. This does not mean that they are always extroverted. Often they are not. Many master students, in fact, are quiet, unassuming people who may be somewhat shy until you get to know them. Once they open up, however, even the shy ones tend to be witty and engaging conversationalists. Although they sometimes are very selective in their friendships, they enjoy the company of others and are fascinated by what they can learn from them. Master students like to inquire, debate, discuss, and ponder out loud in the company of others who enjoy the meeting of minds with equal fervor. They revel in meaningful dialogue with serious-minded people. Without it, they would feel deprived and incomplete.

11. *Sense of Humor.* Although they are at times very serious-minded, the best students usually don't take themselves or life too seriously. They like to have fun and are able to keep things in proper perspective. They realize that balance is important in life. Like most people, they enjoy a good laugh. Unlike many people, they usually have the capacity to laugh at themselves because it takes nothing away from their self-confidence. They are a pleasure to be around because they are so witty. Often, they can tell a humorous story as well as laugh at those told by others. This, combined with their other traits, often endears them to others. Certainly their teachers rarely, if ever, forget them.

12. *Well-Informed.* Knowledge is power. Master students realize this and make every effort to be well-informed. Because they have such a thirst for knowledge, they try to acquire and maintain the best and most up-to-date information possible. They try to stay current on world, national, state, and local events as well as maintain a working knowledge of several subjects—including politics, business, and, for some, even sports and other specialized pursuits.

To keep abreast of things, they have learned that, intellectually speaking, you are what you read. When electronic media are used for both information and entertainment, master students tend to be very selective. The best students are avid readers. They devour newspapers, magazines, and most everything else in print they can get their hands on. Their favorite television programs include those related to news, such as ABC's *20/20* and CBS's *60 Minutes.*

13. *Realistic Attitude.* Master students are, among other things, students of life. They have learned that in order to succeed in school or anything else, we must learn to come to terms with the world as it is rather than how we might wish it to be. There are principles for effective living and principles for being an effective student. These rules apply to us all. There are also, unfortunately, no guarantees. While there is always room for refinement of such principles, we must all operate out of them to be successful. The best students quickly learn what is expected of them from their teachers and courses, face these challenges squarely, and give them their best efforts. In doing so, they succeed.

14. *Optimism.* Master students are optimists. They look at their cup as half full rather than half empty. By always trying to look on the bright side of things, the occasional disappointment or failure can be placed in its proper perspective. We all fail from time to time. We all have setbacks and disappointments. The master student realizes this and tries to turn each negative into a positive. A failure is seen as a temporary setback. Thus it becomes a learning experience, a lesson in life. By taking this attitude, the superior student is able to use each negative experience as an opportunity from which to benefit. This lesson learned then enables this person to improve his or her performance in the future.

15. *Courage.* To become a master student, one has to have courage, the ability to be fearless in the face of adversity. Educational pursuits can be very difficult at times. Master students have the fortitude to rise to each challenge they meet and the gallantry to persevere regardless of the risks taken. The best students risk failure every day. Occasional setbacks are inevitable because of equally inevitable miscalculations. However, to stretch themselves as students and as human beings, master students relentlessly push on beyond the comfortable and familiar into the uncharted regions of the unknown. They impose their light—the human spirit—onto the darkness. In doing so, they exemplify the essence of self-actualization.

Student Success Case Histories

Since the late 1970s, I have given hundreds of ESS seminars to thousands of students in different parts of the United States. There have been many success stories. In preparation for this book version of ESS, some students who recently have been exposed to this skill-based study system were interviewed. These five are fairly representative of the many people whose lives have been changed by learning how to study effectively.

Jeff Vadzemmieks, age nineteen; criminal justice major

Q: **Tell me, Jeff. What type of student were you in high school?**

A: Well, basically I was an average student. I made mainly C's. So you would have to say I was good enough to be considered only average.

Q: **How long have you been in college?**

A: This is my second semester. I'm a criminal justice major.

Q: **How did you do in terms of grades the first semester?**

A: I did extremely well for me. I got an A in Intro to Criminal Justice, a B in Criminal Investigation, a B in Fundamentals of Criminal Law, a B in weight training, an A in orientation, and a C in English Composition I.

Q: To what do you attribute your success?

A: To the ESS study skills. My study habits used to be terrible. I would study for hours and hours at a time and be lucky to get a C on a test. Then early last semester I found out about ESS. Since using it, I now get B's and sometimes an A. So this means I must be doing something right.

Q: What about ESS do you find most helpful?

A: It used to be that I had to rack my brains to study each subject. It seemed to take forever and I didn't comprehend what I was reading. With ESS, it is a lot easier to comprehend the material. It has also helped me break material down into smaller chunks for better understanding. So it has made reading, comprehending, and organizing much easier.

Q: So you have been using the system for about one semester?

A: Yes, sir.

Q: Tell me what you experienced when you first started using ESS?

A: Well, when I first started trying it out, I said to myself: This looks kind of tough. It took me about a month to get used to it because I had a lot of bad habits to overcome. But after I started working at it and practicing the methods, it became much easier to use than the way I was studying before ESS. And the best thing is, it really works.

Q: What type of GPA do you think you will earn this semester?

A: I think I'll get about a 3.5 grade point average this semester.

Q: Would it be fair to say then that you are a more successful student now than before you began using the system?

A: Oh, yes, sir! I'm a much better student now, much better. I got a 3.07 grade point average my first semester because of ESS. When I was in high school, I could never have imagined that I could do this well in college courses.

Q: Do you have any advice for high school students preparing to go to college and for college freshmen?

A: Well, I would like to say this. If you have any trouble studying or taking tests as I did because I was never a good test taker, ESS would be the ideal system to use. In fact, if you are a college student or even a high school student, you must use ESS. It will seem difficult at first and it will take some work. But if you will use it, you will reap the benefits.

Sheila Humphrey, age twenty-three; nursing major

Q: Sheila, could you tell me a little about yourself, something about your background?

A: Well, I'm married. I have a little girl, and another one on the way. I'm mostly a homebody who likes a quiet life at home with my family. I've also never really had a good job. That's why I'm going to school now. I mean, I've worked at Stop-and-Go's as a cashier. However, I'm working on my nursing courses now and plan to go all the way to a bachelor's degree.

Q: How long have you been in college?

A: This is my second semester. So less than a year.

Q: How did you find out about ESS?

A: When I was interviewed for the nursing program, the program director told us that the first level of the nursing program was very difficult. She advised us strongly to get ESS and use it as a system for study. Unfortunately, a lot of students did not use ESS. You can really tell the difference between those who did and those who did not.

Q: What were your grades before you used ESS compared to what they are today?

A: Well, I took the advice of the school and went through the ESS seminar just before I started my nursing program. So I have no before-and-after nursing grades to compare, thank goodness. But compared to other college courses I took before entering the nursing program and my high school grades, the difference is unbelievable. I'm a B+ student now. Before ESS, I was a D and F student in high school and a C student in my first college courses. I just wasn't motivated mainly because I lacked self-confidence and it was hard for me to comprehend the material in school.

Q: What has happened to you as a student since you began using this system?

A: I have learned how to study for the first time in my life, how to put into perspective what I have read. Before I learned about ESS, I would read and read and read. It would just go in one ear and out the other. ESS has taught me how to comprehend what I read and when to write things down. One of my instructors told us when we began our program that by now in our studies, we should be able to design a test for each of our nursing courses. It didn't dawn on me until a few weeks ago what she meant. Now with my ESS skills, I can pick right out of each chapter what is going to be on the test. About 99 percent of the time I can tell almost exactly what is going to be on major exams.

  That's why a lot of students are coming to me and my friends who also use ESS to ask us what to study. And I tell them. "It's right here. All you have to do is learn how to see it." So we keep telling them to get the ESS system and learn it. Some of them keep saying "I don't have enough time." They want me to sit there and show them, do their work for them, and tell them as if it's magic or something. Frankly, I've got other things better to do.

Q: So specifically, ESS has taught you how to anticipate test questions?

A: Absolutely!

Q: Is there anything else in particular it has given you?

A: Yes. With the ESS system, once I have everything organized, I study maybe an hour or so the night before the big exam. Now, I'm making 86's and 89's as typical grades and have a B+ average in all my classes. With some more work on my part, I could be making straight A's.

Q: What would you say to students in terms of what they need to do in order to improve their grades?

A: I've already told them and tell them all the time. They need to use ESS. Some of them think I'm joking. But I wouldn't be doing as well as I am now if it had not been for this system. They think I'm kidding when I tell them I study an hour the night before the exam. So what I would say to students is this: If you have a problem comprehending and remembering your course material, do yourself a favor and use ESS. It will do wonders for your grades.

Joseph Yeiser, age twenty-nine; history major

Q: Joe, could you tell me something about yourself, your background?

A: I guess you could say that I'm just an average person, basically. I was born and raised on the northeast side of Houston, right next to the Fifth Ward. From the time I was fourteen years old, I have worked full-time right up to today. As far as my educational background goes, it was pretty bad. Part of it was my fault and part of it was the school system's fault. Unfortunately, I was born with dyslexia. So I still to this day don't read as well as I should. But I'm gradually overcoming that.

I graduated 248 out of 408 and I considered myself functionally illiterate. I could not fill out a job form after I graduated from high school. Don't ask me how this happened. I have no idea. I'm sure part of it is my fault. But I was one who fell through the cracks and, at the time, was glad to fall through them. I just thought that school was a waste of time because I was working full-time.

Q: What type of work were you doing?

A: Machine-shop work. I started working in the machine shop full time when I was sixteen. By the time I graduated from high school, I was making between 18 and 20 thousand per year. So for an eighteen-year-old, I was making money. And that was over ten years ago.

Q: When did you first attend college?

A: Well, I tried to attend college part of one semester as soon as I graduated from high school. But I was so ill-prepared for it that it was an impossibility. There was no possible way I could have succeeded then because I was so poorly equipped. It is just mind-blowing. It is just unbelievable how poorly prepared I was.

Shortly after graduating from high school, I went on a job interview at an oil company to try to get a better job. The man who was doing the interview looked me dead in the eye and said, "Sorry, we can't use you. You can't read and write. When you learn to read and write, come back and we'll talk to you." Believe me, that was a pretty rude awakening.

Q: What did you do then?

A: I went into the army, believe it or not. They offer GED programs, the opportunity to earn college degrees, and everything in between. I never got to the stage of taking the CLEP tests. But I did take advantage of the high school education courses. So although I had a high school diploma, I took the GED courses anyway. They offered remedial math and reading courses.

Q: And did this experience help you?

A: Oh yes. It helped a lot. It let me know where my biggest shortcomings were: reading, writing, and arithmetic.

Q: So you went into the army and stayed in the army for several years. What was your job in the military?

A: I was a grunt. Actually, when I went into the army, I wanted to be in the infantry. And I got my wish. Every male member of my family had served. So I figured that I might as well do my time too. When I got out of the military after nearly a decade of it, I went straight into college. I had saved almost twenty-one thousand dollars in educational benefits. So here I am.

Q: Tell me about your college experiences.

A: My first three semesters I was still getting caught up with what I missed in high school. I took every remedial course that the college offered. I took four remedial English classes, two remedial math classes, and I'm still not quite caught up. I blame that on poor study habits which I never learned in the first place. So first I had to get caught up.

Q: When did you first start taking actual college-level courses?

A: Last year was my first full year. I was surprised at the difference between the remedial courses and the college-level courses. It was the difference between night and day. I struggled all last year. Last semester it was a struggle. Then, this semester, I found out about ESS and began using it. This system pointed out to me just how bad my study habits were, how bad my organizational skills were. It has helped me a great deal in the past two months.

Q: Could you tell me what your grades were before you started using ESS and what has happened since? Give me some specifics if you can.

A: OK. No problem. I've got lots of specifics. I've had to take English composition twice. I took it again last semester and earned a C. In Biology I also earned a C. Before this semester, I never made higher than a C in anything. And I worked hard. I just wasn't working smart. I didn't know how to do things right. Since using the ESS system this semester, however, I've been able to raise the grades in my courses two whole letter grades. For example, on the last test in history, I made an 88. On the test before that, I made an 82. ESS has helped tremendously.

Q: So you earned a D on the first exam in history?

A: Yeah. I made a 65 on the first test. Then after using ESS, I made an 82 and then an 88. The ESS system has helped me the most with the organization of my notes. That was my biggest problem. Before I learned how to use ESS, I would get ready to study and would have piles of books and notes; mainly just a jumbled-up mess, a hodgepodge. So before, I had to work very hard to just get by. This involved a lot of cramming which never worked for me. But on the last test using my ESS skills, I only had to study two hours the night before. Now, I have a system for studying. I go home every day, go over my notes, and put them in outline form just like ESS says. From there, I just study my completed outline the night before the test.

Q: So you use all parts of ESS including the concentrated study session and other elements contained in ESS—THE ADVANCED COURSE?

A: Yes. I haven't perfected it yet, but I'm getting there. I still have this terrible adversity to . . . It just seems almost sacrilegious to write in a book. But I'm working on it and getting better at it all the time.

Q: What has happened to you since you started writing in your textbooks?

A: I get much more information and understanding out of them. There is no doubt about that because I don't have to go back and look for where I thought I saw something. It helps tremendously to strategically highlight the core material and to write the little summaries in the margins that explain the material.

Q: How have you been doing with developing your skills in writing the comprehensive outline for ESS STEP TWO?

A: As far as creating the final outline, this is the part I'm still a little sketchy about. ESS says to make your outline as small as possible in terms of number of pages. How much information should you try to cram onto one sheet of paper?

Q: As much as possible. How small do you write?

A: Well, I write very small. We had forty-three ID terms in history and I wrote down all of them on eight lines on notebook paper.

Q: You need to get as much information on one sheet as possible and write as small as you can comfortably see. However, you don't want to write so small that you need a magnifying glass to see it. OK?

A: OK. That makes sense.

Q: Let me ask you this. When you first started using ESS, how long was the first comprehensive outline you developed?

A: The first one was about seven or eight pages long. It covered parts of four chapters and my lecture notes.

Q: How long was the last one you completed?

A: Now I'm able to get them down to a couple of pages. Of course, I write very small.

Q: Joe, let's talk about a different but related topic for a moment. Success. Success as a student and success as a person. What would you say are some key characteristics that make for a successful student, or characteristics that lead to success in general?

A: Drive. Self-determination. That's the primary key. If you don't have the drive, you're not going to do it. The second thing is being able to organize your notes. If you can't organize your notes effectively, you're not going to do well. ESS has taught me how to organize myself to get the job done.

Q: What about Joe Yeiser as a person? If you take where you are now at twenty-nine years of age versus where you were at eighteen and what you've learned about life during that time, what characteristics have you discovered lead to success? What does it take to overcome adversity?

A: Hindsight first of all. Being able to look where you've been and learn from past mistakes. People say that hindsight is twenty-twenty, and that's true. But it doesn't do you a damn bit of good if you don't pay attention to it. If you look back on your mistakes and you either deny them or say "I don't care," you're going to make the same mistakes again. I look back on my high school education. When I was going to high school, I considered it a drag. I can only remember one teacher who actually tried to go out of her way to teach me a damned thing. Of course, back then, I was too stupid to listen.

Q: What got you through your battle with functional illiteracy, all those remedial courses, and the long struggle it took to get you to where you are today, a college student?

A: Realizing how stupid I really was. That's the only thing that got me through so far. I've got a long way to go yet. A long way. But I can look back where I was then and where I am now and there's no comparison between the two.

Q: What do you think it's going to take to get you to the next step?

A: That's the scary part. It really scares me when I think about it. But you can't just sit around thinking about it. You have to do it. It's going to take a lot of work. It's going to take probably ten times as much work, for me especially. I still consider myself somewhat underprepared.

Q: So you have found that hard work is an important ingredient in the formula for success?

A: Yes. That's probably factor number three. I mean, if you don't have the drive, you can't do it. If you aren't organized, you can't do it. And if you don't work toward it, you can't do it. Those are three strikes against you right there. If you don't care and you're not organized and you don't work at it, it's just not going to happen for you.

I see people like this in my classes. You can go through the motions and say "Well, Mom and Dad are saying that I should go to school and do this or do that. So I'll do it." Well, that's not drive. *You* have to do it. They can't do it for you. I look back at the way it was before I started seriously trying to educate myself. I mean, I couldn't even vote. Now I don't miss an election. There was a time when I couldn't read the ballot. All the information I got from the outside world was what I could get from the TV and radio. That's just how bad it was.

Q: Then you discovered books?

A: Well, you might say that books discovered me. One day my roommate hit me up the side of my head with a book and said, "Read it!" He was a reader. So one day I picked up the book and tried to read it. I couldn't at first. After a long struggle with reading, I finally got through it. I'll never forget it. It was James Michener's *Caravans*. By now, I've read practically everything Michener has written. I've read Louis L'Amour. Now I don't care what it is. I'll read practically anything and everything except pornography and Harlequin romances. I don't read those.

Q: Has ESS contributed to your appreciation of reading and what you can get from books?

A: It surely has. Well, reading textbooks is . . . For the most part, textbooks are dull. I mean, they will put you to sleep pretty quick. But with ESS, you don't read textbooks the way you read other material. You go through the text and learn to pick out important material, the information you will have to know to do well on the exams. So reading textbooks is not the same as when you read for pure enjoyment. You're doing a job. You're doing what has to be done. ESS teaches you a task-oriented approach to reading, a formula that shows you how to get the most from your reading. Before I knew about this system, the teacher would say, "Read this chapter." I would pick it up and read ten or fifteen pages. Then, the next thing I knew, I'd be sitting there daydreaming. Oh, I was still reading. But I didn't know what I was reading. With ESS, you learn how to dissect the chapter.

Q: Have you used the diagnostic component of ESS?

A: Yes. And I've found that I'm still not using my textbooks as fully as I should. It's still hard for me to spend forty or fifty dollars for a brand-new textbook and write all over it. But I'm working on it and getting better at it.

Q: That is important. The purpose of the textbook is to serve as a tool to help you master the course material, so it's important to use it most effectively by writing in it. Not to do so is like buying a brand-new car and not driving it. I have another question. Has ESS helped you with your self-confidence as a student?

A: Yes. Most definitely. I can remember taking tests from Dr. Bailey a couple of semesters ago. You would walk into his class and just sweat. I would go into his class on the day of the test and literally have the shakes. He would give you a two-hour exam. And he wanted to know everything.

Q: So you had test anxiety?

A: I would say that it was closer to a panic attack. It seemed like half the class was near panic attack. Today, however, it is completely different. I walked in to take a test last week and had no problem. Handling test anxiety now is a lot easier because of ESS. Mostly, that comes with the confidence of knowing that you have had a lot of quality study time and that you know the subject. This does a world of good in relieving test anxiety. One poor woman in Dr. Hall's class the other day almost had a fit. I thought she was going to break down crying and leave the room. I saw her later after the test and she was so fearful about failing it that she was paranoid. It turned out later that she passed it. I should have told her then to use ESS, because it sure took care of my problem.

Q: I take it then that you would recommend ESS to others?

A: You bet I would! After using ESS, there's no way I'll go back to my former study habits. Before ESS, I had never been taught effective organizational skills. I really didn't have much to work with. Therefore my two semesters of taking regular college courses was terrible. I had to struggle like hell to just barely squeeze by. Now, that is no longer the case because I have ESS.

Tamorah Vincent, age thirty-one; business management major

Q: To begin, Tammy, could you tell me something about yourself, your background?

A: OK. I'm thirty-one years old and, prior to last year, had not attended college for ten and one-half years. Last year, I decided to go back to school and get a degree in business management with an emphasis in human resources. My minor most likely will be psychology.

Q: What would you say is your career goal at this point?

A: I'd like to help a company or business operate more effectively and manage people from a human relations standpoint. I'm presently a legal secretary. At my job, I see a lot of mismanagement of people, of time, of details. Many situations could be handled in a much more productive manner to both get the work done and keep people happy.

Q: Since returning to college, how long have you been going to school?

A: About a year and one-half. Two full semesters and one summer semester. I work full time and go to school at night.

Q: How many semester hours do you take each term?

A: Anywhere from six to nine hours. Last semester I took nine hours.

Q: How did you first learn about ESS?

A: I found out about it at the college I attend. Several people were taking the seminars offered in ESS so I decided to sign up for one.

Q: Could you tell me what your grades were before ESS compared to what they are today?

A: Well, my grades before ESS were mainly B's. Not low B's or high B's, but in the middle range. So I was a fairly good student. However, since using ESS, I'm happy to say, I've made straight A's.

Q: What specifically has happened to you as a student since you began using ESS?

A: Several things, really. However, the primary factor for me is knowing how to construct a comprehensive outline to study from for each exam. Having the material from the textbook, my class notes, and other material all in one place has been wonderful. This way, when I get ready to study for the test, I know what to study. I'm no longer having to dig around trying to find information and then pull it all together at the last minute. Now I know how to organize things step by step over several weeks, and all I have to do the night before the test is sit down and study it. This way, all the guesswork has been taken out of it.

Q: Would it be accurate to say, then, that this study approach has helped you anticipate possible test questions?

A: Absolutely. With ESS, I get a well-rounded picture of what my classes are really about, what they encompass, what I need to learn from them. It used to be that I only learned things that I found interesting or that caught my eye. Now I have developed a trained eye. With ESS, I now know how to get everything I need to learn. Therefore I am able to get the full impact of the class, not just sections or bits and pieces of it. In other words, now I get a total learning experience from each class, not just a partial one.

Q: Is there anything else about ESS specifically that has helped you in your studies?

A: The outlining of the textbooks. I was always a pretty good notetaker and kept my notes fairly well organized. But reading the textbook was something else again. I would always put off reading until the last minute. I didn't enjoy reading textbooks because I wasn't getting much from them. It was just page after page after page of "stuff" that all seemed to run together. Now with ESS, however, things are different. I have learned to sit down and read my assignments in segments, "chunk" the material into smaller learning components, outline it, and really understand and retain it. I used to be lost in textbooks and didn't know what I was reading. ESS teaches you how to get down to the core material, find out what's important, and organize it effectively for exams.

Q: What type of time commitment did it take in the beginning, when you first started using the system?

A: It took me, on the average, about three or four hours extra a week compared to the amount of time I was spending before. That was in the beginning. Now the time commitment has been reduced dramatically because I've learned how to use the skills. Of course, even when you master ESS, it does take some time to prepare. This is just the way college is. However, with ESS, you learn to get the most from the time spent. The main benefit is when you do the final study session for each exam. Once I get to this point using the system, I just sit down with my outline and go through it page by page, question by question. Once my outline is completed, I can prepare for any of my exams in just a couple of hours.

Q: If you were advising high school and college students, what would you recommend that they do to improve their grades?

A: I would say to them that the key to success in school is organization and knowing how to pace yourself to get everything done. I think that's the key with ESS. You learn how to organize yourself, especially ESS—THE ADVANCED COURSE. You learn the key steps and skills for effective study and when to use them. This system teaches you how to pull all these elements together. Therefore, if other students want to make good grades consistently all the time, they definitely need to use ESS. I have seen a lot of so-called study books and systems. This is the only one I know of that really works.

Brenda VanDell, age forty; nursing major

Q: Brenda, could you tell me a little about yourself as a person, your background, and why you are currently in college?

A: You could probably describe me as a person who is always learning something new. It seems like I've been in just about every type of business there is. I started out going to beauty school to be a beautician. I went to secretarial school to be a secretary. Then I went to real estate classes to sell real estate and was in real estate sales for ten years. I also went to school to become a dental technician and did that for a while. A few years ago I started my college career part time and earned twenty-five semester hours before I recently began my studies in the nursing program. Now finally I think I've found my niche. For the past few years, I've really wanted to become a nurse.

Q: When you entered, what did you hope to gain from the nursing program? What are your goals now?

A: When I entered, I wanted to be the best. I wanted to gain from the nursing program the ability to provide a higher standard of nursing care than what I saw recently when my mother died. Like many of my classmates, I still want to be the best and to do what I must to make the best grades. However, it is a very tough program.

Q: **How long have you been in nursing school?**

A: I started last fall. So this is my second semester.

Q: **If you had to advise someone about being successful in life or being successful in any particular endeavor, what would you suggest that this person do?**

A: To never stop learning. To never lose the ability to want to know. To be curious. To go into depth. It is not enough to just look at something and take it at face value. It's important to go back and see what makes it work. What makes it work this way? Why do you want to do it this way?

Q: **How did you find out about ESS?**

A: The director of the nursing program recommended it to every student who was interviewed for admission to the nursing school. Many of us, therefore, were interested in finding out about the system and how it worked. I was especially interested because of my daughter, who is also in the nursing program. She didn't do well in high school at all. My main fear was that she would get into college and not know how to study. So we took the ESS seminar together.

Q: **How has she done in her studies since?**

A: The ESS system has helped her immensely. She is now making A's and B's. She just barely made it through high school. Now, however, she knows how to apply the information she is learning. ESS has taught her how to retain the information and apply it. And that is just great. We can both do that now. So it has helped her tremendously.

Q: **What has happened to you in your studies since you began using this system?**

A: Well, I took some college courses before I entered the nursing program and did very well in terms of grades. However, I couldn't tell you now what I learned. I simply could not retain it. I knew it for test purposes only. The ESS system, however, has taught me how to retain the information. I can now apply what I learned in the first level—the first semester—and use it. I still remember what I learned then.

Q: **So ESS has helped you in regard to your long-term memory?**

A: It surely has. It is fantastic. I can recall things. I can relate things and know what's going on. When I see a patient. . . . When I see something on a lab test. . . . For example, if one of their electrolytes is high or low, I can perhaps tell you why. And that's the only way you can give good patient care. You have to know what you've been exposed to in school and apply the information.

Q: **Are you saying then that you made good grades before nursing school, but "crammed" and therefore really didn't retain much?**

A: Yes. Crammed is right. I couldn't tell you much about anything I was exposed to before I started using ESS. I have had biology, political science, history, and so on. But I can't go back and tell you much of anything about these courses. By using ESS,

I now can tell you a great deal about every course I've had since. It has helped me tremendously. I can now read with understanding. My books are no longer just one big yellow mark where I highlighted practically everything I was reading. I now know what to look for, what is important, and how to apply it. I know how to use a highlighter pen strategically. It's a very good feeling. It really is. I generally read my chapters, integrate my book and class notes into my final outline, and study for tests just the way ESS says. Now I can condense fifty to seventy-five pages of reading for a course each week and all lecture notes into a three- or four-page weekly outline.

Q: When you first started implementing ESS—THE ADVANCED COURSE, how was it?

A: Oh it was real hard at first. I just wanted to throw it all against the wall. I think at first I must have had thirty pages of notes for every twenty-five pages I read. So I was a disaster at first because I had so many bad habits and so few skills. But as I went on, I got better at it fast. It has taken me a full semester and one-half to master it, but now I'm just about there. It feels wonderful.

Q: What about your self-confidence level now versus before ESS?

A: My self-confidence level now is very high. When I go into the hospital and my clinical situations, I no longer simply shake like I did the first couple of weeks. I now know what to do for my patients. And it's only because I used the ESS system for my benefit. I now know how to answer the questions my patients may have for me and explain to them why. And that's so very important. They don't like to hear just the definitions. They want to know why this is happening to them. And I can now address their concerns. This is because ESS not only teaches you how to find out what is going to be on a test, but it shows you how to think with the material as well.

Q: Do you have any advice for students as they begin to use ESS?

A: My daughter and I are now making A's and B's on tests, mostly A's. It is hard at first and you may want to give it up. We were both frustrated in the beginning. It seemed at first that all we were doing was reading and outlining. It just didn't seem to come naturally at first because we had so many bad habits. I mean, I'm forty years old and it's hard to break old habits. But like everything else worthwhile, if you stick with it, you will see results. Now it comes so naturally to me because I have retrained myself to do it right. It now only takes me half as much time to study as it did before ESS.

Q: Have you used the Diagnostic Follow-up component that is built into the advanced version of the system?

A: Yes. At first when you use ESS, you make mistakes. But with a little time and practice, it comes to you automatically. The Diagnostic Follow-up has helped to lead me to where I am today.

5 GETTING STARTED: THE ESS PRETEST

Now it's time to get started and to find out specifically how ESS works. However, before moving on to the next part of the book—ESS—THE BASIC COURSE—take a few minutes to complete the following instrument as honestly as you can. This beginning exercise will help you track your progress later in mastering ESS as a total study system.

Completing the ESS PRETEST

Be sure to date this pretest so you will have a record of when it was taken. In addition, write down in the space provided the grades you are currently receiving in the courses you are taking. If you are just beginning a school year or semester, record here your most recent overall grade-point average. When you complete this fifty-item inventory of student behaviors, compute your raw score using the key at the end of the book and record it in the space provided at the top of the pretest. This will be valuable information to have later.

For research and assessment purposes, the ideal situation is for you to take this pretest before being exposed to ESS—THE BASIC COURSE and ESS—THE ADVANCED COURSE. Near the end of the book (Part 4, MASTERING ESS), I will show you how you can assess your progress with ESS and document the changes in your grades.

ESS PRETEST

TODAY'S DATE _____
CURRENT GRADES IN COURSES BEING TAKEN (IF UNAVAILABLE, USE MOST RECENT OVERALL GRADE POINT AVERAGE):

    Course 1 _____; Current Grade _____

    Course 2 _____; Current Grade _____

    Course 3 _____; Current Grade _____

    Course 4 _____; Current Grade _____

(continued)

Course 5 _____; Current Grade _____

Course 6 _____; Current Grade _____

Current Grade Point Average (GPA) _____

COMPUTE AFTER TEST:
RAW SCORE _____ × 2 = _____ **Pretest Score**

Please respond to the following statements about student behavior. If you do engage in the behavior described in each item, circle Y for yes. If not, circle N for no.

Y   N   1. I use a dictionary regularly to look up unfamiliar words.

Y   N   2. I miss more than one or two days from school each semester.

Y   N   3. I am tardy for a class more than one or two times per semester.

Y   N   4. I regard my success as a student to be mainly the responsibility of my teachers.

Y   N   5. I regularly participate in class discussions (make comments/ask questions).

Y   N   6. I rarely sit in the front row in class.

Y   N   7. I almost always complete reading assignments before class.

Y   N   8. I sometimes daydream in class.

Y   N   9. I sometimes find it difficult to stay awake in class.

Y   N   10. I write my class notes in outline form as a regular practice.

Y   N   11. I sometimes use a tape recorder in class.

Y   N   12. I spend at least two hours of study for each hour spent in class (Example: 15-hour course load × 2 hrs. = 30 hrs. per week).

Y   N   13. I find it difficult to have enough time for study.

Y   N   14. I attended the first meeting of each class this semester (or the last school term for which I was registered).

(continued)

Y N 15. I sometimes miss deadlines for class papers/projects.

Y N 16. I sometimes ask teachers I plan to take in the future for a copy of their class syllabus.

Y N 17. I rarely if ever visit the class of a teacher I plan to take for a course next term.

Y N 18. I regularly consult a teacher I respect as an adviser.

Y N 19. I take five to ten minutes to systematically preview each reading assignment before I begin reading it.

Y N 20. I usually can tell specifically which text material is likely to appear on an exam.

Y N 21. Reading text material for class sometimes puts me to sleep.

Y N 22. My mind often wanders when I read textbooks.

Y N 23. I find it difficult to tell which paragraphs in textbooks contain the most important material.

Y N 24. I sometimes read textbook assignments two or three times in order to better learn the material.

Y N 25. Using a highlighter pen to mark portions of the required reading material is not very helpful to me.

Y N 26. I write notes to myself in the margins of my textbooks about the material I have read.

Y N 27. I find it difficult to identify the study aids authors design into their textbooks.

Y N 28. I regularly use Study Guides when they are available with my textbooks.

Y N 29. I rarely if ever outline my reading assignments in the book.

Y N 30. I make regular use of a weekly written calendar to budget study time.

Y N 31. I rewrite my notes taken in class in order to prepare for exams.

(continued)

Y   N   32. Compared with my other activities, I place study at the top of my priority list.

Y   N   33. I prepare for exams by condensing my reading assignments and class notes into a final comprehensive written outline.

Y   N   34. I effectively use "drill and practice" techniques to master all the specific material likely to appear on exams.

Y   N   35. I often put off studying until a day or two before a scheduled exam.

Y   N   36. I am confident with my note-taking skills.

Y   N   37. I usually get at least seven or eight hours of sleep the night before a major exam.

Y   N   38. I perform as well on essay exams as with other types of tests.

Y   N   39. I sometimes experience test anxiety to such a degree that it prevents me from doing my best on exams.

Y   N   40. I seldom make an appointment with my instructor to go over my test.

Y   N   41. I don't know how to use the library effectively to complete research assignments.

Y   N   42. I have an effective step-by-step method for completing term papers that enables me to get good grades.

Y   N   43. I usually take advantage of extra-credit opportunities.

Y   N   44. I don't have a clear understanding of plagiarism and what it involves.

Y   N   45. I have an effective method for writing a résumé to use in applying for jobs.

Y   N   46. I submit written papers to my instructors with few if any errors in grammar or spelling.

Y   N   47. I have a clear understanding of the key parts of an essay.

Y   N   48. I can name at least five memory techniques that I use regularly for effective study.

(continued)

Y   N   49. I usually write two or three drafts in preparing term papers.

Y   N   50. I don't know how to write an effective cover letter to a prospective employer for use in applying for a job.

TO COMPUTE YOUR RAW SCORE ON THIS PRETEST, CONSULT THE KEY PROVIDED IN THE APPENDIX.

PART 2

ESS—THE BASIC COURSE

Twenty Action Principles for Student Success

Quality is never an accident; it is always the result of high intention, sincere effort, intelligent direction and skillful execution; it represents the wise choice of many alternatives.

—Willa A. Foster
Commitment to Excellence

To build upon the general life principles already discussed, you will now be shown a concise but comprehensive system for academic success. This approach to study is called ESS, which stands for Effective Study Skills. It is a skill-based system designed to furnish you with the intelligent direction mentioned above in the quote from Foster. By using it, and all of it, you will place yourself on the road to quality performance as a student.

However, quality performance as a student, employee, parent, or anything else in life also requires the other three ingredients Foster mentions: high intention, sincere effort, and skillful execution. These are qualities and behaviors that neither ESS nor any other study approach can guarantee. They represent internal factors that are the responsibility of each person.

Let's briefly examine these three traits. Although ESS furnishes the needed intelligent direction, the successful student must also exhibit high intention, the deep-seated commitment to succeed and excel in school. In this regard, the most brilliantly conceived system in existence won't work if the desire isn't there and the goal to succeed isn't firmly in place. Then too, the successful person is one who is able to reinforce high intention with sincere effort. Most significant goals require a good measure of hard work and perseverence to achieve. Obtaining a good education is no exception.

Skillful execution is a final ingredient in the formula for peak performance. The person who intends to excel in school or in life's many other challenges must constantly try to improve performance by giving more effort to each task than is merely required. This means mentally rehearsing upcoming tasks, overpreparing for most tasks because of the desire to get things right, and believing strongly in the old adage that practice makes perfect.

If the preceding paragraphs describe you or characteristics you would like to develop, read on. You have the makings of a winner and you will find ESS indispensable in equipping you with the principles and skills you will need to excel as a student. You may already be an A or

B student who, through intuition or trial and error, has discovered some of the principles and skills contained within ESS. If this is so, acquisition of the entire ESS system will make you an even better student. In addition to learning more techniques, you will also learn how to order and prioritize your study skills.

By comparison, if you lack the characteristics of high intention, sincere effort, and skillful execution or the deep-seated desire to develop them, then ESS will be of little or no value to you. Success accrues to doers, not talkers; those who *impose their will* on a goal rather than merely *wish* for it.

As a prerequisite for the successful use of the complete ESS curriculum, you will need to accept and implement the following action principles until they become internalized as values about college life and manifested as everyday student behavior. Some of these principles are obvious. They are very simple and may appear to be common sense. The question you must ask yourself is "Am I applying them to my studies on a continual basis?" Other principles to be discussed are somewhat complex. They will require some time, effort, and skill-building on your part to master.

Even were you to read no further than this section and put into practice only some of these principles, you will enhance your academic performance. However, I hope you will implement all twenty action principles in order to receive maximum benefits. In addition, I hope that you will go on beyond this basic course in ESS to ESS—THE ADVANCED COURSE, which follows in Part 3. If you do and implement the four-step system contained there, the result should lead to superior academic performance within one or two semesters.

6 PRINCIPLES 1–5: THE BASICS FOR STUDENT SUCCESS

GETTING STARTED: How to Survive Your First Week at School

If you're like many students, particularly if you're just beginning studies at a new school or at college, you need to know what to do first to get started. Suppose, for example, you just acquired this book, school begins in a few days, and you don't have the time now to read it from cover to cover. You may have seen this heading in the table of contents and now have thumbed over to this page to see if there are any suggestions that seem helpful. Indeed there are.

There will be plenty of time later to read this book in detail. I urge you to do so as soon as possible. For now, however, it is important that you first complete the checklist that appears below to establish a firm foundation for the school term to come. If you will begin your first semester by doing these nine things, you will be well on the way toward establishing the habits necessary for student success.

The Survival Checklist for Starting Your First Semester

☐ 1. Choose a realistic, balanced class schedule to avoid burnout and class withdrawals later (see Action Principle 2).

☐ 2. Acquire textbooks and a good dictionary to have access to essential course materials (see Action Principle 3).

☐ 3. Attend all classes the first week to get positioned successfully for the semester (see Action Principles 5 and 6).

☐ 4. Read all first-day handouts (class syllabi) to understand the requirements of each course (see Action Principle 5).

☐ 5. Complete all reading assignments to avoid getting behind, which negatively affects grades (see Action Principle 7).

☐ 6. Sit in the front row in each class to stay alert and avoid distractions (see Action Principle 8).

☐ 7. Write comprehensive class notes to get the maximum benefit from class lectures (see Action Principle 9).

☐ 8. Visit the library to learn where to find basic resources that you will need to use later (see Action Principle 11).

☐ 9. Spend at least two hours in outside study for every hour spent in class during the week (see Action Principle 15).

PRINCIPLE 1: Take Responsibility for Your Performance

For any study system to be effective, the student using it must begin with (1) the commitment to succeed and (2) the willingness to implement the principles and learn the skills necessary to make success happen. These ingredients in large part comprise the Formula for Success discussed earlier. In a word, success for any of us requires that we take personal responsibility for it.

College and professional students (such as dental, medical, and law school students) in particular are expected to assume the responsibilities that accompany the academic experience. Most college instructors have neither the time nor the inclination to surpervise students closely concerning the completion of every assignment. Likewise, it is the exceptional instructor who checks on the daily progress of students and their study habits. Therefore the student usually is left to his or her own resources and is expected to take full responsibility and schedule study time carefully in order to meet all requirements and earn acceptable grades.

Those entering college or a private career school for the first time often experience a rude awakening. College, for example, is very different from high school in several respects. Some of these differences are pleasant; some of them can be potentially unpleasant, especially for the immature and undisciplined. Since you are an adult by the time you get to college, you are treated as one. This means no required study halls, no need for hall passes, and no report cards sent home to parents. How you spend your time outside class is left totally to you. If you cut a class or even three classes, rarely will an instructor say anything to you about it. Ah, freedom. How sweet it is!

Of course, freedom has its price, in school as with most everything else. That price is responsibility. Those who use their time wisely to *first* take care of their academic responsibilities will also come in first when the grades are passed out at the end of the school term. Those who foolishly squander their time because they lack the discipline or maturity to do otherwise will also reap what they sow. In most cases, they will earn mediocre to failing grades.

PRINCIPLE 2: Plan What You Take and Finish What You Start

It should be obvious from the preceding discussion that taking responsibility and being successful go hand in hand. One leads to the other. One important aspect of being responsible and successful involves the careful planning of your class schedule and the successful completion of each course. This is one application of the formula for success. If the goal of completing your education is really important to you, it deserves a carefully crafted plan. To successfully use this plan to achieve the goal, you must stick to it with dogged determination.

Plan Your Class Schedule Carefully To ensure academic success, the careful planning of your class schedule is important. It requires close attention each semester. Be sure to *see an academic counselor* before you begin your program of study and *check back with the counselor periodically* to make sure you are still on track. Think carefully about your other time commitments to family, job, and outside activities and *plan a class schedule that is realistic* given other responsibilities. In choosing courses each semester, try to *balance difficult courses with easier ones.* By doing so you will be less likely to overcommit yourself.

Avoid Chronic Withdrawals The W grade (withdrawal) offers you a nonpunitive alternative to an F should special circumstances arise that make satisfactory completion of the course impossible. Note that I said "special circumstances." School officials want you to succeed. They understand that the unexpected can happen. Anyone may experience a serious illness, a family or financial emergency, or an occasional course that just doesn't work. It is for these types of special circumstances that the W grade is designed. So if something like this happens to you, do not hesitate to exercise the W option. Although it will remain as part of your permanent record, it won't affect your grade-point average at most schools. It also is unlikely that one or two W's will hurt you. Even dropping all courses one semester because of a serious illness or other special circumstance will not damage your credibility as a student or as a person.

However, one of the worst habits you can develop as a student is to chronically withdraw from classes *each semester.* This is a very destructive pattern that may harm you in several ways. First of all, chronic withdrawals are a terrible waste of time and money. In extreme cases, some students foolishly squander thousands of dollars in lost tuition and a year or two of their lives by dropping many or even most of their courses each semester. Second, those withdrawals become part of your permanent record. If your transcript shows a string of W's semester after semester as a chronic pattern, you may still be in school, but the damage done to your reputation and credibility may take years to overcome.

Take a look at the actual transcript of Student A on the left (Figure 6–1) from an unidentified college. What does this record say to you about this individual as a student? What would be your assessment of this person's commitment to education? On a scale of one to ten, how would you rate this person's level of maturity? What about his or her degree of responsibility? Does this person appear to be focused on a goal? How about his or her organizational skills? Ability to use time effectively? Planning ability?

Now examine the transcript of Student B on the right. Ask the same questions. Imagine you are a prospective employer and you have received applications and supporting materials from both these students, who are applying for a part-time or even full-time job. In all important respects, they are equal except for their academic records. Which one do you think you would be inclined to hire? Why?

Let's examine another issue related to grades and student records. Imagine for a moment that you are a financial-aid officer at a college or university. Let's say Student B previously was awarded a government grant or loan to pursue a certificate or degree. His or her eligibility is now in question because, according to government and/or school policy, hours attempted versus hours completed may be one criterion used in making an assessment. A time limit for completing a program of study may be another. You have to make the decision regarding whether or not to renew or extend financial assistance? What do you think your decision might be?

The point to be made here is an important one. In this mass, impersonal society in which we live, our accomplishments and the records we amass to prove them are the primary criteria upon which we are judged. Schools we wish to attend, banks with which we want to do business, and employers for whom we would like to work aren't interested in what we say we can do. Anybody can talk a good game. Indeed, the world has a plentiful supply of fools and con artists who do just that by trying to get by on talk alone. Sooner or later, their actions become obvious to most people and they lead sad, empty lives.

What others tend to judge us by is what we have done. Our history. Our accomplishments. The employee evaluations we receive, the bills we pay, and the grades we earn all say to the world who we are as human beings. They tell the world about the standards we set for ourselves, our levels of commitment and responsibility, and many other things. The sooner each of us learns this lesson, the

A COMPARISON OF TWO PERMANENT STUDENT RECORDS

Transcript of Student A

ISSUING CAMPUS	I.D. NUMBER	STUDENT NAME			
BIRTHDATE	SEX	MAIDEN - OTHER NAME			

C A M P U S	COURSE IDENTIFICATION			G R A D E	SEM HRS CR	G P O I N T
	SUBJECT	NUMBER	DESCRIPTIVE TITLE			
	PRIOR SCHOOLS AMARILLO COL 1977					
	PHI THETA KAPPA					
	SPRING SEMESTER 89					
N	ENGL	1311	COMPOSITION I	B	3	9
N	CHID	1314	CHILDREN'S LIT	A	3	12
	HRS COMP EARNED GP GP AVG					
	6 6 21 3.50					
	1ST SUM SEMESTER 89					
N	PSYC	2311	GEN PSYCHOLOGY	A	3	12
N	MATH	1305	+INTRODUCTORY ALGEBRA	A	3	12
	HRS COMP EARNED GP GP AVG					
	6 6 24 4.00					
	2ND SUM SEMESTER 89					
N	MATH	1306	INTERMEDIATE ALGEBRA	A	3	12
N	ENGL	1312	COMPOSITION II	B	3	9
	HRS COMP EARNED GP GP AVG					
	6 6 21 3.50					
	FALL SEMESTER 89					
N	PHED	2311	EL REC GAME SK	A	3	12
N	ART	1320	ART HISTORY I	A	3	12
N	GEOL	1411	PHYSICAL GEOLOGY	A	4	16
N	ENGL	2311	EARLY BRIT LIT	B	3	9
N	MATH	1322	COLLEGE ALGEBRA	A	3	12
	HRS COMP EARNED GP GP AVG					
	16 16 61 3.81					
	*** DEAN'S HONOR LIST ***					
	SPRING SEMESTER 90					
N	HIST	1312	AM HIST SINCE 1877	A	3	12
N	ENGL	2312	LATER BRIT LIT	A	3	12
N	GEOL	1412	HISTORICAL GEOLOGY	A	4	16
N	ART	1321	ART HISTORY II	A	3	12
N	SPCH	1311	PUBLIC SPEAKING	A	3	12
	HRS COMP EARNED GP GP AVG					
	16 16 64 4.00					
	*** DEAN'S HONOR LIST ***					
	MINI 2 SEMESTER 90					
N	GOVT	2314	AM ST-L GOVT I	A	3	12
	HRS COMP EARNED GP GP AVG					
	3 3 12 4.00					

Figure 6-1

Transcript of Student B

ISSUING CAMPUS	I.D. NUMBER	STUDENT NAME		

BIRTHDATE	SEX	MAIDEN - OTHER NAME		

C A M P U	COURSE IDENTIFICATION			G R A D E	SEM HRS CR	G P / G R A D E P O I N T S
	SUBJECT	NUMBER	DESCRIPTIVE TITLE			

```
                    FALL SEMESTER 88
N  GEOL  1411   PHYSICAL GEOLOGY                C*    4    8
N  ECON  2313   MACROECON PRIN                  D*    3    3
N  ACCT  2311   ACCT PRIN I                     W*    0    0
               HRS COMP   EARNED   GP   GP AVG
                7          7       11    1.57
                    *** PROBATION ***

                    SPRING SEMESTER 89
N  MATH  1305  +INTRODUCTORY ALGEBRA            W*    0    0
N  ENGL  1301  +PREP COLLEGE ENGL               W*    0    0
N  GEOL  1412   HISTORICAL GEOLOGY              C     4    8
N  GENB  2315   BUSINESS LAW I                  C     3    6
               HRS COMP   EARNED   GP   GP AVG
                7          7       14    2.00
                *** PROBATION CONTINUED ***

                    MINI 2 SEMESTER 89
C  ECON  2313   MACROECON PRIN                  W*    0    0
               HRS COMP   EARNED   GP   GP AVG
                0          0        0    0.00
                *** PROBATION CONTINUED ***
**PROBATION CONTINUED APPEALS COMMITTEE 896**

                    FALL SEMESTER 89
N  MATH  0305  +INTRODUCTORY ALGEBRA            W*    0    0
N  ENGL  0307  +PREP COLLEGE ENGL               C     3    6
N  ECON  2313   MACROECON PRIN                  B     3    9
N  ACCT  1301   ELEM ACCOUNTING I               D     3    3
N  PHED  1117   AEROBIC ACT                     B     1    3
               HRS COMP   EARNED   GP   GP AVG
                10        10       21    2.10
                *** PROBATION REMOVED ***

                    SPRING SEMESTER 90
N  ENGL  1311   COMPOSITION I                   C     3    6
N  ECON  2314   PRIN MICROECON                  C     3    6
N  ACCT  2311   ACCT PRIN I                     C     3    6
N  MATH  0305  +INTRODUCTORY ALGEBRA            W*    0    0
N  REAE  2311   PRN OF REAL ESTATE              F     0    0
               HRS COMP   EARNED   GP   GP AVG
                12         9       18    1.50
                *** PROBATION ***
```

better off we tend to be. Therefore, as far as your school career is concerned, plan what you take and finish what you start.

PRINCIPLE 3: Develop a Personal Library for Success

Like most areas of endeavor, success as a student requires that you use the right tools. The cornerstone of scholarship is the ability to find key information, learn from it, and use it to increase your knowledge and skills. Whether you are a high school student, private career school student, college student, or graduate/professional student, it is important to establish your own library of key reference sources.

Although it would be ideal to acquire all of these sources today or in the next week or two, this usually is not necessary. Instead, make a concerted effort to obtain one each month. Set as a personal goal the completion of this core library of essential reference sources no later than six months from today. Once you have acquired these books, refer to them regularly.

Books You Should Use for Maximum Student Success

A Collegiate Dictionary   Increasing your vocabulary is an essential component of your education. To assist in this process, you should have and make habitual use of a good college-level dictionary. If you don't have one, you should obtain one *immediately*. Such dictionaries are available at practically all retail bookstores, including college bookstores. When an instructor or author uses an unfamiliar word, you can then look it up to increase your word skills and broaden your understanding.

Although there are many different dictionaries currently available, any of these described below would be a good choice for the student at the high school level or higher:

The American Heritage Dictionary, Second College Edition. Boston: Houghton Mifflin, 1985.

This dictionary contains 200,000 definitions and 3,000 photographs and illustrations.

The Random House College Dictionary, Revised Edition. New York: Random House, 1988.

This resource contains approximately 173,000 entries.

Webster's Ninth New Collegiate Dictionary. Springfield, Mass.: Merriam-Webster, 1988.

Probably the most popular of all collegiate dictionaries, this volume includes 160,000 entries and 200,000 definitions.

A Comprehensive Book on Study Skills   There are several books available that offer the student many valuable study tips. I urge you to examine them carefully and choose the one you feel is the most comprehensive and useful. After you do so, I am confident that you will decide to use the ESS system for student success. Keep this book handy at all times and follow its Principles, Steps, Skills, and Tasks closely. It will furnish you the master plan for getting superior grades.

A Thesaurus   The word *thesaurus* is Latin for "treasure house." A good thesaurus is indeed that for the writer. With it, you will be able to find the most appropriate and precise words to use for given ideas. This will enable you to use the written word with greater clarity and precision. Your grades on papers, book reviews, and other written projects most probably will show it.

I would recommend that you acquire one of the following:

Roget's II: The New Thesaurus. Boston: Houghton Mifflin, 1988.

The Random House Thesaurus, College Edition. New York: Random House, 1984.

Webster's Collegiate Thesaurus. Springfield, Mass.: Merriam-Webster, 1988.

A Book on the Fundamentals of Grammar   The use of correct grammar is essential to anyone wishing to become an educated person. How we speak reflects instantly on our social class and level of education. In addition, it also affects how seriously we will be taken by the listener. When we write, a similar assessment is made by the reader.

Therefore, not only is good grammar necessary to earn good grades in school—through oral and written reports, essay exams, term papers—but it also represents an essential form of power. Without the ability to use language clearly, precisely, and correctly, you stand little chance of being taken seriously as an employee, consumer, or citizen.

Of the many books on grammar currently available, this one is among the best:

Bazerman, Charles and Wiener, Harvey S. *Writing Skills Handbook* (2nd ed.). Boston: Houghton Mifflin, 1988.

This volume offers the most concise treatment of basic grammar that I have found. It provides nuts-and-bolts coverage of the sentence with all its parts and forms, the mechanics of writing, and composition. Condensed into 143 pages, it presents the fundamentals of language usage in a well-organized and easy-to-understand manner.

Two Classic Books on Writing Good writing is a complex craft that requires effective techniques coupled with lots of practice. If you are serious about developing your writing skills, acquire and use these books by Zinsser and Strunk and White. In all honesty, I owe much of my success as a writer and author to the principles I learned in these two brief volumes. The techniques and insight they provide can be invaluable to you as well.

Zinsser, William. *On Writing Well: An Informal Guide to Writing Nonfiction* (3rd ed.). New York: Harper, 1985.

This modern classic is regarded by many experts as one of the two best books ever written on writing. Using a no nonsense, nuts-and-bolts approach, Zinsser explains how to write well in a simple, straightforward manner. His book is an absolute must for students wishing to write A-quality papers. My copy is fraying and dog-eared from regular use.

Strunk, William, Jr. and White, E. B. *The Elements of Style* (3rd ed.). New York: Macmillan, 1979.

Called "the little book" by generations of writers, Strunk and White is the perfect companion volume to Zinsser. In fact, Professor Zinsser recommends that every writer read this brief volume by his colleagues once each year.

A Book on Writing Term Papers (Optional) All the essential steps in writing a research paper are covered in this basic course section of ESS (see Action Principle 13). By first examining the papers of students who have earned A's and then following the ESS format, it may not be necessary to acquire a separate book on this subject.

However, writing term papers in some courses may involve specific applications and specialized formats. In addition, students pursuing advanced academic or professional degrees will have to meet extensive and specialized research requirements. Under such circumstances a separate book on writing research papers is highly recommended. Among the best of these books are:

Lester, James D. *Writing Research Papers: A Complete Guide* (6th ed.). Glenview, Ill.: Scott, Foresman, 1990.

This book is especially useful because it covers how to write research papers on a word processor. It also includes computerized library sources, key reference sources by discipline, and the latest style changes for writing papers according to MLA (Modern Language Association) and APA (American Psychological Association).

Turabian, Kate L. *Student's Guide for Writing Research Papers* (3rd ed.). Chicago: University of Chicago Press, 1976.

This brief volume is considered a classic by many English instructors. It contains all the necessary information for writing an A-quality term paper.

NOTE: If you wish to purchase any of the books recommended above and they are not available at your campus or local bookstore, the store manager usually can order them for you.

PRINCIPLE 4: Actively Choose the Best Professors

Those who wish to get the most from their education should take an active role in choosing the best professors for the courses they take. If you currently are a high school student, you probably have little if any choice in the teachers you must take. However, when you do get to college, this principle will also apply to you. To gain the most from your classes, make sure that you use it.

College professors, like everyone else, vary significantly in competence, temperment, and style. A few are incompetent and hang on due to the inattention of a few equally incompetent school administrators. Some teachers are mediocre. However, most are average to above-average in the classroom. A few are brilliant scholars who publish with regularity and fewer still are master teachers. *The best and the rarest of the breed is the recognized scholar who also is a master teacher.*

The various distinctions among teachers continue. Some professors possess a keen sense of humor, others a dry wit, and a few appear to have no wit at all. Most will provide students with time and direction if asked, some will spend hours working with students on their own time, and there are always a few who won't give students the time of day. Some prefer lecture, others class discussion, and a few like to preach and proselytize. While this certainly doesn't exhaust all the possibilities, it is somewhat representative of the many types of professor.

Before we discuss how you can pick the best professors for you, let's examine two wrong approaches students often use. Some students pick a convenient time like 9:00 A.M. rather than a professor. As a result, they play a kind of Russian roulette with their education. Others blindly take the advice of other students without first ascertaining how competent those students might be to judge.

How to Choose the Best Professors

To choose the best professors for you, take the time a few weeks before the end of a current semester to do the following things (If you are new to the campus and time and distance permit, use these guidelines as best you can):

Accept Student Recommendations Only from A Students   Honor students are better sources than students in general. They are more likely to be interested in obtaining a quality education and want to make maximum use of their time and tuition dollars. Those students who recommend or don't recommend a professor based mainly on how easy or difficult they think the teacher is should be ignored. Such students are only interested in taking the path of least resistance. They shop for the easiest classes in an attempt to muddle through. This is the attitude of mediocrity. It is doomed to failure. Those with such a perspective in our highly competitive world almost always finish last if they finish at all.

Check the Credentials of Prospective Professors   The general credentials of faculty normally are listed in the college catalog. Check on those of the professors whose courses you're thinking about taking. What degrees do they hold? Where did they obtain them? All else being equal, a professor with an earned doctorate will be more knowledgeable about the subject than one with only a master's degree. Has the professor conducted any significant research? Has he or she published in the field? These are all important aspects to consider in making your decision.

Ask a Professor You Respect for a Recommendation   While this can be very helpful, be careful how you approach the teacher. Don't ask a faculty member "Who is the best teacher in the English department?" This approach will make most teachers nervous and uncomfortable. The result for you is likely to be no recommendation whatsoever or one that is not very helpful.

Simply ask in an open-ended fashion: "Whom would you recommend that I take for . . . ?" Even then, some faculty may give you a diplomatic reply such as "We have a fine English [or math, history, psychology] department. Any of our faculty would be good to take." However, if you ask a faculty member you respect and with whom you have some rapport, he or she often will give you a recommendation. A typical reply might be: "Well, you might think about taking——." Most teachers are on your side and want you to get the best education possible.

Make no mistake about it. Faculty know who the best scholars and teachers are at their institution because, in most cases, they have worked with them for years. They also may help answer your questions about the research and publication credentials possessed by the other professors.

Ask for a Copy of the Class Syllabus   If they have extras, many professors (or their teaching assistants) will be glad to give you a copy of the syllabus. Unfortunately, however, some colleges have very tight budgets for duplicating and extra copies just aren't available for prospective students. If that is the case, you might offer to pay for a copy or borrow one so you can take it to the library and make your own copy.

If a prospective teacher won't allow you to see or obtain a copy of the syllabus, think about what this could mean. Is this the professor for you? Likewise, if you obtain a syllabus from professor A that is one page in length compared with the ten-page syllabus of professor B, what might this possibly tell you about each of the two teachers? Such a comparison might be useful in deciding which teacher's class you should take.

Ask to Visit a Prospective Professor's Class   Provided there is room, most professors should feel flattered to have you visit their class. However, if a faculty member turns you down with some arbitrary reason or starts asking a lot of un-neccessary questions, don't take that instructor. These responses may indicate a mediocre, insecure, or rigid individual who would be a poor teacher.

When you visit a class, pay close attention to the professor's style, command of the subject, and degree of organization. Of course, there is no "best" style, and lecture, discussion, and other approaches can be equally effective. However, learning is a very personal thing. Some of us learn best with one style of instruction as compared with others. Also, some of us prefer an instructor with a keen sense of humor while others like a dry wit.

It's all very subjective. But if you like what you see and seem to click with the professor, that should be the best measure of whether you should take that person or another. By seeing professors in action as they actually are in the class-room, you will be in the best position to judge whether their teaching style fits your learning style.

Request an Appointment to Discuss the Subject and Course   In es-sence, this is an interview of the professor. This may be very helpful, particularly for courses in your major field. Once there, ask the professor (or teaching assis-tant) about the subject if you are unfamiliar with it, the course and its require-ments, the research interests or areas of specialization possessed by the professor, and any publications he or she might have.

Since this occurs so rarely, many if not most teachers will be pleased that you cared enough to take an interest. Most likely, they will be glad to tell you what you wish to know. This is useful information for you to have because it may pro-vide clues regarding how the prospective professor may teach the course. Since there are several theoretical perspectives in some academic disciplines, it is very useful for the student to know where the professor is coming from.

This interview will also help you in two other specific ways. First, it will give you a head start on others in establishing rapport with your professor. He or she will most certainly remember you and be impressed by the conscientious way in which you are approaching your education. Second, if the professor is willing to spend a little time with you, this will let you know how he or she regards students and where they fit on his or her priority list.

Unless a professor is extremely busy, such as being in the middle of a book or research project with a tight deadline to meet, he or she should be happy to spend a little time with any student who shows an interest. If busy, he or she should at least be willing to make an appointment to meet with you later at a more convenient time. In most cases, a teacher who can't or won't meet with you is not the professor you want for a course.

There are a few professors at most every college and university who, unfortunately, take a patronizing attitude toward undergraduates. They consider it beneath them to spend much time or energy with students, especially undergraduates. While some of them may be brilliant scholars, they are often lousy instructors who give disorganized, rambling lectures and talk at students rather than to them.

This you don't need. So if you will make an effort to actively choose the best professors rather than playing it hit or miss as many students do, you will be putting your valuable time and tuition money to their best use. In the end, your grades will most likely show it.

PRINCIPLE 5: Follow Instructions

As a student, it is important to recognize that, in most respects, education is not democratic. Of course, at the college level you are free to choose a school to attend provided you meet its entrance requirements and are accepted. In addition, you may elect to pursue any major offered by this school by filing and following the appropriate degree plan. Finally, you often may decide between two or more professors for most courses. Your choosing, however, should be done with care and diligence, because not all professors are alike.

Beyond these areas of discretion, however, you have little control over the formal educational process. Regional accrediting bodies, state legislatures, and college regents set the requirements for each degree or program of study. Academic departments and individual professors do the same for each course.

With this in mind, it is important that you follow the instructions established for each course very carefully to achieve maximum success in school. Unfortunately, it is commonplace for high school and first- and second-year college students to lose points and even letter grades or worse simply because they don't follow instructions.

How to Follow Instructions to Get the Best Grades

These guidelines are designed to help you use instructions constructively to maximize the number of points you will receive. If you will follow them closely, they will assist you in getting the best grades possible.

Always Attend the First Day of Class   Some students mistakenly register late or fail to attend the first day of class. Often, they figure that nothing important will be covered. In truth, the first day of class is the second most important day in the school term (the date of the final exam is the most important day).

It is on this day that the requirements and tone are set for the rest of the term. It is a mistake to assume that the professor will furnish each student with a well-written, detailed syllabus that explains all aspects of the course. A few professors give instructions orally and don't furnish a class syllabus. They expect students to take notes on the requirements. Some give only a very general one-page syllabus and fill in the details verbally. Just as important, students who miss the first class or two usually fail to get the first assignment and often have to play catch-up until at least the first exam is given.

Read Each Class Syllabus Carefully and Refer to It as Needed   Some professors do indeed give their students a fairly detailed class syllabus the first day or week of class. If such a resource is provided, it is your responsibility to ask for one if you register late or otherwise miss the first day. This syllabus becomes the blueprint for the course and is essential to follow. Think of it as a contract between you and your instructor that you agreed to when you signed up for a course. If you don't follow the syllabus closely and lose points as a result, you will have no one to blame but yourself.

Read Exam Instructions Carefully   Particularly with essay exams, pay close attention to what the question requires that you do. For example, you may be asked to describe, explain, analyze, or compare and contrast certain areas of course content. A detailed explanation of how to address these and other kinds of test questions is found in Part 3.

Follow Instructions for Papers and Projects to the Letter   Many instructors have their own format for writing research papers and book reviews and completing other projects. Make sure you understand what is being called for. See to it that your work is organized exactly as stipulated by your instructor. Often, otherwise excellent papers are marked down simply because the student didn't follow instructions. There is no hope of obtaining an A grade or sometimes even a C with most professors unless you do this.

Never Miss a Deadline   Part of the self-discipline required for success in school involves learning to pace yourself and properly manage your time. Most professors will deduct substantially for work turned in late and some will grant no credit at all. Students should understand that the end of the semester is busy for teachers too. Instructors have to set deadlines for students so that they can evaluate all work and meet deadlines imposed on them for turning in grades.

7 PRINCIPLES 6–10: HOW TO GET THE MOST FROM CLASS

PRINCIPLE 6: Attend Every Class

One of the strongest indicators of a conscientious and responsible student is regular class attendance. Almost without exception, students who consistently earn A's rarely if ever miss class. They know from experience that daily attendance is essential to derive the maximum benefit from a course. The student who misses classes should not expect to earn above-average grades and the student who misses excessively should not expect to complete the term with a passing grade. You would rarely miss showing up for work because chronic absence could jeopardize your job; the same principle applies to your class attendance and grades.

Those who chronically miss class say two things with their behavior. First, they do not place school very high on their priority list. This is evident not only by their absence but by some of the excuses they give. In almost twenty years of college teaching, I have heard some amazing stories. They have ranged from, "My neighbor's dog was sick and I had to watch her child while she took it to the vet" to "I was under the curse of the evil eye and had to have my body packed in herbs for several days to ward it off." No, I am not kidding. Second, students often don't realize that, with each absence that ultimately results in their failing or dropping out of school before attaining a four-year degree, they are taking at least fifteen hundred to two thousand dollars out of their own pocket in lost lifetime earnings.

However, the immediate results of missing class are very observable and easy to understand by the end of a school term or semester. When you miss class, you are missing course content that could appear later on exams.

In fact, the *only* way you will be able to remember the critical information likely to appear on exams is to first be exposed to all of it. Therefore, to miss any class is foolish because, when you do, you play a type of roulette with your grade. You miss information that the instructor might introduce that is not in any reading assignment. Some of this material could appear on the exam. When this occurs, you may be subtracting points from your grade before the test is even given.

To prevent this from happening, do just the opposite. By attending every class, you will be setting yourself up for success rather than failure.

PRINCIPLE 7: Complete Required Reading Before Class

Instructors assume that their students have read all appropriate assignments prior to the class session in which such material is discussed. Yet at least half of all first-year college students do not stay current with their assigned reading. They procrastinate and, by doing so, often hear the material cold for the first time in class, which they may or may not understand.

The most successful students complete their reading assignments ahead of time. Consequently, their learning is reinforced when much of the same material is then covered in class lecture or discussion. This way they derive the maximum benefit from each class.

If you will practice this principle as an everyday habit, it will benefit you as well. The results most likely will be increased learning and higher grades.

PRINCIPLE 8: Participate Constructively in Class

Successful students find it advantageous to work with their instructor to create a positive learning environment. Teachers, being human, respond best and usually teach a better class when students meet them halfway by cooperating and participating in class.

How to Participate Constructively in Class

There are several effective techniques for class participation that you can use to gain maximum benefit from your instructors and their classes. The best of these include the following:

Always Arrive at Class on Time   Not only is it impolite and distracting to be late, but you may miss key material in the first few minutes that could appear later on an exam.

Sit in the Front Row   It is very important always to sit on the front row or near the front of the classroom in order to see and hear everything more clearly. Since relatively few students strive for excellence and an A grade, you usually can find a front-row seat. If your instructor uses a seating chart, request to sit on the front row or near the front of the classroom at the beginning of the school term.

Where do you think most A students tend to sit? You guessed it. Most prefer to sit at the front or near the front of the classroom. Where do many if not most F students tend to sit? Again, you probably guessed right. Students who perform the poorest often sit in the back half of the classroom. Although exceptions occur to every rule, observe for yourself the seating locations of students in the classes you are now taking. You will find that these patterns often hold true.

By making it a practice to sit on the front row in each of your classes, you will benefit in several ways:

1. *You will be more alert* and thus less likely to daydream or go to sleep.
2. *The instructor will be more likely to learn your name* and see you as a person instead of a social security number.
3. *You will impress the instructor* as a student who really wants to learn (which is true).
4. *You will be less likely to be distracted* by the fidgeting and whispering of non-serious students, which tends to become more pronounced toward the back rows.

Be Prepared to Take Notes When Each Class Begins   Those who are not prepared when the class starts may lose points on exams because their class notes are incomplete. In addition, they create disturbances—by trying to find or borrow pen and paper—that may inhibit the learning of others.

Avoid Any Conduct Distracting to Other Students   This includes irrelevant conversation, whispering, eating, drinking, chewing gum, and so forth.

Participate Constructively in Class Discussions   Class participation facilitates active learning. This, in turn, translates into higher levels of understanding and retention. The result tends to be higher grades. By contrast, those who rarely if ever participate tend to become passive learners whose attention and interest may wane. Unfortunately, their grades tend to show it.

Ask Questions   In addition to general participation, be sure to ask questions of your instructors, particularly if you don't understand a key concept or point and need further clarification. Instructors are not psychic. They have no special abilities to know when you don't understand something. After the test, they may suspect a problem, but by then the damage to your grade already may have been done. Therefore, if you are confused or don't understand any of the content material, it is your responsibility to ask your instructor for added clarification or explanation.

PRINCIPLE 9: Take Effective Class Notes

Students who perform well take thorough and comprehensive notes in class. This is an essential habit to develop, because many instructors include additional material in their class presentations not found in the text or other required reading. As one professor has stated, "I teach the subject, not the textbook. The text furnishes only the foundation or background for the course."

Even if your instructor doesn't share this philosophy and teaches almost exclusively from the text, students who take detailed notes benefit in two essential ways. First, the class reinforces what they learned from their reading. This ultimately makes preparation for exams easier. Second, students receive valuable clues regarding specific information likely to appear on the exam.

How to Take Notes Effectively

Many if not most college instructors talk at a fairly brisk, conversational pace. Therefore, *do not try to write down every word.* This will not only frustrate you, it will result in a great deal of nonessential information that will have to be sifted and sorted through later. Instead, devise a system for notetaking with which you are comfortable but that also focuses on capturing the essence of the material covered in class. Some of the specific notetaking techniques that are most helpful are:

Listen Actively to Everything Said in Class   By listening carefully to everything the instructor says, you will be able to distinguish the essential information from the elaboration.

Focus your attention on identifying core or essential material. Much of this information—key concepts, principles, theories, and important thinkers and personalities—will be seen again on exams. However, the elaboration your instructor provides *about* key material is also important. Such things as examples, illustrations, and explanations furnished by the teacher may make the difference in whether or not you understand something well enough to answer it correctly on an exam.

Pay Attention to How Material Is Being Presented   Use these auditory and visual cues for notetaking:

1. *Listen for changes in the tone or volume of the teacher's voice.* Although instructors vary significantly in their style of presentation, often there are subtle and sometimes easily recognizable changes in voice tone and delivery when important points are being made.

    Some instructors, in effect, underline key material with their voice by changing the pitch or volume of their presentation. By listening for this, you can often "tune in" to the important material most likely to appear on an exam.

2. *Recognize that repetition of information by an instructor is done so for emphasis.* For example, an instructor may mention a concept, define it for you, and then immediately repeat the definition. You are likely to see such areas of content again on an exam.

3. *Listen and watch for all material presented in alphabetical or numerical fashion.* For example, if an instructor says "There are five types of . . . ," "The first point I'd like to make is . . . ," "Point A," "First of all . . . ," or something similar, you should pay very close attention for two basic reasons. *First,* the instructor is telling you with such language that he or she is about to make a series of points. *Second,* he or she is also informing you that these items of information are important. This is why they are being set apart by a sequence of letters or numbers.

NOTE: If you will now reread the last three sentences, you'll see that I have just modeled the point I was making by the manner in which I made it. Therefore, if you were being given an exam on the Twenty Action Principles for Student Success in ESS, you might get a question like this: "What are the two basic reasons why it is important to listen and watch for all class material presented by the instructor in alphabetical or numerical order?"

4. *Consider anything written on the blackboard (or shown on an overhead projector) to be likely material for exam questions.* Instructors often place this material there for emphasis and explanation to ensure that you write it down and remember it.

Write Notes in a Concise, Organized Manner   Follow these tips for maximum success:

1. *Develop your own form of shorthand.* Practice leaving out nonessential words such as adverbs, adjectives, and prepositions when possible. It is also helpful to develop a system of abbreviations and acronyms that have meaning for you. For example, an American history instructor may use use terms such as American, political, and Monroe Doctrine dozens of times or more. Abbreviations such as *Am, pol,* and *MoDoc* will serve just as well for note-taking purposes. Likewise, you could use the acronym MD for Monroe Doctrine even more efficiently.

2. *Write down core material as completely as possible.* Core material is that which is most likely to appear again on exams. It includes, among other things, key concepts and principles. For example, if your instructor identifies a key concept and writes it on the blackboard, includes it on an overhead transparency, or defines it repeatedly in class, write it down in as complete a form as possible.

NOTE: All of the basic forms of core material you will need to learn how to identify and understand for earning superior grades will be discussed in detail later in ESS—THE ADVANCED COURSE.

3. *Listen carefully when a teacher elaborates on core material and then briefly summarize it in writing.* Most of the content of any class lecture will be in the form of elaboration. *Do not try to write down all of this explanation verbatim.* If, for example, your instructor spends five minutes explaining and illustrating a concept or principle, listen rather than try to write down every word. Then, as you make the connection between the explanation and the core concept or principle, briefly summarize it in only a few words, phrases, or sentences.

4. *Write class notes in an outline form.* Although it will take some time and effort to master the skill of outlining, the rewards will be well worth the effort. You will have the class material in a concise, coherent form and will be able to master it more easily for exams.

NOTE: The skill of outlining course content for maximum effectiveness and straight-A grades is explained later in ESS—THE ADVANCED COURSE.

Do Not Use a Tape Recorder in Class   It is not advisable for most students to tape record class lectures even though some instructors allow it. Although the beginning student who lacks self-confidence and notetaking skills may find tape-recorded lectures self-assuring because "I got it all," such security blankets in most circumstances represent very inefficient and ineffective ways to learn.

If you are an aural learner who learns best by hearing things, then tape and play back the key points you have gleaned from your class notes and your reading assignments. Otherwise, don't use a tape recorder or abandon its use as soon as possible. For most people it is a poor substitute for good notetaking skills and a very inefficient and time-consuming way to learn class lecture material.

PRINCIPLE 10: Take Advantage of All Extra-Credit Opportunities

Some instructors allow students to complete optional projects and provide other opportunities to earn extra credit points. Take advantage of all such opportunities. This is one way to put into practice Lesson No. 10 from Life 101: *To succeed, you must give more than is merely required.*

This principle is so fundamental and simple that it requires little elaboration. Nonetheless, it is important to make a couple of brief points. First, when an instructor offers an extra-credit opportunity to students, it is offered to everyone.

In a sense, it represents a test to find out which students really care about their grades and try to do their very best. Second, those who don't complete such work are often the ones who need extra credit points the most. This tells their instructor that school is not one of their high priorities.

As a college educator myself, I give students an extra-credit option in some of the courses I teach. However, many students each term fail to take advantage of what, in some cases, could make the difference between one letter grade and another.

Students who do complete extra-credit opportunities tend to come disproportionately from two groups, failing students and good to excellent students. Failing students, as often as not, do not seem to fully realize that an F is imminent until a few short weeks before the end of the semester. Then, in a desperate last-minute move, some of them will try to throw something together to keep from failing. Unfortunately, the work usually shows it and it's a case of too little, too late.

By contrast, A or B students often will do extra-credit work to ensure the best possible grade. They possess the attitude of excellence and would be very much disappointed with average grades. As a result, these students rarely if ever make them. If you will adopt their attitude and always take every opportunity to earn extra points, your grades will be higher as well.

8

PRINCIPLES 11–13:
HOW TO USE THE LIBRARY,
ACHIEVE SCHOLARSHIP, AND
WRITE TERM PAPERS

PRINCIPLE 11: Use the Library

There are three main reasons for using the library. First and perhaps most important, the library is where the information produced from human civilization is kept, categorized, and cared for. As a repository for the ideas and wisdom of the ages, it can be a wondrous place in which to lose yourself for a time pursuing any one of a multitude of subjects. I'm sure you have heard the expression, meant quite literally, "You are what you eat." Well, from an intellectual standpoint, "You are what you read." With a steady diet of ideas and information consumed at the library, your mind should develop quite well.

Second, and more practically, the library is the learning-resource center for the school you attend. It is the place where you will find the information necessary to complete book reviews, term papers, and other research projects. In addition, most outside readings assigned by your instructors will be found there.

Finally, the library usually is the best place on campus to study. It is quiet; much of the information you need to finish your assignments is nearby or within easy access; and knowledgeable librarians are available should you need help. If your class schedule is such that you have an hour or two between classes, try to spend it studying at the library. In this way you will make maximum use of your time on campus and your grades will show it.

How to Use the Library

Ask a Librarian By using this section of ESS to develop a basic understanding of libraries, hopefully you won't need assistance too often. However, when you do, don't hesitate to ask a librarian for help. This knowledgeable person often holds a graduate degree and can save you a great deal of time in helping you find what you need.

Unfortunately, some students waste hours of valuable time floundering around in the library looking for something they don't know how to find. Others sometimes get discouraged and leave. In both cases, these students tend to be too bashful, too embarrassed, or too stubborn to ask for help. Don't let this happen to you. Librarians are there to help you. So use their services.

In most cases when you do need help, the librarian you should consult is the **reference librarian.** This person's primary job is to help library users find the information they need. Larger university and government libraries have several reference librarians who are specialists in certain fields such as physical sciences, social sciences, and humanities. For instance, if you are a student at a large university and need help in getting information for a paper in political science, you should consult the social science librarian.

Learn the Rules   On your first visit to the library, ask at the reference desk for a copy of the library rules or policies. Some libraries will include rules on a general information sheet or library guide. In any case, such information will help you use the library effectively. The most important policies will relate to such things as days and hours of library operation, checking out and returning books, overdue books and fines, procedures and costs related to computer searches and the use of other media, and interlibrary loans.

Find Key Locations   At your earliest opportunity, take a few minutes to go on a walking tour of the library. Its physical layout includes several key locations. Find out where they are and learn how to use them. Over the course of several semesters, you will need to use most if not all of them to gain the most from school. They include:

1. *The circulation (loan) desk.* This is where books and other materials are checked out, returned, and renewed. Also, if you wish to check out a book or periodical that is missing from the shelves, this is where you inquire about it.

2. *The reference desk.* One or more reference librarians will be located here waiting to serve you. Both general and specialized indexes and other reference books will be nearby to help you and them find what you need.

3. *The catalog of library holdings (card catalog).* Near the reference desk is where the card catalog or other form of library catalog usually is found. Although libraries today may use several catalog formats, the card catalog is the primary reference source for finding library holdings. Typically, it consists of several large cabinets with numerous traylike drawers. These drawers are arranged in alphabetical order and contain three-by-five cards (on books and related materials) that are alphabetized as well. Many libraries today have computerized catalogs in which library holdings are updated regularly in printout book form or are available online through the use of a computer.

4. *General reference guides.* In addition to the card catalog, several other general reference guides are available to you. They include:
   a. Both general and specialized dictionaries and encyclopedias (such as *Who's Who in the World* or *Encyclopedia of Associations: National Organizations in the U.S.*)
   b. Yearbooks (such as *Guinness Book of World Records*)
   c. Biographical indexes (including *Current Biography*)
   d. Book review indexes (such as *Book Review Digest*)
   e. Newspaper indexes (including *The New York Times Index*)
   f. Periodical indexes (such as *Reader's Guide to Periodical Literature*)
   g. Abstracting services (such as Educational Resources Information Center or ERIC, and *Psychological Abstracts*)
5. *Specialized reference guides.* These include:
   a. Government documents indexes (including *Index to U.S. Government Periodicals*)
   b. Specialized subject indexes (such as *Abstracts of English Studies* or *Humanities Index* in the humanities, *Social Sciences Index* in the social sciences, and *Applied Science and Technology Index* in the natural or physical sciences.
6. *Periodicals.* The term **periodicals** refers to magazines, scholarly journals, and other sources of information published on a regular basis. In the library, some will be bound and shelved like books while others will be stored or displayed as single issues. To find specific periodicals, consult the card catalog or other source of library holdings. One index source to consult for periodicals is the *Reader's Guide to Periodical Literature.*
7. *Microform.* Some periodicals and other materials may only be available in **microform**, a process consisting of several formats in which printed material is reduced and stored on small pieces of film. *Microfilm*, a common form, uses reels or rolls of 35-mm film to store newspapers, magazines, and other materials that are then read through a special viewing machine. Another popular format, *microfiche*, consists of flat sheets of film the size of index cards, each of which can store up to 100 pages of printed material.
8. *Stacks.* This term refers to the rows of shelves six to eight feet high where most of the books and journals owned by the library are stored. In large multifloor libraries with extensive holdings, the shelves on each floor are devoted to one or a few specialized subjects. Browse through the stacks to find the locations of specific types of books, particularly those related to your school major.

9. *Nonbook holdings.* Your library has many resources other than books, magazines, and other printed materials. Some librarians use terms such as *media, AV,* or *audiovisuals* to refer to such nonbook holdings. They include slides, audiotapes, films, videotapes, videodiscs, sound recordings on record and compact discs (CDs), maps, and artworks. In addition, larger libraries have viewing rooms and listening laboratories where you can view a vintage movie or newsreel, practice a foreign language, or listen to a wide range of music.

Learn How the Library's Holdings Are Organized   Most libraries organize their holdings according to one of two major classification systems: the Dewey Decimal System or the Library of Congress System. With either system, **call numbers** are placed both with each listing in the library catalog and on the spine of the matching book on the shelf. To know immediately which system your library uses, examine the call number. If it begins with numbers, the Dewey Decimal System is the one being used. If it begins with letters, the Library of Congress System is in use.

The complete classification charts for both systems are located in your library. However, a brief discussion of each, along with general classification categories, follows:

The Dewey Decimal System.   Smaller libraries often use a classification system developed by Melville Dewey at Amherst College in 1873. Called the Dewey Decimal System, it makes use of ten major categories.

The Dewey Decimal System

Call Numbers	Classification
000–099	General works
100–199	Philosophy, related disciplines
200–299	Religion
300–399	Social sciences
400–499	Language
500–599	Pure science
600–699	Technology (applied science)
700–799	The arts
800–899	Literature, rhetoric
900–999	General geography, history

Within each major category are subcategories divided by tens. For example, **The arts (700–799)** is subdivided as follows:

The Arts

Call Numbers	Classification
700–709	The arts in general
710–719	Civic and landscape art
720–729	Architecture
730–739	Plastic arts Sculpture
740–749	Drawing and decorative arts
750–759	Painting and paintings
760–769	Graphic arts Printmaking and prints
770–779	Photography and photographs
780–789	Music
790–799	Recreational and performing arts

The Library of Congress System   Larger libraries typically use the Library of Congress system. It contains twenty-one major categories arranged alphabetically. Many librarians prefer it over the Dewey system because it allows for the logical classification of many more items.

The Library of Congress System

Letter		Classification
	A	General works
	B	Philosophy, psychology, religion
	C	Auxiliary sciences of history
	D	History, topography (excluding America)
	E	American history
	F	United States local history
	G	Geography, maps, anthropology, recreation
	H	Social sciences
	J	Political science
	K	Law
	L	Education

The Library of Congress System *(continued)*

Letter		Classification
	M	Music
	N	Fine arts
	P	Language, literature
	Q	**Science**
	R	Medicine
	S	Agriculture
	T	Technology
	U	Military science
	V	Naval science
	Z	Bibliography, library science

Each of the letters above may be divided into subcategories by the addition of another letter. For example, when **Q**, which stands for **science**, becomes QB, the classification is for astronomy. In addition, any number from 1 to 9999 may be added to a combination of letters to form additional subcategories. Therefore, QB 46 represents juvenile works (in astronomy) and QB 460 is the call number for astrophysics.

Use the Catalog of Library Holdings (card catalog)   The **card catalog** contains three types of cards. First, there are the *author cards* that contain the library's holdings arranged by author's name in alphabetical order. Sometimes you may need to find a book without a designated author that is published by a governmental agency or other type of organization. In this case, the book will be listed here under the name of the organization. Second, *subject cards* list the books contained within the library by subject area. Third, *title cards* contain an alphabetical listing of books by their titles.

Each card in these three categories contains five important items of information:

1. *Listing entry*. The author (last name first), the subject, or the title of the book appears at the top of the card.
2. *Call number*. Placed in the upper left corner, this number enables you to find the book marked with the same number in the stacks. If the initial REF appears above the call number, the book is located in the reference section of the library.

3. *Bibliographical entry.* Sometimes called the imprint, this appears directly below the listing entry. It includes the author, title, edition, place of publication, publisher, and date of publication.

4. *Collation.* Directly below the bibliographical entry, information appears such as the number of pages contained in the book, whether it includes illustrations, and so on.

5. *Tracings.* Near the bottom of the card, additional information such as the subject headings under which the book is found in the card catalog is included. By examining these headings, you may get some clues regarding the contents of the book.

In addition to the traditional card catalog, your library probably will have its holdings cataloged in other ways as well. Large libraries often have a **book catalog** located on each floor. Now usually bound from computer printouts, a book catalog has the advantages of being portable and easily updated. Another variation is the **COM** (computer output microfilm) **catalog**, a list of holdings placed on microfilm. Since this format also is portable and requires little space, some libraries have these catalogs and COM reading machines placed at various locations.

Finally, the computerized **online catalog** is fast replacing the traditional card catalog in terms of student use. This consists of a computer workstation with a keyboard and screen. To use it, you need only learn a few simple commands. Given the ongoing advancements in computer technology, the day is fast approaching when many if not most students will be able to use an online catalog and other library services at home on their own computers.

Check Out Books Early   If your instructor assigns you a research paper, book review, or other written project, go to the library, find the sources you need, and check them out early in the semester. Remember, several other students may be looking for the same sources. If you wait until only a few days before the assignment is due, many of them may already be checked out.

Use Other Libraries   If you can't find the information you need at your school library, don't hesitate to use others. Most communities in America have a public library and one or several college libraries nearby. College instructors are rarely sympathetic when a student says "I couldn't find much information."

One way to benefit from the resources of other libraries without leaving your own is to make use of an **interlibrary loan**. Check with your reference librarian to see if your library has this service available to students. If it does, books or other materials you need, but which are unavailable at your library, may be borrowed from another institution at a nominal charge. Some libraries have agreements established with other area libraries just for this purpose. In other instances, it is often possible to obtain a book on loan from a major library hundreds of miles away.

PRINCIPLE 12: Practice the Ethics of Good Scholarship

Intellectual honesty is one of the important hallmarks of successful students and scholars. The best students also tend to be the most ethical in that they subscribe to a code of conduct that guides their behavior both in and out of the classroom. It is important for them to know that they earned their grades and credentials honestly and independently without asking for inappropriate help or taking unfair advantage of other students or anyone else.

As citizens and consumers in the larger community and society, it is also important for them to feel assured that the physicians, accountants, technicians, clerks, teachers, and others whose services they use have earned their grades and credentials in a legitimate manner. Consequently, ethical behavior and accountability for students at all levels of education is in the best interests of practically everyone.

You can set a good example for other students with regard to intellectual honesty by acting on these two precepts:

Carry Out Important Student Responsibilities on Your Own Taking exams and writing research papers is your responsibility alone; avoid using inappropriate outside assistance. Likewise, try to guard against providing any such assistance to those who may try to corrupt you by getting you to assist them in some form of cheating. If, for example, you are taking an exam and someone tries to look at your paper, use a cover sheet, move to another location, or tell your instructor.

Always Assign Proper Credit Where It Is Due Particularly in the completion of research papers, it is important to give credit to the ideas and research of others. The word *plagiarize*, for example, is defined as "to take and use as one's own the writings and ideas of another" (*American Heritage Dictionary of the English Language*, 1977, p. 1001).

In the world of academic and professional writing such behavior is not only unethical but illegal as well, with the accused subject to charges of literary theft or copyright infringement. For college students, gross plagiarism on a research paper normally carries a penalty ranging from a zero on the paper or an F in the course to dismissal from school.

Therefore, always be sure to use quotation marks, citations, and so forth in order to properly assign credit. If you have any doubt how to do this, consult your English instructor for assistance or purchase a style manual for preparing theses and research papers from your college bookstore.

PRINCIPLE 13: Prepare Term Papers as if Applying for a Job

Both getting a good job and writing a good research paper require a similar attitude about the task at hand. This attitude is reflected in Lesson 10 from Life 101: *To succeed, you must give more than is merely required.* Let's examine briefly how this life principle is applicable here.

Those who succeed in obtaining full-time positions in the labor force realize that appearances count in applying for and interviewing for jobs. In the competitive world in which we live, few employers will hire those who turn in incomplete and sloppy applications and résumés and dress and act inappropriately in interviews. Successful applicants are those who take extra steps to convince the prospective employer that they are the best person for the job. From the employer's vantage point, those who exhibit such characteristics also are more likely to take pride in their work and do an excellent job.

High school and college students also live in a competitive world in terms of grades. To get the best grade on a research paper, book review, or other written project, appearances also matter. Those who earn A's almost always take extra pains to make sure all written work is neatly typed with correct spelling, grammar, and punctuation. You should never expect to obtain a job interview with a handwritten or poorly typed résumé with errors and smudges; the same applies to getting good grades on school papers.

Professors may read hundreds of papers each semester. They assume, and rightly so, that the best ones almost always stand out from the crowd in appearance and form as well as in content. Students who take pride in how their work looks usually take the same care in making sure the content of their work is superior as well.

Excellence is an attitude and a habit. Those who practice it adopt it as a way of life and are constantly trying to do their best and improve upon what their best is in all areas. This attitude is reflected in the quality of work people do. Employers recognize this quality in the job applicants who are hired. Professors look for it in the few students who earn A's. If you will apply this principle, this will help you earn A's too.

How to Write an A-Quality Research Paper

Required research papers are designed as exercises to produce a trained mind and a thinking person. To complete these exercises successfully involves learning an organized process to discipline the mind and become an effective scholar. Once you have mastered the steps and skills that go with this process, you will not only be a more effective learner but will also receive the best grades.

There is a fairly standard formula for writing research papers that get A grades (see Table 8–1). If you follow it without deviation, you will receive superior grades too. It is always important to keep in mind that A grades don't just happen; they must be planned. Here is the plan to follow.

Before You Start

1. *Learn and follow instructor requirements.* Most instructors have specified requirements for written papers. Make sure that you know and follow them closely. Such guidelines typically include a range of acceptable topics, required elements and general directions, the number and type of required sources, and a specified deadline.

2. *Examine A papers.* The best way to fully understand the standards used to grade your paper is to examine some A papers. Unfortunately, many students write blind. They often make assumptions about what constitutes a good paper without testing their perceptions against reality. By choosing to write their papers in the dark, they often receive poor grades. To avoid falling into this trap, ask your instructor if you can see some examples of A-quality papers. If this is not possible, ask students who have received A's on papers if you can see their work.

Table 8–1—The Ten Steps in Writing a Research Paper

1. Select a topic
2. Establish a purpose
3. Write a preliminary thesis statement
4. Gather information and take notes
5. Write a final thesis statement
6. Construct a working outline
7. Write the first draft
8. Edit and revise
9. Write the final draft
10. Prepare and present the completed paper

3. *Allow adequate time.* Start papers and projects early in the term and turn them in early if possible. You will need the last few days before the end of the semester to prepare for final exams. By pacing yourself carefully, you will be able to give your work the careful attention an A paper needs. Quality is not something that can be hurried.

Once you have accounted for specific requirements, standards of quality needed to get an A, and the time necessary to do it, you are ready to begin. Here is what you do, step by step.

Step 1: Select a Topic   The **topic** is the field or subject on which you wish to write. Topics for research papers are varied. They can range from abortion to the Versailles Treaty of 1918, from photosynthesis to Sigmund Freud. If your instructor doesn't assign a topic, choosing one sometimes can be difficult.

How to Select a Topic   To simplify the choosing of a topic, carry out the following tasks in order:

1. *Choose a general topic you like (if possible).* As long as you stay within the guidelines established by the instructor, it usually is best to choose a topic in which you have some interest. In the final analysis, your paper is more likely to get written and written well if the topic intrigues you. Depending on the course, examples of general topics might include the Civil War (American history), human physiology (biology), the Lake Poets (English literature), or deviant behavior (sociology).

2. *Consult general sources on the topic or topics you are considering.* Sometimes students devote several hours to a topic and have much of the preliminary writing done before realizing that they have chosen an unworkable subject. It may be too general, too specific, or of little importance. Sources may be difficult to find or practically nonexistent.

   To avoid such problems, read a general article or two about the topic to see if it has merit for you. (An encyclopedia article on the general topic is a good place to start.) As you read, examine how the authors approached the topic, the subheadings they used, and their bibliography. Doing this should provide you several useful clues about how to decide on a specific topic and organize your paper. If it doesn't, consider changing topics.

3. *Decide on a specific topic.* In making such a decision, keep three issues in mind. First, the topic should have a *clear relationship to the course* in which it is required. Second, it should be manageable given the nature and level of the course and the time available for the paper's completion. In other words, don't bite off more than you can chew. Guard against choosing a

topic that is either too general or too specific or technical. Also make sure that sources for your topic are both plentiful and available. Third and most important: Take care that the topic is *satisfactory to your instructor.* If you have any doubts, be sure to ask.

Step 2: Establish a Purpose   It is not enough to simply choose the *What* or topic of your paper. You must also develop a central purpose by deciding *How* you will treat the topic. The **purpose** in a formal research paper is the specific approach you intend to use in writing on a specific topic. As such, it represents the unifying theme that gives the paper focus and direction.

Five Popular Approaches to Purpose   Depending on the topic, you may decide to use one or a combination of several different approaches in developing the thrust of your paper. Common purposes used in term papers and other written class projects include chronology, explanation, analysis, comparison, and persuasion.

1. *Chronology.* Refers to the tracing of the topic from one point in time to another. Example: The development of sociological thought in Europe during the nineteenth century.
2. *Explanation.* Divides the topic into component parts, describes them, and then cites causes or reasons why they are important to the overall topic. As such, it does not represent true investigative research. Rather, it is designed to report on, review, or summarize the research of others. Examples: Book reviews and article reviews.
3. *Analysis.* Involves the presentation of facts about key aspects of the topic, the amassing of evidence to explain and support the facts, and the presentation of conclusions based on the evidence and facts. The analytical approach involves the determination of causes or reasons that explain the topic. It includes the identification of important elements related to a topic coupled with an explanation of how they interrelate and should be prioritized. Examples: An examination of factors leading to the Great Depression (history); An analysis of hormones as a physiological factor affecting sexual functioning in humans (biology).
4. *Comparison.* Refers to an examination of two or more elements of a topic in terms of similarities and differences. Example: A comparison of the psychoanalytic and behaviorist approaches in psychology.
5. *Persuasion.* Requires that the writer take a position on an issue or topic and argue convincingly through the use of good evidence and sound logic. Un-

like chronology, explanation, analysis, and comparison (used primarily to inform the reader), the persuasive purpose seeks to sway the reader to the writer's point of view. Example: The threat of world overpopulation on the future of humanity (English composition, sociology, speech).

NOTE: Depending on the course and instructor, some of these purposes may be more appropriate than others. If in doubt, ask your instructor.

Step 3: Write a Preliminary Thesis Statement   In one sentence, write down your planned topic and specific purpose as clearly as you can. This will serve as a guide as you proceed to gather your sources. Recognize, however, that this statement is designed mainly to get you started. In all likelihood, your final thesis statement will be modified and perhaps changed altogether once you have had the opportunity to examine available sources.

Step 4: Gather Information and Take Notes   Next, you need to gather information from appropriate sources and take effective notes. Before doing so, however, it is important to understand the nature of scholarly research and the nature of sources that should be used.

The Nature of Research   To write a genuine research paper, the writer must begin with neutrality or objectivity about the subject. In keeping with the spirit of the scientific method and the rules of evidence observed by most disciplines, scholarship represents an orderly process of discovery, critical thinking, and interpretative evaluation by the student. The result is increased knowledge and insight about the topic discussed.

The Nature of Sources to be Used   Always use the best and most up-to-date sources available. The grade given your paper will be based in part on the quality of your sources. Professional and academic journal articles and books written by respected scholars with legitimate credentials are appropriate. Popular periodicals such as *Reader's Digest* usually are inappropriate in formal papers. If used at all, they should be used sparingly. In addition, nonscholarly periodicals, books published by interest groups with a biased editorial position, and those written by pop writers, journalists, and clergy are also inappropriate in most cases. If in doubt about the suitability of any source, ask your instructor.

Especially for papers on social issues, up-to-date sources are essential. For instance, a paper dealing with the disease and issue of AIDS would be considered poorly researched if the most recent citation listed in the bibliography was two or three years old.

A Step-by-Step Guide to Gathering Information Gathering information involves consulting the most appropriate sources at a good library. This perhaps can best be accomplished by performing several tasks in this sequence:

1. *Consult the subject index in the card catalog.* Every library has a card catalog with subject, title, and author (name) indexes. Find your topic in the subject index. Then examine the sources listed.

2. *Prepare source cards.* Using a three-by-five-inch index card for each book, write down the call number, title, and author of each source you want to examine. To save yourself additional research time later, also write down the place of publication (city and state), the publisher, and the year of publication. Then, armed with your completed source cards, go to the stacks to find them.

   NOTE: Be sure to keep all source cards, for now. They will come in handy later.

3. *Conduct a citation search from available books.* As you examine these books derived from the subject index, look carefully at the citations or references used by the authors. References most likely will be found in the bibliography. Make additional source cards from those citations that interest you. With articles from journals and other periodicals, be sure to include the title of the article, the name of the journal, the date or month and year of publication, volume number, and page numbers.

4. *Consult the author (name) index.* After completion of the citation search, return to the card catalog and look through the author index for the books you have listed as likely sources. If you find some of these books listed in the holdings of the library, record the necessary call numbers on your source cards. Then return to the stacks. As you find some of these books, conduct a citation search of the bibliographies and continue the process until you are satisfied that you have sufficient sources.

5. *Conduct a citation search of available articles.* This should be done in two steps. First, go to the periodicals section of your library, find the articles you have already listed from your citation search of available books, and examine the references or bibliographies used by their authors. This should help you identify more articles and books that you can examine. Then consult the appropriate index or indexes to find additional up-to-date articles you might wish to use. In most cases, you can find much of what you need by using one or more of these indexes:

Reader's Guide to Periodical Literature (usually only appropriate for finding articles in science-related periodicals such as *Physics Today, Psychology Today, Scientific Review,* and *Science Digest*)

Arts and Humanities Citation Index, 1977–present

Science Citation Index, 1961–present

Social Sciences Citation Index, 1966–present

6. *Consult the reference librarian for additional source materials.* For example, most college and university libraries today have computer-search capabilities. Your reference librarian can explain which database searches are available, how much they cost, and how to use them.

Advanced Applications   The preceding six-step method usually is best for high school students and first- and second-year college students. Those more experienced with the library needing to conduct advanced research may find it best to modify this approach to suit their particular purposes. For instance, a graduate student doing thesis research might wish to begin with one or more computerized database searches and use such additional specialized sources as *Dissertation Abstracts.*

How to Take Notes   After gathering together your sources of information, you will need to organize your material and take detailed notes. These guidelines should prove useful in setting up your note cards.

1. *Use large note cards.* Because they will hold more information, it is best to write detailed source notes on four-by-six or five-by-eight-inch index cards.

2. *Place only one idea or item on each card.* It will be easier to organize information later if each note card only contains a single idea or item of information. If, however, you wish to write notes on the same idea from three or four different sources, use a separate card for each source and label accordingly. For example, you could label the first card A, the second card B, and so on.

3. *Label each card clearly.* This should be done as follows: First, print in capital letters the author's name in the upper-left corner of the card along with the page numbers from which the material came. In the upper-right corner, print in capital letters the idea or item written about on the card. Finally, if you write on the back of the card, be sure and write the word *over* in the lower-right corner. This will help ensure that nothing is overlooked later.

4. *Write notes in complete form.* It will save you time later if you write all notes in complete sentence and paragraph form. If you think you may want to quote something directly, place this material in quotation marks and record

the page numbers carefully. Good writing takes much time and careful editing. The more complete your notes, the easier it will be to write a good first draft later.

5. *Convert source cards into bibliography cards.* Find each three-by-five source card that corresponds to a larger note card and separate it from the rest. Take *these* source cards, place them in alphabetical order, put a rubber band around them, and keep them in a safe place. These are the bibliography cards you will use later to construct the References or Bibliography section of your paper.

Step 5: Write a Final Thesis Statement   Once you have decided on a topic and purpose and you have gathered and recorded information from your sources, the next step is to formulate a thesis statement. A **thesis statement** is a one-sentence scholarly declaration that explains in summary form how the paper will be written. Put another way, it serves as an organizing device to give your paper unity and direction.

Writing an effective thesis statement involves combining the topic and purpose in a focused way to establish specifically how the paper will unfold. Doing so provides an investigative thrust to the paper that will lead, in many cases, to the emergence of conclusions. This example illustrates how a thesis statement emerges out of the first four steps:

Topic: Propaganda

Purpose: To examine the development of propaganda during the twentieth century.

Thesis Statement: Twentieth century propaganda has evolved most notably in certain countries and has taken very specific forms because of a variety of factors.

Three Characteristics of an Effective Thesis Statement

1. *It should be a declarative sentence* that explains how a specific topic will be handled. A thesis statement that simply restates the topic or purpose with no additional specifics is of little value.

2. *It should provide a reason why the topic is to be discussed.* Does the statement indicate that the topic has significance? Does it point toward an explanation of the topic? A topic simply tells us "What." A thesis statement goes one step further and explains to us "So what." It helps show why this topic has importance.

3. *It should emerge from the information and evidence gathered through re-*

search. A proper thesis statement is based on the information compiled on note cards from the sources consulted.

Step 6: Construct a Working Outline Most good writers use an outline to give their writing focus, clarity, and direction. It keeps them organized. As far as research papers are concerned, the best ones almost always are written from an outline.

You can use an outline in two ways to receive the best grade. First, it will help you to organize your thoughts so that you can deliver a paper that says something with clarity and punch. Second, you can show your outline to your instructor to get feedback regarding how you plan to handle the topic. Some instructors will be glad to look at your plan for the paper and may provide you with valuable input.

How to Construct an Outline for a Term Paper

1. *Begin with the thesis statement.* Write your thesis statement first. It will provide the rationale and direction for the outline to follow.

2. *Examine and organize your note cards.* First, read the note cards you developed at Step 4. Their convenient size and concise form will be invaluable to you because all materials needed for constructing the outline and writing the paper are now at your fingertips. You no longer need the heavy and bulky books and journals from which you took notes.

   Second, arrange your note cards in the order in which you plan to discuss key ideas and items of information in your paper. Once organized in this manner, these note cards can be used to construct a working outline without much difficulty.

3. *Decide on how much depth to use.* The amount of depth to place in the outline is a matter of student or instructor preference. In some cases, a listing of major topics and subtopics is sufficient. In other instances, students may find it more useful to write a sentence or even an entire paragraph under each heading. However, you may find this principle helpful: Generally speaking, the more in-depth the outline, the easier it is to write the paper.

4. *Use outline notation.* For organizational purposes, major headings in your outline should begin with Roman numerals, first-order subheadings with capital letters, and so forth. Depending on course requirements, most college term papers will vary in length from five to twenty pages. Therefore use the number of heading and subheading levels most appropriate to the length of the paper.

   The following example shows too many levels of detail for most college papers because there aren't enough pages available to develop all these points. However, a graduate-level paper twenty-five to forty pages in length or longer would benefit from an outline this detailed.

I.
  A.
    1.
    2.
      a.
      b.
        (1)
        (2)
          (a)
          (b)

NOTE: Each heading level must have at least two headings of equal value. A Roman numeral I requires a II, an A necessitates a B, a 1 must have a 2, and so on. In addition, all periods should align:

I.
II.
III.
IV.
V.

Step 7: Write the First Draft Writing the first draft of anything substantial is similar to being a high-wire performer on a tightrope. It can be challenging and exciting but scary at the same time. To face an empty page knowing that whatever you write on it ultimately will be seen and evaluated by others can evoke similar feelings.

However, a first draft is not a final performance. It is only a practice session. It is aimed at developing on paper the ideas that eventually will lead to the final polished product. Just as the aerialist must walk the tightrope and fall off several times to develop a routine, you must get your ideas down in written form to develop your paper. Mistakes in spelling, grammar, syntax, punctuation, and sentence form will be made because they are a part of the process. This happens to the best of writers as they write, rewrite, and rewrite until their work is acceptable for presentation. There will be time later to polish and refine the manuscript. The important thing at this point is to start writing.

Guidelines for Writing the First Draft   The first draft is written from the note cards and outline. As you proceed, follow these guidelines:

1. *Allow adequate time.* Good writing is rarely hurried. Try to begin your first draft at least a few weeks before the paper is due.

2. *Write a preliminary title.* An effective title has three characteristics. First, *it is clear.* It states the topic and its scope in a manner understandable to the reader. Second, *it is brief.* A wordy title may bore or confuse the reader from the outset. Third and most important, *it should be interesting.* The title should capture the reader's attention and engage his or her interest.

3. *Write the first draft in three parts.* Term papers should include one or more opening paragraphs (*introduction*), the main section (*body*), and one or more closing paragraphs (*close* or conclusions). The opening paragraph should be based on the thesis statement. Thus it should introduce the topic to the reader and tell how "the story" is to be told. The main section of the paper should be developed from the note cards and the outline. The closing paragraph should summarize the points developed in the main body of the paper. Any conclusions made should flow logically out of that discussion.

4. *Use a format that allows for revision.* To be of maximum benefit, the first draft should be planned with revision in mind. This requires the right format. Use good-quality paper that can be erased easily and place only one paragraph on each sheet. This will make it easier to insert additional material later if necessary. In addition, write on only one side of each sheet. As you do so, use double or triple spacing and wide margins.

5. *Use the resources for effective writing.* Elsewhere in ESS (Principle 3) you were advised to develop your own basic library of resources for increased student success. This is a time to use these key books, which include a collegiate dictionary, a thesaurus, a book on grammar, two books on writing, and this book on ESS. As you write the first draft, consult them as needed.

6. *Follow the conventions for formal writing.* Here are some of the more important ones:
   - Use only complete sentences.
   - Define important terms when they are used in a specific way. Example: A paper on the matriarchal family should define what is meant by this family form when it is first introduced.
   - Write in third person. (Appropriate: It was; Inappropriate: I feel)
   - Write in the correct tense. (Discuss historical events in the past tense; refer to scholars whose work remains in print in present tense. Examples: James Johnson writes; Juanita Torres says)

- Write to your audience. (A term paper writes to scholars and should be formal. By contrast, this book on ESS was written for students and is designed to be conversational and informal.)
- Use transitional words and phrases to unify ideas presented in different sentences, paragraphs, and sections of your paper; these include *also, consequently, in addition, nonetheless,* and *therefore.*
- Avoid the use of large, complex words when simple ones will do. Examples: Use, not utilize; pay, not remunerate.
- Avoid the use of colloquial and slang expressions (except for emphasis and in quotation marks).
- Avoid personal pronouns in scholarly writing (I, you, we, ours).
- Avoid humor or satire (unless called for by the nature of the paper).
- Use appropriate documentation. Be sure to use a style of footnoting and/or documentation that is acceptable to your instructor. The MLA (Modern Language Association) style is favored by many English instructors, while the APA (American Psychological Association) style is preferred by many instructors in the behavioral and social sciences.

  Regardless of the style used, it is important to cite sources accurately and place all brief quotes within quotation marks. Longer quotes should be set apart from the main text in indented blocks. Quotations should be used sparingly. As a general rule of thumb, no more than 5 to 10 percent of the content of a research paper should be from quoted material.

Step 8: Edit and Revise Once the first draft is finished, set it aside for a day or two before attempting any revision. Good writers usually distance themselves from their work after each draft in order to approach revision later with greater objectivity. One of the hallmarks of an effective writer is the ability to view one's own work critically with fresh eyes. Good writers are therefore also good editors who will revise and revise and revise until they are satisfied with the final product.

Guidelines for Effective Revision To produce a better paper, use these techniques to revise the first draft. Remember that editing and revising are two separate processes that occur simultaneously. To edit is to check, to revise is to make changes:

1. Check for logical flow.
2. Check for factual support.
3. Check for style and form.
4. Polish the paper sentence by sentence.

5. Read the entire draft and make final revisions.

6. Proofread the revised first draft.

7. Have someone else proofread the revised first draft.

Step 9: Write the Final Draft   As with Step 8, wait a day or two before continuing further. This will provide the time necessary to put some distance between you and your work. The result will be heightened objectivity that should allow you to improve the paper. Although changes at this stage mainly are refinements, they may add significantly to the quality of your writing. This in turn could make the difference between a good and an excellent paper, a B or an A grade.

Guidelines for Writing the Final Draft   The final draft is written from the revised first draft. Proceed as follows:

1. *Write the final draft.* You will find that, even at this stage, you will make slight changes and refinements that will add polish to your paper. As you proceed, make sure that each footnote or citation in the text corresponds to an entry in the bibliography.

2. *Proofread the final draft by reading it aloud.* Good writing sounds good. It has a smooth cadence or rhythm. Likewise, poor writing becomes very obvious when read aloud. Such problems as incorrect sentence structure, poor grammar, inadequate transition, and lack of clarity or direction become readily apparent when heard by the ear. Even more effective than reading aloud to yourself is to read your paper to someone else. This way, you and a partner can critique the paper together.

3. *Make any final revisions.* By this point in the process, revisions probably will be minor. Nonetheless, you may wish to make a few.

4. *Write the ancillaries in presentation form.* These include the final title and title sheet, the final thesis statement and outline (if they are to be turned in with your paper), and the bibliography, arranged by author in alphabetical order.

Step 10: Prepare and Present the Completed Paper   Quality writing—whether it results in a term paper, an article, or a book—emerges in steps, in layers. The effective writer, therefore, is like the miller who, through several repetitions of grinding and sifting, transforms coarse grain into fine powdery flour. To write a quality term paper involves a similar series of steps: topic, purpose, thesis statement, outline, first draft, revised first draft, final draft, revised final draft, completed paper.

Of these, the final phase of writing a term paper involves the careful typing of the revised final draft and its presentation to the instructor. Always keep in mind that an A paper should look like one. The quality of our work both in appearance and content reflects on us as people.

Guidelines for Completion and Presentation

1. *Type the completed paper from the revised final draft.* If the paper is to be typed into a computer or word processor, use an easy-to-read font such as Chicago or Times Roman. Always print the paper on a letter-quality printer, preferably an ink jet or laser printer. If you prepare the final copy on a daisywheel printer or typewriter, use a new black ribbon for the best appearance. Regardless of whether you use a computer or typewriter, prepare the presentation copy on white bond paper (8 ½ by 11) with a rag content of at least 25 or 50 percent.

2. *Add all ancillaries.* Make sure your title sheet includes: Title of paper, your name, your instructor's name and title (Dr. Robert T. Jones; Professor Nancy A. Smith), the course number and title, the name of your school, the semester or term (Fall, Spring, Summer I, Summer II), and date of presentation. If the outline is to be included, insert it after the title page. The bibliography should be arranged alphabetically by author and placed at the end of the paper.

3. *Proofread for the final time.* In most cases, minor errors are easy to correct, particularly if the paper has been prepared on a computer. The paper presented to your instructor should be in letter-perfect form if possible.

4. *Make a photocopy for yourself.* Since papers do occasionally get lost, play it safe by making a copy. Also, writing anything well is a creative process that requires lots of hard work. It's always nice to have a record of your endeavors for future reference.

5. *Place in a folder for presentation.* Any superior product deserves an attractive package. Therefore, place the results of your best efforts in an A-quality folder.

9 PRINCIPLES 14–17: THE HOWS OF FINAL EXAMS, TIME MANAGEMENT, MEMORY TECHNIQUES, AND CRITICAL THINKING SKILLS

PRINCIPLE 14: Study Smart for Final Exams

Especially at the college level, an entire semester's work in a course tends to build toward the final exam, which represents the culmination of several months of effort. Many instructors give comprehensive finals that cover the entire semester from the first day on. In any event, final-exam scores constitute a major part of your grade. In many instances they count more than anything else.

Many students procrastinate in their studies and allow the final-exam period to sneak up on them. When this occurs, it is often easy to become overwhelmed by a week or so of intensive testing, much of which may include material from early in the semester. Other students sometimes lose the resolve and energy to study late in the semester, particularly in the spring after a long academic year. They appear to lose steam and fizzle out precisely because they didn't pace themselves carefully as they progressed through the school year and term. Come exam time, these students offer too little, too late and get poor to failing grades as a result.

Don't let this happen to you. Instead, focus your study efforts early in the semester toward preparation for the final exam, particularly if it is comprehensive. Later in the book (in ESS—THE ADVANCED COURSE) you will be shown precisely how to prepare for various types of exams.

For now, however, follow these general guidelines. First, as you progress through the semester or term, *keep your study notes for each exam* in each course and store them in the same place for easy retrieval later. Second, and most important, *start your study for final exams well ahead of time.* Final-exam week is a hectic time, and many students who end up with mediocre or failing grades do so because they are overwhelmed due to their own lack of organization and procrastination. You can avoid this by organizing your time and materials carefully and studying smart.

PRINCIPLE 15: Practice Effective Time Management

Effective study is a serious enterprise that requires an adequate amount of time in order to achieve academic success. The time required to be properly prepared varies according to such factors as the degree of student interest in the courses taken, the level of course difficulty, and the extent to which a student knows, understands, and uses effective study techniques.

Most successful students look upon a full course load of twelve to sixteen semester hours or more as a full-time job responsibility. They have learned that A grades require a significant amount of commitment and work. Therefore, *you will need to spend approximately two hours of study outside class for every hour spent in class in order to succeed and excel in college* (fifteen hours in class per week plus thirty hours of study per week = forty-five hours per week). Graduate or professional school may require even more time.

True, you might be able to muddle through and earn passing grades with a smaller time commitment. But if you wish to excel in school and get the A grades, you usually will need to put in the recommended amount of time.

In addition to spending enough time at study, the successful student must budget study time just as one might manage limited financial resources for a business or family. Therefore, just as one must manage money effectively to pay the rent or car payment each month, effective student time management also must become an ingrained habit practiced on a continual basis.

To say that time is one of our most valuable resources is an understatement. In truth, the effective use of time is an essential requirement for achieving meaningful goals in any area of life. Used wisely, it can help ensure success. Squandered carelessly, it will guarantee failure.

The most successful students are those who have learned how to prioritize their time and harness it as an ally in their pursuit of excellence. They *know* that time devoted to school is valuable, act accordingly, and consequently do things well and on time.

Mediocre-to-poor students, by contrast, allow time to slip through their fingers like sand through an hourglass. This is evident when they habitually say "Something came up," "I ran out of time," "I didn't have enough time," or "I had to do something else."

Such statements sometimes are little more than lame excuses used in an attempt to gloss over irresponsibility. "Things" always "come up" when we don't plan our time effectively. As far as "running out of time" is concerned, the A student and the F student have the same twenty-four-hour day. Someone who says "I had to do something else" is really saying (1) "I don't know how to plan my time," (2) "My studies really aren't that important to me," or both. Most college instructors will not be sympathetic. Neither will most employers, who sometimes hear the same excuses from equally unmotivated and irresponsible employees.

How to Manage Study Time Effectively

To make time an ally instead of an enemy, it is imperative that you take on certain values, acquire the necessary tools, and engage in particular forms of behavior. Earlier we discussed the formula for success. As you will recall, the first step necessary for any form of significant success requires that we make a commitment to a meaningful goal. Step two involves the development of an effective plan to achieve the goal. The third and final step requires that we persevere by sticking to the plan.

Therefore, to become an effective time manager—like every other Principle, Step, Skill, and Task outlined in this book—will require that you first make a personal commitment to it as a meaningful goal. I am now going to give you an effective plan you can use to achieve this goal. All you will need to do for effective management of your study time is follow it.

Establish a Workstation for Study   The most successful students have a designated place for study. In fact, some of these students claim that this is one of the secrets to academic success. If you also want to perform well in school, you should do the same.

To be an effective student you must consistently put in the necessary amount of time. This responsibility is easier to fulfill when you have a quiet, comfortable place to study free from distraction and interruption. For maximum effectiveness you should study in the same place most of the time. Being creatures of habit, we humans typically are more comfortable and effective in completing important tasks when we have a special place in which to do them.

Think of how much our lives are organized already. Most of us have special places in which we carry out a variety of functions. We usually sleep in the same bed in the same room and go to bed at about the same time each night. If this routine is disrupted, we lose sleep or don't sleep as well.

When you attend class, you probably sit at the same desk or in the same part of the classroom each time. If you currently are employed at a full-time or part-time job, you probably conduct your work in the same office or at the same workstation each day during the same hours. We all tend to do these things in the same places, at the same times, and often in the same ways because we find the results rewarding.

This principle also applies to the effective use of study time. What is ironic is that many students let study time escape them precisely because they haven't established a special place to study along with definite timelines for doing so.

Home Usually Is the Best Place to Study   Usually the best place to establish a workstation for study is at home (or perhaps in your dorm room at school if your building is quiet). A spare bedroom or even a corner of your bedroom can easily be turned into a study area. All that is required is the addition of a desk and chair, a small bookcase, and, if there is room, a set of file drawers.

Also Consider the Library   If you have a large or busy household—particularly if small children are present—and you can't have a quiet room to yourself, a nearby library is the next best choice. Larger public and university libraries sometimes have available a small number of private study carrels. These private enclosures are ideal for study, although the best ones with lockable doors normally have a waiting list and require a monthly rental fee.

Equip Your Workstation with Needed Study Tools   Many students waste a great deal of their time trying to obtain resources they need for a particular study assignment. Many of these resources can be placed at your workstation for easy access and reference when needed. Although the following list is designed for a home study location, many of these items also can be stored at a lockable library study carrel.

1. *An electric typewriter or personal computer.* Most instructors require that research papers, book reviews, and other class projects be typed. Since the best students normally edit and revise their written work at least one or two times, the personal computer, if affordable, will save you the most time. While the initial dollar investment is significant, a personal computer will save you hundreds of hours in editing and typing time over the course of four years at college.

2. *Your personal library for success.* Earlier, I gave you a select list of recommended books you should acquire and keep handy for easy reference. It includes a collegiate dictionary, this book on ESS, a thesaurus, a book on the fundamentals of grammar, and two classic books on writing by Strunk and White and Zinsser. Place them at your workstation for study and refer to them as needed.

3. *The necessary study supplies.* A typewriter will require paper, spare ribbons, correction fluid, and so on. With a computer, you will need an adequate supply of disks, paper, ribbons, or toner for your printer, and so forth. In addition, you will need to put together a list of essential supplies that I call the **study kit.** These are tools or aids you will need periodically as you study. It is important that you keep your study kit "stocked." This will prevent you from wasting precious study time having to go buy any of these items at critical times immediately before a major exam.

   The study kit should include: writing paper or notepads, several ballpoint pens and sharpened pencils, a pencil sharpener, a stapler and a box of staples, a staple puller, a hole puncher (for adding material to a ring-binder notebook), two or more ring-binder notebooks and paper, three-by-five index cards, five-by-eight index cards, scissors, tape, paper clips, a ruler, file folders (for storing study material such as syllabi, class handouts, and project research related to each class), one bottle of household glue, and several presentation folders (for research papers, book reviews, and so on).

Plan Your Study Week Like a Work Week   From a time-management perspective, your study week should be planned like a work week for which you are paid wages. In most occupational situations you usually go to work each day at a certain hour and leave to go home at a specified time. If you don't do this, you will not be paid and could lose your job.

This same principle also applies to study. Particularly if you are taking a full load of courses, you should set aside sufficient time each day for study. This will take self-discipline on your part because, unlike most job supervisors who supervise your activities, your instructors will not manage your study behavior.

Divide Daily Study into One- or Two-Hour Appointments   As a student, you are on your own. To maximize your performance and get the best grades, it is necessary to *make and keep daily appointments with yourself for study.* If you don't, time will elude you, your grades will probably suffer, and you possibly could fail.

If, for example, you are assigned a chapter or two each week in a given course, divide this work into two or three study sessions or more. As a general rule, *you should not study more than one or two hours at a time without a break.* Although there are exceptions, most people begin to lose concentration after a couple of hours of intensive study. After a brief break of only ten to fifteen minutes most students can continue to study at a high level of efficiency for another hour or two.

Know Your Best Times to Study   It is important to try to plan your study sessions at times in which you will be most alert and ready for study. There are night people and there are day people. We each have our own body chemistry and biological clock. You will get the most from your study sessions if you tune in to your body and plan accordingly.

Use Dead Time Productively   Let's assume that you are a busy person with many responsibilities. This can make it difficult to use your workstation for study all the time because you are on the go. Yet, no matter how busy you are, you probably are faced with a great deal of dead time.

No doubt you have heard someone use the expression "I've got some time to kill." **Dead time** consists of periods of time that we tend to spend unproductively while we wait to do something else.

Most of us find it easy to waste or "kill" time in dozens of ways: Waiting an hour or two while a mechanic fixes our car, waiting thirty minutes outside in the car while a relative or friend is inside a store shopping, or waiting twenty minutes for someone to arrive to pick us up. Likewise we wait for buses and important phone calls and we sometimes wait in line for an hour or more to get tags for our car or tickets for an "important" concert we want to attend. Most of us even spend several hours each year in special rooms for wasting time called waiting rooms while we wait for doctors, dentists, lawyers, accountants, counselors, and other professionals to see us.

Time is a precious resource. Once gone, it can never be recaptured. When significant amounts of time are "killed" because of our own inattention, we inhibit our ability to develop our potential as human beings. What is tragic is that many of us do this unconsciously. If we don't actively harness time to work for us, we can get trapped by dead time and squander it. The expression *killing time* is so appropriate here. By developing the habit of not using it productively, we may find ourselves "killing" what our future could be.

Those who are most successful have learned how to minimize dead time. Corporate executives and consultants who must travel often take their work with them on the plane. It is common to see them reading a report or writing on a notepad or laptop computer. When they travel by car, many have car phones or make use of voice-activated cassette recorders to dictate memos and record ideas. They also may participate in meetings at meals and work in their hotel rooms at night.

Many of the best students use similar techniques to, in effect, do two things at once. You can accomplish the same. By careful planning you can take a textbook, lecture notes, or other study materials with you when you are faced with dead time. Although you should use a primary workstation for study at home or at some other convenient place, you should also possess the flexibility to study wherever and whenever you have the time. This way you will use time most productively to get better grades rather than waste or "kill" it.

Avoid Getting Too Comfortable   One of the potential drawbacks to using a room at home as your primary study workstation is that you may get too comfortable for effective study. If you study in a bedroom, the bed can be very tempting. So can an overstuffed easy chair. Never try to study while lying down, especially while lying on a bed later in the day or evening. This is almost certain to cause you to go to sleep within thirty minutes to an hour. Sitting at a desk in a firm but comfortable straight-back chair with good lighting is the ideal way to study.

Do Not Allow Others to Distract You from Study   If you are a high school student or college freshman, some of your friends will almost certainly try to lure you away from your studies with something fun to do. Let's face it. Studying for an upcoming exam can't hope to compete from a fun standpoint with a ball game, a movie, or just hanging out with the guys or girls. However, being successful as a student means placing studies first and recreation second. If you are a full-time student, school is your primary responsibility. With careful planning, you should have time for both.

If you have family responsibilities, discuss with your family members the importance of adequate study time in getting good grades. This may be difficult if you are a parent with small children who is trying to go back to school. I would be the first to say that it is also important to spend adequate quality time with your loved ones, particularly children. Please do so. However, if time is planned carefully and you don't overcommit yourself with your various activities, you should be able to fulfill all important obligations.

Use the ESS Time Management System   Busy and productive people use calendars or other time-organizing devices. This way they are able to establish and use time benchmarks to keep track of when they should carry out various responsibilities. If you will do the same, you too will be able to get the most out of each day, week, month, and semester. This will help prevent the alternative, allowing time to slip away with nothing to show for it.

The ESS Time Management System is placed here for your use (see Figure 9–1A). It consists of a one-page Weekly Study Schedule that you can use to effectively plan and coordinate the time you spend engaged in various activities. By making adequate copies of this form and using one sheet for each week in the school term, you can organize your time in weekly increments for the entire semester. Two copies of the time management system form are in the back of this book for your convenience.

Use of this form will have an extra benefit beyond helping you get good grades. It will also be good practice for a career. Because time literally is money, time management is increasingly being stressed in the business world. Wasted time translates into lost productivity, higher labor costs, and either higher-priced products or lower profit margins, or both. Corporate CEOs and their top-level managers are keenly aware of this. They realize that, to stay competitive in the international marketplace in which they now find themselves, efficient management of human resources is essential.

Consequently, today's corporations, businesses, and even some governmental agencies and funded organizations encourage or require their professional and support staffs to use time-management systems very similar to the one provided here with ESS. Getting into the habit *now* of scheduling your study time and treating hours blocked out for study as appointments will make it much easier for you

ESS TIME MANAGEMENT SYSTEM
Weekly Study Schedule

Fall/Spr./Sum. Semester, 19____			Week Ending Saturday _____								
Courses This Term Listed by Code Number		Month - - - - - - - - - - Date →	**Day of Week**								**Notes: Things To Do This Week**
Course	Code No.	Hour	Sunday	Monday	Tuesday	Wednesday	Thursday	Friday	Saturday		
	1	8-9									
	2	9-10									
	3	10-11									
	4	11-12									
	5	12-1									
	6	1-2									
	7	2-3									
	8	3-4									
Other Activities Listed by Code Letter		4-5									
		5-6									
		6-7									
Activity	Code Letter	7-8									
		8-9									
In Class	C	9-10									
Work Obligations	W	10-11									
Extracurricular Activities	E	11-12									
Tests Scheduled This Week					**Papers or Projects Due**						

Figure 9-1A

ESS TIME MANAGEMENT SYSTEM
Weekly Study Schedule

(Fall)/Spr./Sum.   Semester, 19_90_   Week Ending Saturday _29_

Courses This Term Listed by Code Number		Month _SEPT._	Day of Week							Notes: Things To Do This Week
		Date →	23	24	25	26	27	28	29	
Course	Code No.	Hour	Sunday	Monday	Tuesday	Wednesday	Thursday	Friday	Saturday	
AM. HISTORY 8-9 MWF	1	8-9		C	C	C	C	C		① get format for research paper from Dr. Hall on Tuesday.
COLL. ALGEBRA 9-10 MWF	2	9-10		C	C	C	C	C		
E. BRIT. LIT. 10-11 MWF	3	10-11		C	C	C	C	C		
INTRO. PSYCH. 8-9:30 T-TH	4	11-12		5	4	5	4	5		
SPEECH 9:30-11 T-TH	5	12-1								
	6	1-2		2	E	2	E	2	E	
	7	2-3		2	4	2	4	2		
	8	3-4		3	4	5	4	2		
Other Activities Listed by Code Letter		4-5		1	1	1	5	W		② get oil changed in car on Saturday.
		5-6		1	1	1	W	W		
		6-7					W	W		
Activity	Code Letter	7-8			3	3	W	W		
		8-9			3	3	W	W		
In Class	C	9-10			3			W		
Work Obligations	W	10-11								
Extracurricular Activities	E	11-12								

Tests Scheduled This Week	Papers or Projects Due
Test in Algebra on Friday. (Chapters 1, 2, 3, 4)	① Research Paper Due in History on Nov. 10th. (Begin work this week.)

Figure 9-1B

to make the transition to the realities of work in business, support, and professional occupations.

As you read the instructions below, examine the specimen provided in Figure 9–1B. It should prove useful as a guide in setting up your own study schedule. Be advised that it probably will take you twenty or thirty minutes the first time you plan your week using this system. However, once you get used to planning your time and you practice using the form a few times, this process typically will take only ten or fifteen minutes per week—or less. If you decide to stick basically to the same weekly study schedule, the form can be filled out in five minutes. The chief benefit will be this: Use of this schedule and the small investment of time it will require should save you several hours of wasted time each week.

Instructions for Using the ESS Time-Management System

1. Fill in the semester, year, and week ending date at the top of the Weekly Study Schedule Form.

2. List the courses you are taking this term in the order that you attend classes in each of them during the week. For example, if this semester the first class you attend each week is American History 1301 at 8:00 A.M. on Mondays, Wednesdays, and Fridays, list it in the space provided next to code number 1. If the second class you attend each week is Early British Literature at 9:00 A.M. MWF, it should be listed next with the code number 2. Proceed in this manner until all courses are listed.

3. Write the code letter C (which stands for "in class") in the time blocks each week that correspond to days and times you are in class and thus unavailable for outside study. If, for example, you are taking a fifteen-hour course load, then fifteen hourly time blocks during the week should be filled in with the letter C.

4. If it is necessary that you work part-time or full-time at a job while attending school, place the code letter W (for "work obligations") in the hourly time blocks that correspond to times each day you are unavailable for study. Otherwise, outside study time should be your top work-related priority.

5. Place the code numbers that correspond to each course in the time blocks during the week that you plan to use for study in each of them. For example, if College Algebra was listed with the code number 4 and you wished to study that subject from 7:00 P.M. to 9:00 P.M. on Monday and Wednesday evenings and from 9:00 A.M. to 11:00 A.M. on Saturday mornings, insert the number 4 in the appropriate hourly time blocks for those days.

6. To emphasize time planned for outside study, use a lightly covered highlighter pen (such as yellow or light orange) to fill in each hourly time block

set aside for this purpose. Be careful, however, that the color used not be so dark that it obscures the course code numbers.

7. *Optional.* If you wish, you also may use the code letter E to keep track of time designated for extra-curricular school activities.

PRINCIPLE 16: Use Effective Memory Techniques

Success as a student requires that you be able to acquire, understand, organize, retain, and retrieve large amounts of information. The best students understand this and work hard to develop effective memory techniques. Since a good memory is primarily a skill, you can do the same. All it will require is a little effort and practice on your part. Before discussing specific memory techniques, however, let's briefly examine the nature of memory.

What Is Memory?

Memory refers to the location of information retained in the mind along with the ability to retrieve it. A computer analogy is helpful in explaining how it works. Information is stored in the memory of a personal computer in much the same way it is retained in the human mind. When using a computer, you activate a three-step process of entering, saving, and calling up and/or printing information.

Once acquired or entered into a computer, information is categorized into named files, where they are saved for efficient storage and retrieval. These files act as memory cues to tell you where specific items of information are located. To retrieve any stored information, you issue the correct command to the computer. Then the file with the needed information is opened and appears on your screen.

The human memory works in a similar way, although it is much more complex. The effective use of the human mind involves the same three-step process of acquiring, storing, and retrieving information. In addition, each of these steps has its own set of characteristics and related problems. Unlike its mechanical counterpart, however, the mind has an almost infinite number of memory locations where information may be stored in both short-term and long-term memory.

Behavioral scientists are just now beginning to understand how human memory works. It is perhaps best viewed as a continuum. **Sensory impressions** that continually bombard our consciousness appear at one end, selective short-term memory as we move toward the middle, and selective long-term memory as we approach the other end.

For students, the immediate task at hand is to effectively develop short-term memory sufficient to do well on exams. If this is done well, long-term memory also tends to be maximized. **Short-term memory** consists of information that is usually retained for only a few seconds, particularly if it is not regarded as important and is not repeatedly rehearsed. Remembering a phone number long enough to write it down is a typical example. Most of what is learned in school for exams is an extension of short-term memory that is retained for only a few days or weeks.

Long-term memory consists of information that is retained for months and years and perhaps even for a lifetime. We remember long-term the sensory experiences that have made the strongest impressions on our minds.

The Three Stages in the Memory Process

Memory develops as a three-stage process that can be briefly explained as follows:

Stage 1: Memory Acquisition (Encoding)   The first step in the memory process is initial learning or acquisition. Cognitive psychologists sometimes refer to this as encoding. Without this capacity, humans would live in the perpetual present. Since each of us is constantly being bombarded with sensory impressions—colors, images, sounds, smells, and numerous others—the inability to be selective in filtering and retaining information would deprive us of our humanity. Sensory inputs would literally go in one ear and out the other. Consequently we would have no recollection of what happened in our lives last month, last year, or during our childhood.

One key to effective memory acquisition is the **principle of meaningful classification.** This refers to the ability to focus attention on important pieces of information and place them into meaningful categories. However, if this is not accomplished in a disciplined way, much of the information we wish to acquire may be lost or distorted. Untrained observers are very susceptible to such distortion and therefore are unreliable. This is indicated by the differing descriptions of purse snatchers and other assailants often given by eyewitnesses. Their descriptions vary because, at the time of the incident, their attentions were focused on different things.

As a student, your first memory task is to focus your attention on the course content (sensory inputs) from which exam questions are most likely to come. To do so effectively, you must be exposed to *all* the course content. This means, among other things, reading every text assignment, attending every class, and taking good notes (see Action Principles 6, 7, and 9).

Then, as you read every assignment and attend class, your second task is to distinguish between core material and elaboration material in your reading and class activities. You will only remember what you acquire or encode as **critical**

information. To distinguish this critical information, it is imperative that you learn to ask yourself certain key questions about the course content to which you are exposed: What is important here? How do I know it is important? What does this concept, principle, or theory actually mean? What different categories should I use in classifying this information?

Information that you have consciously decided is important and meaningful will be easier to remember later.

Stage 2: Memory Storage   Once information has been acquired or encoded, the next step is to store it in the mind for later retrieval.

Stored information takes the form of what psychologists call **memory traces.** Some psychologists assert that these memory traces are stored in different parts of our minds according to distinct categories of memory: procedures (how to ride a bicycle or operate a computer), semantics (vocabulary, simple facts, rules, and concepts), and episodes (life events and experiences).

When information is learned well or is newly acquired, it is often easy to remember in complete form. But information that is not learned thoroughly is often easily forgotten. Likewise, the passage of time can cause a memory trace to fade or decay. This is evident when a person returns to visit a city he or she once resided in several years ago. Streets and places that were once known intimately now have to be checked on a city map. Likewise, you may encounter persons with whom you attended school ten or twenty years ago and recognize their faces but fail to remember their names.

To maximize the strength of memory traces that are stored in the mind, it is important to implement the **principle of distributed practice.** Psychological research consistently has shown that it is easier to store or memorize information in several spaced-out study sessions than in one or more massed sessions. Put in simple terms, cramming is a very ineffective way to study. You will remember far more material if you use several one- or two-hour sessions spaced over several days or weeks instead one or more marathon sessions lasting several hours each.

Stage 3: Memory Retrieval   The last step in the memory process is the ability to remember or retrieve information that was learned and stored. To maximize the ability to remember, it is helpful to understand the **principle of selective reconstruction.** Psychological research has shown that remembered information is, in effect, a reconstructed reality based on what information is learned initially and how it is stored. What we remember, therefore, is selective, not total. We usually cannot remember and relive a total experience or learning situation from the past, only selected aspects of it.

What we do remember tends to be based on two essential activities. First, we decide at the time of initial learning what is to be defined as critical information.

Then we make decisions as to how that information is to be stored and classified into memory categories or clusters. In so doing we may cluster information in a variety of ways at various levels of complexity. Some simple examples might include function (Fords and Nissans are motor vehicles), location (Nashville and Memphis are in Tennessee), chronology (the Civil War and World War II), rank (corporal and general), and quantity (quart and gallon).

If you understand this principle and organize your course content into meaningful categories for selective reconstruction later, your exam scores will rise because you will be able to retain and retrieve more information. If you don't, your base of information will be too general and superficial to recall.

This is why the lockstep, passive reading of an assignment in a text or other source tends to be a waste of time. Many students simply start at page one and read straight through to the end of an assignment without any active preparation or attempt at meaningful classification. Then they have difficulty remembering much of anything. Don't let this happen to you.

Students usually are required on exams to retrieve or remember information in one of two specific ways. First, they may be asked to demonstrate **recognition,** the ability to identify information which one has been exposed to previously. Instructors mainly use multiple choice and true-false items to test for recognition. Second, students may be tested for **recall,** the ability to remember and reproduce detailed information which one was exposed to previously. Essay questions typically are used for this purpose. Generally, essay items are considered more difficult because (1) they require demonstrated organizational and writing ability and (2) they provide the student the fewest clues for making a response.

Ten Techniques You Can Use to Improve Your Memory

1. Developing the Intent to Remember   Have you ever observed an avid twelve-year-old baseball fan who can tell you which teams dozens of athletes play on, the positions they play, their batting averages or strikeout standings, the team standings in each division, and other assorted baseball facts? What about the fourteen-year-old who has memorized the lyrics to dozens of pop rock tunes and can tell you all sorts of detailed information about various rock groups and entertainers? And then there's the forty-year-old television follower. This person perhaps can remember Lucy Ricardo's maiden name, identify all the kids on *The Brady Bunch* and *The Waltons,* or give you the plot lines and major characters on several current daytime dramas. What's their secret? How do they remember all this information? What techniques do they use? Well, their secret really is fairly simple. Each of them has the intent to remember.

Of all the memory techniques available, the most important one has to do with harnessing your will to learn and remember. Effective learning is active, not pas-

Table 9–1—Ten Techniques for Improving Your Memory

1. Developing the intent to remember
2. Seeing the big picture
3. Chunking
4. Distinguishing core material from elaboration material
5. Linking: The use of acronyms
6. Visualization
7. The pegboard system
8. Spaced repetition
9. Outlining
10. Overlearning: The final study session

sive. You must say to yourself, out loud if necessary, "This is important. I need to learn this. I will remember this." If you don't see school as important and the desire to work diligently to get good grades isn't firmly in place, all the memory techniques in the world won't help you much. So make an active positive affirmation to learn the content material in each of your courses. By taking your studies seriously you'll be amazed at how much you'll remember.

2. Seeing the Big Picture Before you embark upon mastering any learning task, it is important to first get a broad overview of it. Effective study is like going on a trip. To reach your destination, you must first know where you're going. When faced with a reading assignment, *preview* the material to be learned before you begin by examining the table of contents and major headings. At the beginning of each class, *listen* carefully to see if the instructor presents a preview or overview of the lecture to follow. Many good lecturers do this to position the listener for the material to be covered. As you prepare for each exam, *focus on the big issues* first. *Ask the big questions* and be prepared to answer them. Then, within each general topic, *focus on the specifics,* such as the more specific issues, concepts, and principles.

This process will allow you to get more from the course content because your study will have purpose and direction. By focusing first on the big ideas, the major benchmarks in your journey through the course material, you will be taking the first step toward mastering the principle of meaningful classification.

3. Chunking After obtaining a big-picture view of the course content to be learned, divide content material into smaller wholes or chunks for better retention. By doing so, you will be implementing the principle of meaningful classification. Here are a few specific applications of chunking. First, when course content is covered in class, try to *identify and record the major points* presented in class lecture and discussion. Then, *divide each of the major points into a few secondary points.* Finally, *do the same with your text and other reading assignments.* Most textbook chapters are divided into several major headings. Each of these tends to be further divided into several subheadings. Organizing course content into smaller meaningful chunks will enhance your ability to store and retrieve information.

4. Distinguishing Core Material from Elaboration Material   As you divide course content to be learned into smaller chunks, it is important to distinguish important core material from less important elaboration material. To remember anything for a significant period of time we have to acquire or encode it as important in the first place. If we don't, it will evaporate from our memories in seconds or minutes, like faces we briefly look upon in a crowd and then promptly forget.

There are many terms for what needs to happen during the acquisition stage in the memory process. Harry Lorayne, a popular writer on memory techniques, calls it the principle of original awareness. As a behavioral scientist and professional educator, I prefer *the principle of meaningful classification.*

Regardless of the terminology used to describe it, this is what you need to do. As you read and attend class, make a concerted effort to separate core material most likely to appear on the exam (key concepts, principles, theories, and so on) from elaboration material (such as examples and illustrations). As you identify such critical information, ask and answer key questions about it—Who? What? When? Where? Why?—so that it will have meaning for you. This way, you will be able to meaningfully organize both core material and the elaboration that explains it. You will be more likely to remember it later by using this process.

5. Linking: The Use of Acronyms   After you place content material into smaller meaningful chunks and separate core material from elaboration, there are a variety of association devices you can use to improve your memory. One of these involves the use of acronyms to link important elements within a chunk. An *acronym* is a word formed when the first letters of other words are linked together. For instance, FBI is an acronym for Federal Bureau of Investigation. The acronym HOMES can be useful in a geography course for remembering the Great Lakes: Huron, Ontario, Michigan, Erie, and Superior.

Three Ways to Use Acronyms for Improved Memory

a. *Use a familiar word to link a list of elements.* Suppose that for an upcoming history exam you need to know the identities of (1) the big-three Allies and

(2) the members of the Axis Pact during World War II. The Allies consisted of Britain, America, and Russia (the Soviet Union), or BAR, while the Axis nations were comprised of Japan, Italy, and Germany, or JIG. The acronyms BAR and JIG may be useful as memory devices here.

b. *Use a humorous or intriguing sentence or story to link two or more acronyms together.* Suppose in the same history course you also need to know the names of the leaders of both the Allies and the Axis nations. The Allies were headed by Churchhill (Britain), Roosevelt (America), and Stalin (Russia), or CRS, while the Axis countries were led by Hirohito (Japan), Mussolini (Italy), and Hitler (Germany), or HMH. With the understanding that any or all of this information could be called for on an upcoming exam, you could use the following example: Mr. CRS arrived at the BAR at midnight and danced a JIG with Mrs. HMH. If additional information needed must be learned, you could add more acronyms and sentences to the story. For example: At ONE, Miss JGS arrived and TEN minutes later a SHOT rang out.

c. *Use a string of nonsense acronyms linked by hyphens.* Consider the following lists of numbers:

403796187   7134584050   376180208

By themselves, these three groups of numbers are meaningless. Memorizing several such strings might be a difficult task. However, if you (1) consider the context in which these numbers appear (meaningful classification) and (2) use the memory devices of chunking and linking (further application of meaningful classification), the task becomes much easier.

Lists of Numbers Placed into Meaningful Categories

Social Security No.	Telephone No.	Zip Code No.
403-79-6187	713-458-4050	37618-0208

In such cases as these, the hyphen is used customarily throughout the United States to both chunk and link long strings of numbers for effective recall. No doubt you have used this technique unconsciously to memorize the phone numbers of several close relatives and friends.

This same principle also applies to the use of acronyms in mastering long lists of items in a chunk of academic course content. Consider this example that could apply in a survey course in physics, biology, psychology or any other any scientific discipline:

Chunked and Linked (Hyphenated) Acronym		Course Content to be Learned for Later Recall
PR–HD–OAR		The Seven Steps in Conducting Scientific Research
P	=	1. **Problem:** Statement of the research problem
R	=	2. **Review:** Review of pertinent literature
H	=	3. **Hypotheses:** Statement of hypotheses
D	=	4. **Design:** Research design
O	=	5. **Observation:** Making observations (gathering data)
A	=	6. **Analysis:** Analysis of the data (testing of hypotheses)
R	=	7. **Reporting:** Reporting the results

6. Visualization   One very effective association technique is visualization, the creation of mental pictures about information one wants to recall. The old expression "A picture is worth a thousand words" is true. Most of us can indeed remember information more effectively if we learn to visualize it as a mental picture. This is because, in doing so, we are able to take something complex and abstract and place it in a form that is simpler and more concrete. The mind can acquire and retrieve information more easily when it is filed in a memory category as a picture.

To test the effectiveness of visualization, try this experiment. If you are in your twenties or older, go and get one of your old high school yearbooks. If you are under twenty, a family photo album with pictures of you and your family when you were a child will work. Now, open the yearbook or photo album and look at some of the pictures. No doubt, viewing these pictures will trigger many memories. If you focus on these pictures for very long, your consciousness will be flooded with vivid images and experiences of times past: relationships, events, sights, sounds, and perhaps even smells. These pictures act as retrieval cues to help you remember.

While you can't take photographs regarding course content into an exam to help you remember details, you can create mental pictures of important material as you study. These images will be triggered in your mind when you see key words or phrases (memory cues) on an exam. Once these mental picture files have been opened, you will then be able to retrieve or remember much detailed information.

As you use mental pictures to help you remember course content, two devices in particular will help you create the strongest association. First, create vivid images with a lot of detail. Exaggerate the features of objects, people, and other living things. Use strong colors or wild patterns. Could you, for example, easily forget a green-and-yellow-striped building or a purple-polka-dotted duck? All you have to do is to associate such images in a mental picture with items of information you need to learn and later retrieve.

Second, make use of action. A mental picture of that same striped building swaying back and forth to the beat of tom-toms or that polka-dotted duck driving a motorcycle would be hard to forget. Research has shown that the more vivid and action-oriented the mental picture, the greater its effectiveness. Try it. It will work for you as well.

Two Ways to Use Visualization for Improved Memory

a. *Use mental pictures to link word pairs or other paired content items.* Often in your courses, you will be required to match together certain paired words or other paired items of information. If you take a language course, for example, you will be asked to match Spanish, French, German, or other foreign words with their English equivalents to build your foreign language vocabulary.

Suppose you are taking a beginning Spanish course this semester and you need to remember the meaning of *el mar* (the sea), *dinero* (money), and *saber* (to know facts or information). Although you eventually will learn these by rote through repeated recitation, here are some mental images you could use to recall them initially:

Spanish Term	English Definition	Mental Image for Recall
el mar	the sea	A swimming **mar**lin wearing a sweatshirt with the letter **C**
dinero	money	A man at Joe's **diner** eating a hotdog made of rolled **money**
saber	to know (facts or information)	A man holding a **saber** to the chest of another man who then says, "I **know** the facts. I'll tell you."

Or suppose you are taking a political science, economics, or sociology course and are required to match several prominent individuals with the ideas or theories they originated. Let's say one such example is Karl Marx, who originated the class conflict theory of history. You could visualize a bearded man with **Karl** on his sweatshirt fighting a duel in a **class**room with a **convict** (rhymes with conflict) using ink felt-tip **markers**.

b. *Use the loci method to link together elements of course content.* Perhaps the oldest memory-retention approach in recorded history is the **loci method,** attributed to the ancient Greeks. In Latin *loci* means locations. With this approach, one creates a mental picture of a meaningful location such as the layout of a baseball field or the floor plan of one's home. Several items of information that need to be recalled are then mentally associated with certain reference points in the overall mental location.

If, for instance, you were using a baseball field as a visualization device, you could mentally place items of information at first base, second base, third base, and home plate. If you needed more locations, you could use the pitcher's mound, center field, and the outfield.

The location method has a variety of applications. It is sometimes used by public speakers and corporate presenters who wish to make lengthy presentations without notes. Students also can use this approach in several ways, including the presentation of oral reports.

Suppose you wish to recall a block of course content containing five major points. In addition, each of these major points has four or five minor points subsumed under it. To file this material into meaningful memory categories, you could mentally walk through your home. The five major points would be located in five main rooms. They would emerge in order as you progressed first into the living room and then entered the kitchen, the den, the bathroom, and, finally, your bedroom.

As you paused in your journey through the living room, the four or five minor points located under the first major point could be stored in order mentally and then retrieved from the couch, the chair, the table, the television, and the far corner. Likewise, the minor points listed under the major point located in each of the other rooms could have similar reference locations.

7. The Pegboard System Another useful form of association is the pegboard system, a fairly sophisticated approach that includes some visualization. This technique, developed by psychologists G. A. Miller, E. Galanter, and K. H. Pribram in 1960, has been used more recently by several popularizers, including Harry Lorayne and Jerry Lucas in *The Memory Book* (1986). Essentially, it involves the use of a memorized list of nouns or pegwords that are matched with their respective numbers in a list (such as one = sun, two = shoe, three = tree, and so forth). These pegwords are then associated with a list of items one wants to memorize.

Suppose you need to remember elephant, giraffe, and rhinoceros, in that order. With your pegwords fully memorized, you can visualize an *elephant* lying in the *sun* (with sunglasses and swimsuit, naturally), a *giraffe* wearing one tennis *shoe*, and the *rhinoceros* sitting in a *tree*. The more ridiculous the association, the easier it is to remember.

It might help you get comfortable with this approach if the first few pegwords rhyme with the numbers in the list they represent. However, this is not necessary. Any noun will do so long as you are able to match it to the number it represents. Consider these examples:

1. Sun	6. Sticks	11. Kevin	16. Team
2. Shoe	7. Heaven	12. Elves	17. Bean
3. Tree	8. Skate	13. Earth	18. Figure eight
4. Door	9. Sign	14. Sour cream	19. Crime scene
5. Hive	10. Pen	15. Dream	20. Penny

Mastering the pegboard system, then, involves a two-step process. First, you develop pegwords (nouns) that stand for numbers (1, 2, 3, 4, 5, 6, 7, 8, 9, 10) and memorize them. You can use the pegwords listed above to get started or devise your own. Begin with the first ten. However, with a little work and practice, you can learn twenty pegwords and then develop fifty or a hundred such terms. Think of them as titles or names for memory files. Second, take a list of items you need to learn. Finally, construct a mental association of each memorized pegword with the corresponding term or other item of information you wish to recall. By doing this, you will be able to place information in each of the memory files you may wish to call up or remember later. Mastery of this technique requires only a few hours of your time and some periodic practice.

Suppose you needed to learn the twentieth-century U.S. presidents in chronological order. This is how they might be stored in your memory for later retrieval using the pegboard system.

No. Peg Word	Item to Learn	Mental Image for Recall
1. Sun	McKinley	**Mack** and **Cindy** lying in the **Sun**.
2. Shoe	T. Roosevelt	A **Teddy** bear wearing one **shoe**.

No. Peg Word	Item to Learn	Mental Image for Recall
3. Tree	Taft	Building a **raft** from a **tree.**
4. Door	Wilson	In the **will,** the **son** inherits a **door.**
5. Hive	Harding	**Lard** being stuffed into a bee **hive.**
6. Sticks	Coolidge	Using ice to **cool sticks.**
7. Heaven	Hoover	**Hoover** vacuum cleaners in **heaven.**
8. Skate	F. Roosevelt	**Frank** the **rooster** on roller **skates.**
9. Sign	Truman	A **blue man** wearing a peace **sign.**
10. Pen	Eisenhower	A **pie sent** to **Howard** containing a **pen.**
11. Kevin	Kennedy	**Ken** and **Edie** have a pet walrus named **Kevin.**
12. Elves	Johnson	**John's** two **sons** are Texas **elves.**
13. Earth	Nixon	**Richard** is **fixing** the **earth** dam.
14. Sour cream	Ford	**Fording** a stream of **sour cream.**
15. Dream	Carter	A **car** full of **peanuts** in a **dream.**
16. Team	Reagan	**Ray guns** to equip the Moon **team.**
17. Bean	Bush	A green **bush** with a large red **bean.**

8. Spaced Repetition Remember the twelve-year-old baseball fan with an encyclopedic memory of baseball facts. Do you think this young person consciously makes use of such sophisticated memory techniques as linking with acronyms, visualization, and the pegboard system? If your answer is no, you're probably right. The same is also true for teenagers who know the ins and outs of rock music and middle-aged TV and movie junkies who can tell you the name of Roy Rogers' horse (It was Trigger. Oops! I just couldn't resist!) and ten thousand other things. How then do they know and remember so much information? What is their secret? The answer is really quite simple once you analyze it. First, they have a passion for the subject, the intent to know. They pay attention. As a result, they engage in seeing the big picture, chunking and separating core material from elaboration intuitively. They use simple forms of such techniques as linking and visualization intuitively as well. They pick up and use these techniques unconsciously because of their desire to learn. However, there is a second major component to their super memories. They practice, practice, and practice.

Spaced repetition of important information is one of the most important of all memory techniques. Baseball fans remember so much mainly because they talk about it regularly with other fans. They go to baseball games; the younger ones collect and swap baseball cards; and they read baseball magazines. Through such ongoing rehearsals their memory traces regarding baseball are strengthened and reinforced.

As a student, you can use the same technique to retain the most information and get the best grades. Spaced repetition of key course content is essential to maximize learning. This is why cramming is so inefficient and, ultimately, unsuccessful. With only one or two brief exposures to the material, important course content will evaporate quickly from memory if it is retained at all.

VERY IMPORTANT: THE FOUNDATION FOR ESS—THE ADVANCED COURSE AND SUPERIOR GRADES

The careful reading of *all* text assignments ahead of time before class provides you one exposure to course content. Attending *all* classes and taking effective notes provides a second. Careful consolidation of *all* text material and class notes into a comprehensive outline for exam preparation represents a third repetition. A final study session the day before a major exam offers a fourth.

What I have just said in the brief box is the key to both effective memory retention in school and getting the best grades. It forms much of the foundation for ESS—THE ADVANCED COURSE which follows in Part 3. If you will read the advanced course carefully and use it, you will find yourself on the path to straight A grades.

9. Outlining   The mind will most efficiently grasp material that is organized by topics and subtopics into an outline. An outline, in essence, helps establish meaningful categories of information for effective memory storage and retrieval. Think of what a jumbled mess this book would have been had I not organized it into learning chunks by identifying parts, headings, subheadings, and listings. It would have been largely incomprehensible. The same thing is true of textbooks and lecture notes that you need to organize. This is best done in the form of an outline.

Here is what you should do for maximum retention of course content. First, look at how your textbook authors have organized each chapter into major topics and then outline this material in your textbooks. Second, write an outline from any outside readings. Third, write your class notes in the form of an outline. These then beome preliminary outlines for later study. Finally, develop a comprehensive outline from these preliminary ones for each exam in each course. Each final outline will represent the source document from which you will study for each major exam. While this may seem difficult until you master certain outlining skills, the results will be well worth the effort.

10. Overlearning: The Final Study Session The highest achievers in almost all fields of endeavor are those who overprepare for each task. The same applies to students who wish to learn the most and get the best grades.

A final concentrated study session is an effective way to maximize the likelihood of getting good grades. On the day before each major exam, you should pull together all the course content on which you will be tested. The most efficient way to accomplish this is through a final study session with a comprehensive written outline. By having prepared such an outline as you progressed through the weeks leading up to each exam, you will be freed from having to move back and forth between textbook, outside readings, and class notes. Assuming you developed this outline correctly, you should be ready for the exam when you have mastered all the course content it contains.

PRINCIPLE 17: Develop Critical Thinking Skills

Although the ability to retain and recall large amounts of information is essential to becoming an effective student, a good memory alone is not enough. In other words, being a good student requires more than the simple regurgitation of facts on an exam. One must also be able to take factual information and use it as a critical thinking tool to address key questions and solve problems. Key questions include: What does this information mean? What is my interpretation of it? Why is it important? How can I apply it to this particular situation or problem on the exam to earn the best possible grade?

Several years ago, I was engaged as a consultant by a major corporation to conduct a series of training seminars for marketing executives at the Xerox International Center for Training and Management Development in Leesburg, Virginia.

Those who go to the Leesburg facility, considered by some as the world's finest training complex, live on the premises for the duration of their stay.

As I arrived to check in that first evening, I was impressed by a prominent sign in large block letters placed over the arrival and information desk. It said simply THINK! (This, by the way, has long been the unofficial corporate motto of IBM.)

If I could give only one word of advice to anyone seeking success in school, career, relationships, or life in general. I would say the same thing: THINK! Think long. Think hard. Think smart. Think big. But above all else, THINK! Our capacity for thinking separates us from the lower animals. Thinking coupled with the right attitudes and actions separates winners from losers, both in school and in life. Indeed, the way each of us and our society handles the important challenges that face us in the future will depend on how well we learn to ask questions, solve problems, and, in other ways, think clearly and critically.

Yet critical thinking is not taught as a required course, or even as a separate course, by most of our nation's public schools and colleges. It also is not treated as a high-priority issue by a large number of American government officials, taxpayers, parents, and teachers. And it is not even mentioned in many study skills books and programs that attempt to do what ESS does.

The result, unfortunately, contributes to the poor condition that characterizes American education today. According to numerous comparative studies, students in many industrialized nations are outthinking and outachieving our students at all levels by a significant margin. The 1983 report *A Nation at Risk: The Imperative for Educational Reform*, issued by the National Commission on Excellence in Education, serves as one example. The following is a brief excerpt:

> Our nation is at risk. Our once unchallenged preeminence in commerce, industry, science, and technological innovation is being overtaken by competitors throughout the world. . . . What was unimaginable a decade ago has begun to occur—others are matching and surpassing our educational attainments.
>
> If an unfriendly foreign power had attempted to impose on America the mediocre educational performance that exists today, we might well have viewed it as an act of war. As it stands, we have allowed this to happen to ourselves. . . . We have, in effect, been committing an act of unthinking, unilateral educational disarmament. . . .
>
> International comparisons of student achievement, completed a decade ago, reveal that on 19 academic tests American students were never first or second and, in comparison with other industrialized nations, were last seven times. . . .
>
> Many 17-year-olds do not possess the "higher order" intellectual skills we should expect of them. Nearly 40 percent cannot draw inferences from written material; only one-fifth can write a persuasive essay; and only one-third can solve a mathematics problem requiring several steps (1983, pp. 5–9).

What Is Critical Thinking?

The fallout from such reports on American education has generated a national debate. Part of the controversy has centered around critical thinking. What is it? When should it be taught? How should it be taught? Can it be taught? Experts do not agree on the answers to any of these questions, but one thing is clear. There is not enough critical thinking occurring among our students at all levels. All too often, students are conditioned by their teachers to give the right answers rather than ask the right questions and make effective arguments.

Critical thinking refers to the willingness (attitude) and ability (skill) to use systematic and objective methods to solve problems. In other words, to think critically is to solve problems in an effective manner. Scientists and other scholars make their living this way. So do corporate executives and managers, marketing and sales professionals, lawyers, accountants, computer analysts, athletic coaches, and many other people. The most successful students, the leaders of tomorrow, also must develop these skills. You can be one of those leaders if you will develop and use the critical thinking skills and steps I'm about to show you.

How to Develop Five Essential Skills for Critical Thinking

Discussed below are five key principles for critical thinking. Use them regularly and you will develop valuable skills. Equipped with these tools, both your effectiveness as a student and your awareness and insight as a person will be greatly enhanced.

Skill 1: An Active Process of Questioning The first prerequisite for critical thinking is the realization that the world is a complex place and there are problems to solve. It is to have insight, to see possibilities, to ask questions. Therefore, critical thinkers tend to be an incurable skeptics. They look at the world with some wonder and want to go beyond the obvious and accepted to find out what really makes it work.

On a practical level, genuine thinkers search for meaning; they do not blindly accept what others say. Instead, key questions are posed: "What does this mean?" "Does it make sense?" "Is it correct?" Thinkers ask these and other questions, if only to themselves, about practically everything.

For critical thinkers, truth is never something to be accepted simply because someone says it is so. Instead, it must be sought out, examined, and tested. Thinkers take the position that you must seek in order to find, question in order to know.

In the final analysis, truth tends not to be a thing, fixed and unchanging. Rather, it results from a continual process of discovery, a never-ending search for meaning. Accept this principle and practice it regularly and you will become a more skillful thinker too.

Skill 2: A Systematic Method of Reasoning   Critical thinking includes two dimensions of what philosophers and scientists often call logic. The two basic kinds of logic are called deductive reasoning and inductive reasoning.

Deductive reasoning (sometimes called analysis) involves the movement from general questions or statements about some aspect of reality to more specific ones. Suppose, for example, you asked the question "What caused the Great Depression of the 1930s?" This is a general question about a decade-long phenomenon during the twentieth century.

As you analyze or deduce further, you ask more specific questions. "Was there one cause or several causes?" If you find several causes, you might ask "How should I classify or evaluate these causes?" "Were there both primary and secondary causes and, if so, which were which?" "What were the basic factors that accounted for each cause?" "Were there both immediate triggering causes and underlying historical causes?" "What characteristics or factors were important concerning each of these?"

This is deductive or analytical thinking in which a general phenomonen is dissected by dividing it into smaller parts. To engage in this form of critical thinking is one way to arrive at answers or explanations.

Inductive reasoning (sometimes called synthesis) involves the movement from specific questions or statements about some aspect of reality to more general ones. It represents an effort aimed at finding a general, larger truth from one or more smaller ones; to arrive at a whole by combining several parts. The central question asked by the inductive thinker is "Does this specific part have meaning or application to a larger whole?"

Suppose you were a person who wanted to build a race car to win the Indianapolis 500 automobile race. To meet this challenge as a critical thinker, you would have to arrive at the right synthesis of elements. Race-car drivers call this the winning combination.

Using inductive reasoning, you would have to ask and answer a lot of specific questions to solve this problem. Questions about the engine as one component. Questions about each of many others: the power-to-weight ratio, the chassis, the gearing, the design of the body, the driver, the pit stops, the race strategy, and many more. Only then—if the inductive reasoning process was carried out just right and you had some race-day luck—might your car win the race.

Skill 3: The Ability to Develop Rational Arguments   An argument is based on an assertion about the characteristics or causes of one or more objects or phenomena. Other terms commonly substituted for assertion include *premise,* *proposition, assumption,* and *hypothesis.* Some examples of assertions might include these: The United States has a sound economy. The planet Venus is incapable of supporting life. Hemingway was a more successful novelist than Faulkner.

As the beginning point in the presentation of an argument, the assertion is, in effect, a hypothesis or educated guess. However, the true scholar starts the critical-thinking process before beginning to develop an argument.

The assertion or hypothesis emerges from a set of preliminary questions and the gathering of facts. Then, if the thinker believes a particular line of argument is worth pursuing, an assertion is made. This hypothesis is then tested and evidence is gathered. Finally, after the evidence has been evaluated, conclusions are made.

Five Basic Steps Used in the Development and Testing of Rational Arguments
Rational arguments emerge out of a five-step critical-thinking process summarized here:

1. *The identification of the problem.* You identify a problem by asking one or more general questions. In doing so, you begin the deductive reasoning process (from general to specific). This may involve exploring possible preliminary assertions. Example: What is the state of the American economy? Is it mainly sound? Is it mainly unsound? Preliminary assertions to be explored: The United States mainly has a sound economy. The United States mainly has an unsound economy.

2. *The establishment of preliminary facts* (called *review of the literature* in science). As you continue to move from general to specific, you begin to ask more specific questions. You search for factual evidence that points to possible answers. What have other investigators found? How did they define their terms? How did they gather their facts? What do these facts say? Do the findings of other scholars point to the need for more specific research?

3. *The development of an assertion* (called *hypothesis* in science). As a result of the preliminary fact-gathering process, you deduce to a specific but tentative conclusion. This becomes the assertion and signals the true beginning of the rational argument process. The assertion or hypothesis represents the springboard for verification and additional investigation. Example of an assertion (hypothesis): The United States basically has a better economy than countries A, B, and C in terms of variables X, Y, and Z. The statement of such specifics in the assertion is made possible by the gathering of preliminary facts that seem to point in a particular direction.

4. *The objective gathering of evidence* (called *testing a hypothesis* in science). Once the assertion or hypothesis has been made, it has to be fully tested. To do so, the critical thinker must ponder how best to ascertain whether or

not the assertion has merit. What is the best approach to use in gathering evidence in an objective and systematic way? In science, for example, there are many ways to gather evidence: The survey, the case study, the experiment, and others. Once this issue is decided, the evidence is then gathered.

5. *The evaluation of results.* Once the evidence is in, what does it say? Was the assertion supported or not? Were some aspects or variables included in the assertion supported while others were not? The critical thinker must address these and other questions. At the end of the evaluation process, the critical thinker will then decide whether to continue inquiry about the argument in question, abandon it, put it aside for the time being, or modify and refine it.

Skill 4: The Ability to Understand Rational Arguments   To be an effective thinker, you must also recognize sound thinking and rational arguments when they come from others. Does an argument offered by another person follow the five steps mentioned above? What are some specific indicators that this is or is not the case? To be more specific, what basic assertion or premise is being made? What logical or objectively gathered evidence is offered to support the assertion? What conclusions are given? Are the conclusions adequately supported by the line of argumentation or evidence presented?

Skill 5: The Ability to Identify Faulty Arguments   One of the hallmarks of an educated person is the ability to identify faulty arguments. The world is full of those with untrained minds who, although their motives may be innocent or benign, will try to persuade us with arguments containing errors in reasoning or factual information, or both. In addition, there are those who will intentionally mislead us if we let them. These people, whose ranks include some politicians, advertisers, and other propagandists, stand to gain in a practical way from exploiting the ignorance of others. Beware of such individuals. Their game is to beguile with half-truths and intellectual "hat tricks."

How to Identify Faulty Arguments   We tend to be fooled by faulty arguments because of four main factors: (1) our lack of knowledge, (2) the appearance or enthusiasm of the persuader, (3) the position or authority possessed by the persuader, and (4) our own inattention.

Here are eleven of the more common forms of faulty arguments. Both English and Latin names have been provided:

1. *Appeal to emotion (ad populum).* This approach, a favorite of propagandists, seeks to incite in a person certain emotions—love, duty, fear, and others—as a diversionary tactic to avoid presenting objective evidence.

Examples: The message that buying a certain car, beer, or breakfast cereal will promote sex appeal, adventure, or athletic prowess; the idea that not buying a particular product will result in loneliness or not voting for a specific candidate will lead to higher crime rates.

2. *Appeal to pity (ad misericordiam).* This represents a special form of appeal to emotion. Here, the persuader tries to evoke sympathy as a tactic to obscure the valid evidence and conclusion related to an argument. Example: The high-level corporate or church official convicted of income tax evasion or misuse of funds who meets with reporters at a press conference surrounded by spouse and children.

3. *Appeal to authority (ad baculum).* The message here is that might makes right. Something is seen as true simply because someone in high authority said it was so. Implicit in this approach is the subtle (and sometimes not too subtle) threat that the receiver might experience adverse consequences if he or she does not accept the "wisdom" of the person or persons in authority.

4. *Appeal to the person (ad hominem).* This form of faulty reasoning involves launching a personal attack concerning some aspect of a particular person—such as appearance, morality, character—rather than a focus on the merits of the argument itself.

5. *Use of false or irrelevant authority (ad verecundiam).* Those who use this approach try to claim that a person who has expertise in one field is also an authority in another when no such expertise exists. This is another diversionary tactic aimed at avoiding the presentation of valid evidence in support of the argument. Example: The use of a famous baseball player to sell fast food or pickup trucks.

6. *Overgeneralization.* Sometimes called prejudice, overgeneralization occurs when a person comes to a general conclusion without adequate evidence to support it. Thus, to overgeneralize is to jump to a conclusion. When this faulty form of inductive reasoning is applied to others, it often results in stereotypes—sweeping conclusions about a category of people that have little or no basis in fact. Examples of overgeneralization: "New Orleans is the friendliest town in America." "The Chinese are intellectually superior to Germans."

7. *The fallacy of relevance (non sequitur).* This is a faulty argument in which the conclusion does not follow logically from the assertion. Example: "Henry Smith has been happily married for thirty years. Therefore he will make a fine senator."

8. *The fallacy of false cause (post hoc ergo propter hoc).* Some people at times

mistakenly conclude that one event is caused by another that immediately preceded it simply because of their order of occurrence. Event A happens. Then event B happens. Therefore A caused B. While the nearness of the two events in time may make for an interesting circumstance, this alone is not sufficient to demonstrate a cause-and-effect relationship.

9. *Jumping on the bandwagon.* This approach asserts that an argument is correct because many people agree that it is so. Such a go-along-with-the-crowd mentality attempts to define truth by popularity or majority rule. Example: "Since most people don't vote, voting is a waste of time."

10. *The red herring.* Just as a red herring placed in front of a bloodhound might throw him off the real scent, a similar situation may occur in the presentation of an argument. The red herring fallacy is a device in which an irrelevant issue is introduced to distract the receiver from the main argument. Example: "Cruelty to animals is unfortunate, but abuse of the elderly is really what's important."

11. *Circular reasoning (petitio principii).* Also known as begging the question, this argument uses a conclusion that simply restates the assertion. Although the statement is valid, it adds nothing to our understanding. Example: "The murder rate in our nation's capital is a serious problem because so many people are dying each year."

10 PRINCIPLES 18–20: HOW TO CHOOSE A MENTOR, WRITE A RÉSUMÉ, AND GET SUPERIOR GRADES

PRINCIPLE 18: Choose a Teacher to Serve as a Mentor

The most successful students often choose a teacher they highly respect to serve as an adviser or mentor. Ideally, this professor will be someone in your major field. If you choose such a teacher to act as your counselor and friend, take every opportunity to work with this scholar and seek his or her guidance. While a school counselor can be very helpful and offers several valuable services, the best counselor of all, particularly at the college level, is a professor in your major field.

Such a mentor can provide you invaluable information about which courses to take and, should you plan additional education, which colleges, graduate schools, or professional schools to consider. If you do plan to pursue additional study, your mentor may have key contacts at certain schools who might help you if you need a recommendation for being accepted.

Some college professors engage in outside consulting, original research, and writing articles and textbooks. If you get the opportunity, volunteer to assist your mentor in some of these activities—with or without pay. This can be a very special experience that few students, especially undergraduates, get or take the opportunity to participate in. Yet you may learn as much or more about your chosen field from these endeavors as you will from classroom instruction.

PRINCIPLE 19: Learn to Write a Résumé for Success

A few academics who have not kept pace with the changing realities and needs facing today's students (as well as many casual observers) may wonder "Why discuss how to write a résumé in a study skills book? It doesn't seem to belong." Here is my response.

Why This Topic Should be Included in Study Skills

Education doesn't occur in a vacuum. Students do not consist merely of one-dimensional roles interested only in nuts-and-bolts tips directly related to getting through school. Instead, they are multidimensional human beings with life concerns and challenges that range far beyond the hallowed halls of the educational institutions they attend. Most students are concerned with what happens after basic schooling has been completed. Among other things related to life outside school, they seek answers to two fundamental questions: "How do I use my education to get a good job? and "What do I need to do to get an interview for the job I want?"

One of the main reasons for going to school is to prepare for a career or to gain career advancement. Yet, if you don't know how to effectively present yourself to a potential employer, all your years of study and hard work may go for naught. Take a good look around you at those who are employed. You will undoubtedly notice some people with a year or two of college and perhaps even a few college graduates who don't seem to be getting ahead. They appear stuck in dead-end jobs. In some cases, part of the reason for this may be that these individuals don't know how to package and market themselves to prospective employers.

In addition, many students need to work part-time or full-time to help support themselves and their families while pursuing their education. The demographic characteristics of college students have changed significantly over the last several decades. In the recent past, the typical American college student was an eighteen- to twenty-two-year-old white, native-born individual from a middle- to upper-middle class background who attended school away from home at a regional state-supported public university or private liberal arts college.

The student population attending our business and technical schools, colleges and universities today is different in composition. Increasingly, many are nontraditional students such as housewives, retired persons, dislocated workers, minorities, foreign nationals, and single working parents.

Close to half of all college freshman in the United States today attend local community colleges, and many of them work. In addition, many university students today also hold part-time or full-time jobs while attending school. I especially identify with these working students. As an undergraduate myself twenty years ago, I matriculated at a university thirty miles from my home, commuted back and forth each day by car for four years, and paid my way through school by working at night. Had I known when I entered college how to write a résumé, I might have been able to get a better-paying job while in school, work fewer hours each week, and experience an easier time with my studies.

Nonetheless, only some high schools and colleges offer a practical course that shows students how to write a résumé to get the best jobs. And even fewer freshman orientation courses for first-year college students address this issue. Perhaps this is because résumé-writing is not a study skill directly related to academic success as measured by grades. However, *one direct measure of student success is getting a job while in school or after the formal educational program is completed.* Therefore, in response to many requests from both students and employers over the years, I have included the fundamentals of résumé writing in this section of ESS.

What Is a Résumé? Why Is It Important?

A **résumé** is a record of a person's life or job history in capsule form. Its main purpose is to serve as a marketing tool to get you an interview. In truth, most employers won't even consider applicants without résumés for the better jobs. In our competitive world they will also cast aside résumés that are sloppy and poorly done. Therefore what the résumé includes, how its contents are presented, and its overall appearance and form are very, very important.

Your résumé serves you like a goodwill ambassador. It speaks for you as your representative. Research has demonstrated that the typical employer with a stack of résumés to examine looks at each one only for a few seconds. The best ones are placed in a separate stack for further examination. The rest are set aside and not considered further. Therefore take care that your résumé leaves a good impression.

As a matter of principle, you should present a résumé to a prospective employer each time you apply for any type of job. Even if you are a high school or college student trying to get a part-time job at little more than minimum wage, you should have a résumé. Why? Because, other than the fact that it makes a good impression and may get you the job, you need the practice.

Good résumé-writing is a craft, an art form. I can only show you the fundamentals. In all probability, it will take a few trial runs before you are good at it. But oh what a valuable skill to have!

How to Prepare a Successful Résumé

Always Have an Updated Résumé Handy   The average person will hold at least eight or ten different jobs during his or her lifetime. Even if you are currently employed and relatively happy in your work, one never knows when a significant opportunity might come along. Those currently employed often have the most bargaining power when such opportunities occur. Since they are successfully employed and have experience, they often are the most desirable applicants to prospective employers. Always be prepared with a current résumé should an opportunity come your way. As a general rule of thumb, it is wise to update your résumé at least once a year.

Include a Cover Letter   Remember how it feels to get a letter addressed to Occupant or Resident? A résumé without a cover letter leaves the same impression. Lying there by itself, it appears cold and impersonal. Always include a brief cover letter. It will provide you another selling opportunity and will personalize your application. Since many job applicants, particularly younger ones, don't know to do this, it may give you an edge over some of your competitors.

The Dos and Don'ts of Writing a Cover Letter

1. *Personalize it.* A cover letter should always be addressed to a person within the hiring organization, usually the department or division head who will make the hiring decision. Most likely, it will be this person who will do the interviewing. If all else fails, you can phone the personnel office to get the identity of this person.

2. *Keep it brief.* Most experts recommend a single page with a maximum of two hundred words.

3. *Say something about the organization.* Interviewers are impressed by detail people who do their homework. This shows that they care and take pride in their work. Say something in your opening paragraph that lets the interviewer know that you are informed about his or her organization (its history, current projects, or future goals). Example: "I read with great interest recently in *The Wall Street Journal* that your company is embarking on. . . . "

4. *Match your skills to the organization's needs.* Finish that same first paragraph by showing how your interests, qualifications, or accomplishments match the needs of the organization. Then expand on this theme in the next paragraph by mentioning key points in your résumé that strengthen your argument.

   You have the opportunity in a cover letter to mention one or two strengths that may or may not have been included in your résumé. This way you can tailor your application to special organizational needs that a general résumé is not designed to address. After all, the central question on every hiring official's mind is "What can this applicant do for us?"

5. *Use positive, action-oriented language.* Your language should be formal and professional in tone but positive and action-oriented.

   First, you should appear enthusiastic. Don't say "I read that your company. . . . " Say instead "I read with great interest that your company. . . . " In the minds of most interviewers, enthusiasm translates into energy and productivity on the job. Sterile, stilted language will tend to create a similar impression about you.

   Second, in speaking of your skills or accomplishments, use action-oriented verbs and phrases to get and hold the reader's attention. Don't say

"I was a salesperson for the past two years at XYZ corporation." Say instead "During my two years at XYZ corporation, I increased sales in my territory by 38 percent." *Increased* and *38 percent* are what the hiring official wants to see.

6. *Use a close that creates an opening.* An effective cover letter should end on a positive note that opens the door for further contact. In the final paragraph, it often helps to include a phone number where you can be reached. In addition, use language such as "I would welcome the opportunity to discuss this position with you in person." This indirect request for an interview tells the reader that you are serious about the position and not just going through the motions.

7. *Avoid the Don'ts.* The cover letter should not contain any of the following: misspelled words or improper grammar; handwriting except for the signature at the end; references to salary past, present, or expected; negative comments or excuses about anything.

Stick to One Page To be effective, the résumé must be brief and to the point. Since busy executives will spend only a few seconds surveying each one, help them out by not bogging them down with less important detail. This is one instance in which less is better. In fact, some hiring officials discard altogether résumés longer than two or three pages. Understanding this, you will be more effective if you keep your résumé to one page.

The only exception to this rule would apply to individuals who perhaps, by middle age, have amassed a long list of notable accomplishments in specialized fields. Particularly in the professions, such achievements may require enumeration and brief elaboration. However, even in these cases (which include some corporate executives, lawyers, and college professors) the experts recommend a two-page limit.

Organize by Chronology and Achievements Many books have been written about how to construct résumés. Some show how different types can be used for different situations. Résumé styles include the chronological method (dates of employment, past and present), the functional approach (duties and accomplishments), and the combined method (the best of both types).

In most circumstances, the combined method is the most effective. You should therefore list in reverse chronological order (most recent first) your education and work histories along with a brief explanation of your duties and accomplishments in each job.

Use an Effective Step-By-Step Format In formatting your résumé, don't waste precious space by using a title such as **Résumé** or **Vita**. Besides taking up an unnecessary line, it is redundant. The purpose of this document will be obvious to the reader.

The Contents of an Effective Résumé

Your single page should include these categories of information in the following order:

1. *Name, address, and phone number.* This should be centered at the top of the page with perhaps your name in boldface.

2. *Objective.* If you are clear in your occupational goal, a brief statement about the job you wish to obtain can lend focus and direction to your résumé. If you are unsure about which job you wish to pursue, omit this section.

3. *Education (and training if applicable).* Since employers are almost always interested in education, this should follow next. If your job experience is extensive, make your education section brief to save room as shown by these two examples:

1988–1990: 42 semester hours completed toward B.A. degree in finance, Lake Superior State College.

B.S. —Duke University, 1981—Political Science.
Management Training: Internal training, IBM—1990, 1988, 1986; Summer institute, University of Texas, Austin—1984; Xerox Learning Systems Courses—1983, 1982.

If you plan to send résumés out of the region, include the city-state location of your college (Example 1). Include outstanding academic distinctions such as magna cum laude or a high GPA (Example 2).

If you are a recent college graduate with little job experience, place more emphasis on education by using more space and stressing any notable educational achievements:

1991: Bachelor of Arts Degree in Sociology, University of Chicago.
Graduated Magna Cum Laude with a 3.70 Grade Point Average. Special area of interest and concentration: Marriage and the Family. As a senior, assisted two professors in research on divorce, the results of which will be published in an upcoming issue of *Family.*

---

4. *Experience.* All relevant past and present work experience should be summarized here. Items for each position held should include dates of employ-

ment (beginning with current or last position held), job title, and a list of duties performed. When possible, describe duties using *action verbs and phrases*. Here are some examples of action verbs that may be useful in describing duties performed:

achieved	established	prepared
administered	expanded	produced
analyzed	implemented	promoted
conducted	improved	provided
coordinated	introduced	reduced
created	maintained	restructured
designed	managed	scheduled
developed	negotiated	supervised
directed	organized	trained

If meaningful accomplishments have resulted from any jobs past or present, you can carry this process one step further by using action phrases to pinpoint your achievements. This approach will make the greatest impact on prospective employers. Hiring officials are mainly interested in what you have done, not what you say you can do. Here are two examples:

Developed three sales training programs that were implemented nationally by the corporation.

Restructured department comprised of 15 employees to one consisting of 12 employees with a 20% gain in productivity and no loss in morale.

---

5. *Awards, Honors, and Activities.* Include as few or as many of these categories as you have items for or feel will strengthen your image as a superior applicant. The purpose here is to show that you have leadership ability and are achievement-oriented. Of course, if you have no significant awards and honors, this section might simply be called Activities. Relevant awards and honors include prestigious scholarships (Rhodes, National Merit, Truman, and so on), dean's list, honor societies (Phi Beta Kappa, Phi Kappa Phi, and others), *Who's Who* listings, and professional achievements or community service awards. Relevant activities would also include offices held or accomplishments made in professional associations.

It is a good idea to be active in student organizations while at college, if possible. It is even better to hold an office—president, vice president, secretary, treasurer. In addition to providing you some valuable experience in learning how organizations function, it can be used on a résumé. Particularly for a college student or recent college graduate with little or no job experience, having been an officer in practically any student or occupational organization indicates initiative, responsibility, good interpersonal skills, and leadership potential.

Sample Résumé   Now examine the sample résumé of Leon DaVinci in Figure 10–1. As indicated, he is a second-year journalism student about to become a junior. He is seeking some hands-on experience at a commercial newspaper. Notice how he "markets" his experience although it is clear that he has no employment history related to journalism. By seeking it now, he will be in a good position later to get a professional job after he graduates. Leon has already learned the importance of building up one's résumé over time with documented experience and accomplishments.

Items You Should Not Include   For most jobs, personal information about you is irrelevant. It not only takes up valuable space, but it also may play to possible prejudices of the hiring official. Therefore, omit from your résumé such items as date and place of birth, marital status, ethnic or racial background, religious affiliation, and health. Also leave out reasons why you left any previous job, any reference to salary (former or expected), hobbies, and membership in social or fraternal organizations.

I once knew an extremely well-qualified man who applied for a marketing position at a well-known corporation. On his résumé he listed his hobbies as hunting and skeet shooting. He didn't make the cut for the interview. Later he found out that the hiring official was opposed to hunting and hated guns because his son had been accidently shot and killed the year before by a deer hunter.

Consider another example. What do you think your chances would be in getting an interview if you mentioned any health problems? So don't take the chance. Don't provide any information unrelated to the job that is not specifically asked for. It might ruin your chances before you have had the opportunity to interview for the position.

In addition, don't include references or language that refers to references such as "References supplied upon request." The place for the listing of references is on a job application form. If the prospective employer doesn't use such a form and is seriously interested, you will be contacted to provide such information.

Items You Might Consider   There are a few optional items that sometimes enhance the effectiveness of a résumé. First, if you are clear on your career objective (long-range plan), it might be useful to include it. If used, it should appear as the first category below your name, address, and phone number. Second, em-

SAMPLE RÉSUMÉ

Leon T. DaVinci
605 Mona Lisa Lane
Tulsa, Oklahoma 74115
(405) 111-0000

CLEAR OBJECTIVE

OBJECTIVE: A summer internship position with a city newspaper.

EDUCATION: 54 Semester Hours Completed toward a B.A. degree
in Journalism, University of Tulsa. 3.42 GPA

EXPERIENCE: 1990-1991. Assistant Editor, -- University of Tulsa
Student Newspaper.
Wrote a weekly "Critics Corner" column that
reviewed two current films.
Supervised the work of five student reporters.
Developed a four-step time management
system to help reporters meet deadlines.
Trained three new reporters in the use of Microsoft
Word and various graphics and desktop publishing
software for use with the Macintosh SE.
Assisted the Editor with letters to the Editor.

CLEVER WAY TO POSITION
RELATED EXPERIENCE
EVEN THOUGH THIS WORK
WAS WITHOUT PAY

EXCELLENT USE
OF ACTION VERBS

THESE TWO POSITIONS
SHOW PROGRESS AND
GROWTH OVER TIME

1989-1990. Reporter -- University of Tulsa Student Newspaper.
Wrote a weekly sports column (football and track).

**EMPLOYMENT
HISTORY:** 1989-90. Waiter -- Toni's Italian Restaurant (Full-time
Summer Job)
1988-89. Stock Clerk/Casher -- Kroger (Part-time;
Senior Year in High School)

**HONORS/
ACTIVITIES:** Dean's List -- Three Semesters; University of Tulsa
Secretary-Treasurer -- Journalism Club, UT.

DEMONSTRATES ACHIEVEMENT
AND RESPONSIBILITY

Figure 10-1

ployers are usually impressed by a military record, particularly if it includes training and/or experience related to the job being filled. Third, a listing of current
memberships in professional or occupation-related organizations may be helpful,
particularly if you need something as filler to take up space. This shows that you
are active and conscientious concerning your occupation, which may impress a
prospective employer.

Use Flawless Spelling and Grammar   From the perspective of many prospective employers, there is no acceptable excuse for misspelled words and poor grammar. The message this sends them is that this applicant is careless and sloppy and takes little pride in his or her work. If this person takes so little care in the application process, what type of employee would he or she make? Unfortunately, the answer tends to be a foregone conclusion and, in many cases, this person is excluded from further consideration.

Use a Layout that Says "Quality"   Think of your résumé as a commercial aimed at promoting you (the product) to a prospective employer (potential buyer). To be effective, it must say quality in appearance as well as in content.
Follow these guidelines for maximum impact:

1. *The résumé must be typed* in a clean, crisp typeface such as Times Roman that is easy on the eye.
2. *Section headings should be in boldface* for visual appeal.
3. *Spaces should be left between sections* to aid in eye appeal and readability. This way, the reader can scan, separate, and pinpoint specific sections more easily.
4. *The final résumé should be letter-perfect*—no mistakes in spelling, grammar, or syntax. It also should be razor-sharp, with no stains, smears, or smudges.
5. *Top-quality bond paper should be used,* with at least 50 percent rag content, preferably in white or ivory. Contrary to popular myth, strong colors and pastels don't impress most employers. Rather, they are distracting and appear unprofessional.

To ensure the best quality appearance, your résumé either should be typeset and printed on an offset press or entered and formatted on a computer and printed using an ink-jet or laser printer. Since the per-copy price drops as more copies are printed, order at least fifty to a hundred. This way, you will be sure to have enough.

PRINCIPLE 20: Use ESS—THE ADVANCED COURSE: A Proven System for Getting Superior Grades

If you apply the preceding nineteen action principles to your studying, you will be well on your way toward becoming an effective and responsible student. These principles serve as both conceptual and skill-based guideposts that, when followed, will furnish you the student with important "things to do" in order to improve performance. To be most effective, they need not be implemented in any particular order so long as they are all used.

However, to develop maximum potential as a student, a specific set of study skills needs to be developed and practiced in a particular sequence as a total learning system. This is where the rest of ESS comes in. Part 3: ESS—THE ADVANCED COURSE identifies (1) the essential skills needed to obtain peak performance as a learner in an academic setting and (2) demonstrates how to use them in a simple four-step process. These four Steps build on the Twenty Principles explained in the part of the book you have just completed.

By working hard and devoting a semester or two toward the complete mastery of the Steps and skills taught, the advanced course will place you on the road to straight A's. Within a few short weeks after putting it into practice, you should experience significant if not dramatic improvement in your ability to grasp and master course material. This ultimately can lead to unlimited academic success. If you're up to this challenge, the journey to straight A's—along with all the provisions needed for the trip—begins after the next page.

PART 3

ESS—THE ADVANCED COURSE

A Proven System for Getting Superior Grades

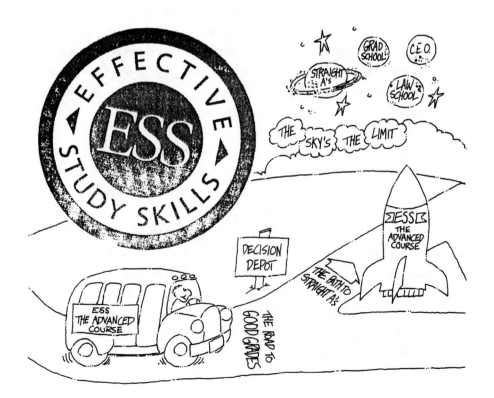

The first two sections of this book provide the tools you will need to be an above-average to good, and at least fairly successful, student. If you continue to practice the life lessons and study principles discussed in ESS—AN INTRODUCTION and ESS—THE BASIC COURSE, you should be able to graduate, obtain a job, and hopefully have a happy, productive future.

THE REST OF THIS BOOK IS INTENDED MAINLY FOR THOSE WHO ARE SERIOUS ABOUT EARNING STRAIGHT A'S. If you are satisfied with B's and C's and maybe an occasional A (as long as it doesn't take too much effort), read no farther. Much of what you read beyond this point—with exceptions such as techniques for taking tests and dealing with test anxiety—will be unnecessary.

However, if you are determined to earn straight A's and learn the skills for unlimited academic success, then ESS—THE ADVANCED COURSE is for you. With some work and dedicated application on your part, it will provide you all the essential tools you will need. These tools for excellence—which build upon many of the principles already presented—are interwoven into a skill-based, four-step system. You might think of this system as an after-burner or power booster for unlimited success.

Well.... you didn't quit reading as I suggested a couple of paragraphs ago. Perhaps then you are one of that rare breed of student who really has an earnest, deep-seated desire to excel in school and put in the work necessary to get superior grades.

If this describes you, I have two brief things to say as we begin. First, Welcome aboard! You should find this part of the book a fascinating trip. What I'm about to show you, if used and developed properly, will empower you to go as far as your desire to achieve in school will take you. Second, I hereby challenge you to develop your potential by learning this system and harnessing its power. To do so will take some close reading, a little patience, and some work on your part. The rewards, I assure you, will be worth it.

CHAPTER

11 THE FOUR STEPS IN THE STUDY CYCLE

ESS—THE ADVANCED COURSE is based on a single simple premise: *Superior performance in school results from the most effective use of each study cycle.* The term **study cycle** refers to the period of time during which all course content for a given exam in each course must be learned. Thus the period from the first day of class until the date of the first exam in each course is a study cycle. If that same course involves three major exams, there are three study cycles. A semester-long course with three major exams and a comprehensive final exam might be seen as having one major sixteen-week preparation period divided into four distinct study cycles: Exam 1, Exam 2, Exam 3, and the Final.

To use ESS—THE ADVANCED COURSE successfully you must learn to think in terms of completing a study cycle for each exam you take. Completion of each cycle involves carrying out three and possibly four essential steps. These steps focus study efforts in the most effective way for maximum results. As a result you develop a variety of study skills as you master course content in steps or stages and use time in the most efficient way possible.

Many high school and beginning college students do not think in terms of study cycles. Instead, they focus their attention on the exam—which, at the beginning of the school term, seems far far away. These students will often say or think to themselves "I've got a major exam in four weeks. The final exam is several months away. I've got plenty of time."

Unfortunately, such statements probably mean that these students have no plan or system for study. In addition, time has a way of escaping us if we don't watch and use it carefully. When this happens, the results tend to be very predictable. By not having a plan and allowing time to get away, some students procrastinate and end up cramming for exams. This leads to poor performance and mediocre to failing grades.

Most advanced students (college juniors and seniors, graduate and professional students) and almost all superior students who earn the best grades have learned to avoid this trap. They tend to think in terms of a study cycle and have an effective plan for regular study.

ESS—THE ADVANCED COURSE is designed to furnish you such a plan for using each study cycle for maximum success. It represents the result of more than a decade of research, testing, and refinement through working with more than two thousand college students who served as research subjects.

As we saw earlier in ESS—THE INTRODUCTION, there is indeed a Formula for Success that really works. Excellence in any area of endeavor involves a three-step process: (1) commitment to a meaningful goal, (2) the development of an effective plan to reach it, and (3) the perseverance needed to put the plan into practice and reach the goal. Then, to challenge our abilities and grow as people, each of us should set a higher goal and start again. This is what writer Ben Sweetland meant when he said "Success is a journey, not a destination."

Your goal is to excel as a student and earn A's in all of your courses. If you really have committed yourself to this goal and are therefore willing to place your studies as a top priority and work hard to develop the necessary skills, ESS—THE ADVANCED COURSE is the action plan that can take you as far as you wish to go in higher education. More specifically, *if you continually implement all four steps as a total system in exactly the same way and order in which they are explained, you should experience significant if not dramatic improvements in both study skills and grades.*

This system will work effectively in almost all courses in the typical college curriculum, including anthropology, business and accounting, biology, botany, economics, geology, geography, philosophy, political science, psychology, and sociology. With some fine-tuning by the student, ESS can also be adapted for use with such subjects as chemistry, English, physics, and mathematics.

The advanced version of ESS is designed to divide each study cycle into four steps:

**ESS—THE ADVANCED COURSE: A Proven System for
Getting Superior Grades**

STEP ONE: Textbook Usage Skills

STEP TWO: Content Organization Skills

STEP THREE: Exam Preparation Skills

STEP FOUR: Diagnostic Follow-up

Each of these steps contains a number of skills and skill elements or tasks that are first identified and defined and then explained in terms of why they are necessary and how they should be used (see Figure 11–1). For example, in STEP ONE: Textbook Usage Skills, the skills of Active Reading, Identification of Core Material, Topical Mapping, Chapter Outlining, and Time Management are identified and explained in the order in which they are to be used. In addition, many of the skills discussed contain related concepts that help make the explanation of each one clear and understandable. Tasks the student will need to perform to acquire the skills are also explained.

It is important to remember that ESS—THE ADVANCED COURSE builds on the principles taught in the earlier parts of the book. Along with these other major

ESS—THE ADVANCED COURSE
The Four Steps in the Study Cycle

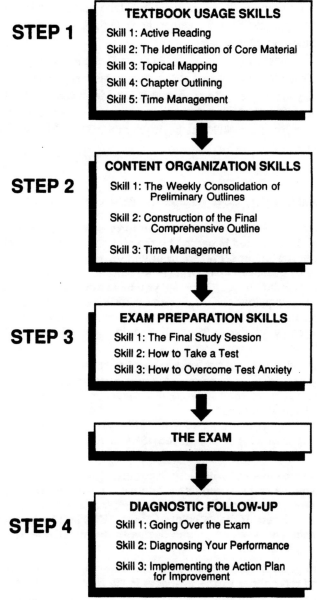

STEP 1

TEXTBOOK USAGE SKILLS

Skill 1: Active Reading
Skill 2: The Identification of Core Material
Skill 3: Topical Mapping
Skill 4: Chapter Outlining
Skill 5: Time Management

STEP 2

CONTENT ORGANIZATION SKILLS

Skill 1: The Weekly Consolidation of
Preliminary Outlines

Skill 2: Construction of the Final
Comprehensive Outline

Skill 3: Time Management

STEP 3

EXAM PREPARATION SKILLS

Skill 1: The Final Study Session
Skill 2: How to Take a Test
Skill 3: How to Overcome Test Anxiety

THE EXAM

STEP 4

DIAGNOSTIC FOLLOW-UP

Skill 1: Going Over the Exam

Skill 2: Diagnosing Your Performance

Skill 3: Implementing the Action Plan
for Improvement

Figure 11-1

components, it represents a comprehensive, skill-based learning system that must be implemented in the following manner for maximum success: *Use the first three steps in* ESS—THE ADVANCED COURSE *every time you prepare for a major exam in each of your courses.* If, for example, you take a political science course that contains three major exams and a comprehensive final, you will need to use the system four times in that course.

STEP FOUR: Diagnostic Follow-Up, should be needed only during the first semester or two as you develop mastery of the skills. This component is essential the first few times you use the system because it provides a way for you to diagnose your progress with the skills and pinpoint areas of strength and weakness. However, after mastery of the skills has been achieved, STEP FOUR should be regarded as optional.

VERY IMPORTANT: HOW TO USE THE REST OF THIS BOOK

This section has been developed to reinforce or take the place of ESS seminars (1) conducted in person by the author and other certified seminar administrators or (2) recorded in various formats. If you have attended one of these seminars or have a recorded version of it, you should have little difficulty. Otherwise, you have not experienced the benefits of ESS explanations, skill demonstrations, and illustrative transparencies used in the seminar format. Therefore, follow these instructions carefully to derive the full benefit from ESS—THE ADVANCED COURSE:

1. *The advanced course in ESS contains FOUR STEPS that are to be completed each time you progress through a study cycle. Once the total system is mastered, STEP FOUR—Diagnostic follow-up—becomes optional as needed.*

   Each Step, in turn, is divided into Skills that are to be learned and used in their proper order. Each Skill is further divided into Tasks that are to be used generally in the same way.

2. ESS is extremely meaty, with very little filler. It is therefore to be studied carefully and savored like a fine meal at a four-star restaurant, not wolfed down on the run like a burger at a fast-food joint. If the sheer richness of the ESS diet of Steps, Skills, and Tasks starts to overwhelm you, slow down and deal with the material a section or a heading at a time.

3. If you find yourself getting lost in detail, take the ESS material in chunks and refer either to the overview in Figure 11–1 or the table of contents in the front of the book. This way you will retain a big-picture perspective.

12 STEP ONE: TEXTBOOK USAGE SKILLS

Have you ever found yourself reading an important school assignment and being unable to stay awake, even though you received plenty of sleep the night before? Did you find yourself nodding off every fifteen or twenty minutes?

Have you ever read a text assignment and then, in the middle of it, suddenly realize that you had been fantasizing or daydreaming for several minutes? Did you imagine yourself engaged in some activity like sailing in the Gulf of Mexico, hunting moose in the Maine woods, or moving across the dance floor with the latest movie heartthrob?

If either of these scenarios is familiar—particularly if such episodes have recurred—you may have experienced a problem that afflicts many students called the passive reading syndrome. This problem tends to be troublesome to those who must read academic and technical literature. It is particularly frustrating to first- and second-year college students who, in making what is often an abrupt change from high school to college, are unfamiliar with the special qualities and challenges of such material.

Simply defined, the **passive reading syndrome** is unfocused academic or technical reading with low comprehension and retention. It occurs when the reader (1) lacks a clearly identified goal concerning the reading material at hand and (2) does not use the techniques necessary to set and attain it. For students who fall into this trap, passive reading involves going through the motions of reading with very little learning taking place. Have you, for example, ever read a textbook chapter and then thought to yourself or said to others "I read it, but I don't remember much of anything about it."

If this has happened to you, you may have done what many students try to do to remedy the situation: just read it again. Many high school and college students consequently experience some frustration with textbooks. The material seems to wash over their brains like waves on a beach. It doesn't sink in and have much impact in terms of learning. In some cases students find that, after rereading a chapter for a second or even third time, they still don't retain much of the material.

It is easy to drift into a pattern of passive reading with text material for several reasons. First, many of the courses taken in high school and college are required rather than elective. Therefore, because students may not be interested in the subject matter contained in some of these courses, they tend to have the same initial reaction to the text materials required for them. In contrast, one usually reads a novel or magazine because of active interest in such things as the story or subject, theme, characters, or the author's writing style.

Second, a few textbooks are unduly tiresome and poorly written. This is because authors of such texts, although they may be brilliant scholars and leaders in their respective fields, are trained as academicians to generate new knowledge rather than as teachers and writers to communicate it effectively.

Third, many beginning students fall into the passive reading habit because no one has taught them otherwise. Some parents and public-school educators, for example, have been far better at preaching to students about the importance of diligent study than they have been at showing them in a step-by-step, hands-on manner how to do it. In many cases, they too have been frustrated because, before ESS came along, effective hands-on approaches that really worked have been extremely difficult to find.

So, for these and other reasons, many students arrive at college without some of the attitudes and techniques they need for reading success. Consequently they find much of the material in textbooks difficult to understand and retain.

By implementing STEP ONE, however, you can learn to (1) clearly identify the important material in any textbook or reading assignment and then (2) retain it to excel on exams. When Textbook Usage Skills become fully mastered, some students discover an additional benefit. Not only do their grades improve because they have learned and retained more, but they also develop a love and appreciation for learning they didn't have before.

When this occurs, the required courses you thought you wouldn't like can become more interesting and, in some cases, enjoyable. Even the occasional poorly written text can be effectively used for maximum learning.

Textbook Usage Skills are the ones acquired first in ESS—THE ADVANCED COURSE. This is because, in most cases, the first important task your instructor gives you on the first day of the term is a reading assignment. This assignment and others that follow are important because, in first- and second-year college survey courses especially, the textbook usually furnishes the foundation for the course and represents a primary source of course content over which the student will be tested.

To master the effective use of textbooks and other required reading material, you must acquire four basic skills: Active Reading, Identification of Core Material, Topical Mapping, and Chapter Outlining. They are to be used with each reading assignment in their proper order. A fifth skill, Time Management, is to be used simultaneously with the rest to tie them together. This sequential use of all steps and skills contained in ESS—THE ADVANCED COURSE is absolutely essential. This is because ESS is designed to increase and reinforce learning all along the way as you prepare for each exam.

To first obtain an overview of STEP ONE, take a moment to briefly review the five basic skills of successful textbook usage that appear below. As you do, remember that although these elements are called Textbook Usage Skills, they apply to all forms of reading you will be assigned in school. After you review STEP ONE, we will discuss each skill and how to use it in detail.

STEP ONE: Textbook Usage Skills
Skill 1: Active Reading
Skill 2: Identification of Core Material
Skill 3: Topical Mapping
Skill 4: Chapter Outlining
Skill 5: Time Management

SKILL 1: Active Reading

As a high school, private career school, college, or graduate/professional student, you must approach text assignments differently than any other form of reading. For instance, compared to novels that you might read for pleasure, academic reading assignments lack the suspense and plot development that so often capture the attention of fiction readers. Some college texts are rather dry and matter-of-fact in their presentation. This is because they are designed with a different audience and set of objectives in mind.

Of greatest importance is the fact that, unlike other forms of reading, you will be tested about textbook material and evaluated on the basis of how much of its important contents you retain. Therefore it is essential that you acquire the skill of active reading as an effective means of mastering the content of these materials.

For the purposes of ESS, **Active Reading** is focused reading with (1) a clearly identified goal and (2) a set of effective steps or procedures used to attain it. As a student, your goal in dealing with textbooks and other reading assignments is to identify, categorize, and fully understand the various content material for which you will be held responsible on exams.

Active Reading is the first and most important textbook usage skill you will develop. Your success in acquiring and using the other four skills of Identification of Core Material, Topical Mapping, Chapter Outlining, and Time Management will depend on your active reading ability.

Active Reading is task-oriented. It includes a set of step-by-step procedures or tasks you will need to follow. By completing them you will learn how to identify and master the material over which you will be tested.

It is perhaps best to handle reading assignments on a chapter-by-chapter basis because these are the types of reading increments most often assigned by high school and college instructors. Each textbook chapter or other reading assignment should be actively read using these procedural tasks:

> **Skill 1: Active Reading (by chapter or assignment)**
> **Task 1: Conduct a Reading Preview**
> **Task 2: Chunk by Chapter Section**
> **Task 3: Engage in Paragraph Classification**
> > **Core Material paragraphs**
> > **Concepts**
> > **Principles and Theories**
> > **Important Men and Women**
> > **Additional Forms**
> > **Elaboration Paragraphs**

Task 1: Conduct a Reading Preview   Your first task as an active reader is to preview the material you plan to read. The **reading preview** is a brief examination of the reading assignment prior to reading to obtain a big-picture view. It provides the student clues as to how the central idea or theme presented by the chapter or assignment will be explained.

A reading preview will help you get positioned for the reading ahead and thereby avoid the problems faced by many high school and beginning college students. Often they approach their reading assignments like other nonacademic forms of reading. That is, they blindly plunge forth into a chapter with no focus or direction. Then, after completing it, they find that they don't know where they've been, why they've been there, or what they were supposed to have learned.

How to Conduct a Reading Preview: Two Useful Techniques

1. *The table of contents method.* Most authors of high school and first- and second-year college texts place a brief outline of each chapter either in the table of contents (at the beginning of the book) or at the beginning of each chapter. These outlines intentionally furnish you, the reader, a set of guideposts to follow in acquainting yourself with the chapter's key idea, theme, or topic and the material contained within as organized by headings and subheadings. Before reading an assignment, take a few minutes to study this outline to get a "big picture view" of the reading to follow.

Write down a few questions or ideas to summarize what you think this chapter is about and what needs to be learned. As you progress on to reading the chapter, your reading can be focused on answering these questions and expanding upon key ideas.

2. *The " in-chapter" approach.* If there is no chapter outline in the table of contents or the beginning of the chapter or if you find it more effective, take a few minutes to first concentrate on the title and then thumb through the chapter. As you do so, pay close attention to the manner in which the material is divided into sections and subsections and topics and subtopics. Most high school and first- and second-year college texts are designed to assist you in this respect. Their authors use headings and subheadings in raised print and boldface type to distinguish the major sections and subsections of the chapter.

An Illustrative Exercise Using the Table of Contents Method   To demonstrate how this is done, let's take a moment to conduct a reading preview of Chapter 1 from a popular American history textbook. This is from the table of contents for *American History: A Survey,* (7th ed.) by Richard N. Current, T. Harry Williams, Frank Freidel, and Alan Brinkley (New York: Knopf, 1987):

Ask the big questions. Before actually reading such a chapter, ask as many of the following questions as possible in the order that seems most appropriate, given the material at hand: Who? What? When? Where? Why? As you formulate these questions, be sure to write them down for future reference. You might see some of them again on an exam.

Using the chapter outline above, let's start by examining the chapter title. *What* two worlds were colliding? In the main headings—The Civilizations of America and Europe Looks Westward—the authors provide us valuable clues. The answer? America and Europe were the two worlds colliding.

When was this collision of cultures and nations taking place? Look at the clues: **The New World Before 1775**, Christopher Columbus, The Conquistadores, The Spanish Empire, The First English Settlements. Since this text is for a college survey course in American history and the authors know the reader has had history in high school, the answer is fairly obvious. You should already know when Columbus sailed (1492). You should also know when Cortéz, De Soto, and other conquistadores were first in Mexico and the southern United States claiming territory for Spain (early 1500s). Finally, you should know when the first English colonies were established in America (early 1600s) and when the English colonial period ended for all practical purposes (1776). The answer to our question, then? America (various native American tribes) and Europe (various nations including England, France, Holland, and Spain) were in conflict with one another from approximately 1500 to 1775.

Likewise, a continued examination of the headings and subheadings in this chapter outline will allow you to answer or partially answer several other questions including these: *Why* were the Europeans coming to America? *Who* were the principals involved in the collision? *Why* were they in conflict with one another?

The Benefits of a Reading Preview   Think of the insight and focus you can derive from this simple five-to-ten-minute exercise.

First, you get positioned for the reading to follow. You now know what to expect as you progress through the chapter. You know what to look for, what's waiting for you around the next page, and what you need to obtain additional information about.

In addition, a reading preview helps you anticipate exam questions. By placing the key ideas in the chapter in the form of questions and then seeking detailed answers in your reading, you are well on the way toward becoming an active and effective learner. Later you can build on this and other skills to handle advanced reading at the senior, graduate, or professional level.

VERY IMPORTANT

It is important that you begin to use this task of Reading Preview *now* with this book on ESS. It is designed to be about as technical in parts as many first- and second-year college textbooks. This way, you get a realistic and valuable introduction to what it takes to effectively deal with academic and technical material.

Go now to the ESS table of contents to get a big-picture orientation as to where your Active Reading with ESS is going to take you. As you progress through this part of the book, also refer back periodically to the outlines provided with each Step and Skill in ESS—THE ADVANCED COURSE. These are integrated into the text to help you retain the big picture with ESS and stay on track.

If you don't do this and merely refer back to these outlines from time to time to stay focused, much of what you read from this point on will go right over your head. If this occurs, you probably will become discouraged, put down the book, and never master the advanced version of ESS.

If, on the other hand, you treat this book like any other college textbook and apply the ESS system to it first as you go along, this will help ensure that you master the system. The result should be academic excellence and superior grades in school.

Task 2: Chunk by Chapter Section   Imagine that you are now in the following hypothetical situation. You are reading a textbook chapter. You are somewhere in the middle of it. Then, suddenly, you find yourself thumbing over to the back to see how many more pages are left to read. "Whew!" you say to yourself. "There are eighteen more pages to go. Will I ever finish this darn thing?" Has this or something similar ever happened to you? If it has and textbooks generally have not been pleasant to deal with, take heart. Nothing like this ever has to happen to you again.

Researchers who study how learning takes place have found that we learn best in small increments or "little wholes." Some learning theorists refer to this process as chunking, the dividing of larger learning tasks into smaller ones.

Therefore, once your reading preview is completed, you then need to proceed on to **chunk by chapter section** (or heading), the next active reading task. This is a process in which a larger amount of content material (as represented by a textbook chapter) is divided into smaller increments or sections for more effective learning.

When you engage in any complex activity, whether it's climbing a mountain, building a house, or mastering academic reading material, success will come more easily if you have a plan of attack—a blueprint, a strategy to follow. Just as a successful mountain climber doesn't merely grab some equipment and start climbing, the successful student shouldn't just pick up a textbook and start reading without a detailed plan of action.

When you conduct your reading previews you will notice that, depending on the subject, the authors of most high school and lower-division college texts divide each chapter into three or four, five or six, or sometimes seven or eight major sections or chunks. This division of the chapter into smaller learning components is designed for your benefit to assist you in clearly understanding the main topic presented in the chapter.

Consequently, you need to focus your reading on these sections or chunks taken one at a time. By regarding each as a little whole you will be able to build—step by step—toward a complete and thorough understanding of the entire chapter.

Task 3: Engage in Paragraph Classification   As you focus your attention first on one section or chunk of the chapter and then another, you will next need to learn and implement paragraph classification, the most important task in Active Reading. This most crucial aspect of Active Reading represents a very important study skill in its own right.

Paragraph classification involves the analysis of chapter content at the paragraph level to distinguish core material from elaboration material. You might think of this as chunking at the paragraph level.

So, as you begin to read a chapter and concentrate your efforts initially on the first chapter section or chunk (represented by the first major heading), you also need to focus attention on each paragraph to determine whether it contains basically core material, elaboration, or, in some cases, both.

Core Material Paragraphs   **Core material** is the essential course content that forms the basis for exam questions. In high school and college courses core material may come from several sources—the textbook, the instructor's lectures, and additional sources such as a book of edited readings, material placed on library reserve, and so forth. (This is discussed at length in ESS: STEP TWO.) In the context of active reading discussed here, core material refers to all essential course content in a textbook.

A **core material paragraph** is any paragraph in a college text or other reading assignment that introduces a key portion of content which could appear again on an exam. Such paragraphs may also contain some elaboration designed to explain the meaning of an essential concept or other form of core material to the reader. However, they should be distinguished from elaboration paragraphs, which serve largely a different purpose: to illuminate and expand upon essential material.

Such core material forms the foundation of both the course and the exams upon which the final course grade will be determined. Since core material paragraphs are typically (1) fewer than those designed to clarify and elaborate and (2) most important for study and test purposes, the ability to distinguish them from elaboration paragraphs is essential to mastering the skill of active reading.

The Different Types of Core Material   Also important to the student is the ability to recognize and understand the different types of core material (see Table 12–1). These include concepts, principles and theories, important men and women and their contributions, and additional forms that relate to the specific nature of some courses and disciplines.

Concepts are key terms an author uses for important ideas, which usually involve very precise definitions. They represent agreements among scholars concerning the meaning of the phenomena they investigate. For example, the ancient Greeks were among the first to conceptualize love precisely. They agreed on three concepts of love: *philos* (long-lasting deep friendship), *eros* (sexual attraction), and *agape* (nondemanding spiritual love).

Principles and theories consist of the structuring of meaningful relationships among concepts and facts at different levels of complexity and scope. Examples might include Bowden's reflex principle of real-world markets in economics or binary fission theory in biology.

Important men and women are listed and discussed in course material in terms of their contributions to such areas of human endeavor as history, the humanities, and science. You may need to know, for instance, about the contributions of Charles Babbage in a computer-science course, John Maynard Keynes in economics, and B. F. Skinner in psychology.

Core material may also take several **additional forms**, depending on the subject or course involved. For example, a particular formula or group of formulas or equations would represent special forms of core material in algebra or calculus.

Table 12–1—The Basic Types of Core Material (The Sources for Exam Questions)

1. Concepts
2. Principles and theories
3. Important men and women (history, humanities, science)
4. Additional forms (e.g., formulas in algebra; phyla in biology)

Likewise various systems (skeletal, digestive, respiratory) and their elements along with phyla and their categories and subcategories would represent core material in biology.

Elaboration Paragraphs **Elaboration material** consists of examples, illustrations, explanations, and additional forms of detail that clarify and expand on the core information presented in a text or other required reading. Although elaboration material may not be the focus on most exams, it is nonetheless very important. It breathes life into core material and makes it meaningful.

If the student, for example, is adept at identifying and memorizing definitions or lists of core material without understanding (1) what the core material means and (2) the relationships between and among different concepts, principles, and theories, he or she may do poorly on exams.

College-level work is higher education. This means that, in many cases, students will be expected to demonstrate the analytical skills of critical thinking. They will be expected at times to analyze, synthesize, compare, and contrast different forms of core material on exams. In addition, they may be asked to apply what they have learned to a novel situation in order to test their critical-thinking ability.

An **elaboration paragraph** is any paragraph in a required reading assignment that explains, illustrates, clarifies, or otherwise expands on core material. Because such paragraphs act to expand on and flesh out the skeleton presented by core material, they tend to be more numerous. They consequently comprise the bulk of most high school and first- and second-year college texts.

As a guideline or rule of thumb to follow, there tend to be at least one or two (and sometimes more) elaboration paragraphs for every core-material paragraph, depending on the course taken and the author's style of writing. This is important to know because core material needs to be dealt with differently from elaboration material for effective textbook usage.

SKILL 2: The Identification of Core Material

This textbook usage skill employs and builds directly on the skill of active reading. The overlap, in terms of the use of skills in subsequent components and steps in ESS, is designed to build study-skill acquisition to a mastery level as soon as possible. Thus skills are first introduced and then applied cumulatively. This provides constant reinforcement as the student progresses through the various steps and skills included in the system.

The skill of Active Reading therefore has several mutually reinforcing applications. In addition to being applied to textbook material, it also allows the student to effectively master all forms of course reading, such as library assignments on reserve. Elements of it—such as the ability to distinguish core material from elaboration—can also be used to more easily master and implement the active listening skills used in taking comprehensive class notes (see ESS—THE BASIC COURSE, Principle 6).

Identification of Core Material represents a process whereby all essential information from the textbook that could appear on the exam is clearly identified. This is an extremely important skill to master because, with this ability, you can reduce the most voluminous reading assignments to a very concise form for effective exam preparation. To master this skill, it is important that you complete these tasks:

> **Skill 2: The Identification of Core Material (likely to appear on an exam)**
>
> **Task 1: Fully Implement Active Reading**
>
> **Task 2: Use the Learning Aids in the Text**
>
> > **Aids Within Each Chapter**
> >
> > **Aids at the End of Each Chapter**
>
> **Task 3 (Optional): Use the Student Study Guide**
>
> **How to Use Study Aids: A Few Words of Caution**

Task 1: Fully Implement Active Reading   First, you must fully implement the skill of **Active Reading,** already discussed. In short, this involves the tasks of (1) conducting a reading preview, (2) chunking by chapter section, and (3) paragraph classification with each reading assignment. This allows you to divide the reading material into smaller and smaller units for easier learning.

At the most elementary level of active reading you must learn to separate core material paragraphs from elaboration paragraphs. In doing so you will be able to identify key concepts, principles and theories, important men and women, and perhaps other forms of core material likely to appear on an exam.

Once this is done correctly, not only will you be able to dissect a reading assignment, you also will see how the various elements of core material at the paragraph level combine and build to make up the key chunks or sections of a chapter. This will allow you to develop a clear understanding of the chapter as a whole. This is how you implement the skill of active reading.

Task 2: Use the Learning Aids in the Text   If you are a high school student with plans for college or a first- or second-year college student, Tasks 2 and 3 will have particular value for you.

To facilitate identification of core material that may appear on exams, you should make use of the **learning aids** contained within most high school and first- and second-year college texts (see Table 12–2). Authors place these aids there to

Table 12–2—Learning Aids Often Found in Textbooks

Aids within Chapters	Aids at the End of Chapters
1. Chapter outlines (beginning of chapter and/or table of contents)	1. Chapter summaries
2. Chapter headings and subheadings (point the way to core material)	2. Glossaries of terms (often with definitions)
3. Boldface and italicized words	3. Review questions
4. Terms defined in margins	4. Suggested readings

help students identify much of the essential material they will be tested on later. Such aids may appear both within and at the end of each chapter.

Aids Within Each Chapter   Learning aids within the chapter include chapter outlines, headings and subheadings, boldface and italicized words, and key terms defined in the margins. Some authors place *chapter outlines* at the beginning of each chapter. This allows you to conduct a reading preview without having to check the table of contents. *Chapter headings and subheadings* do the chunking for you by dividing chapter content into key sections and subsections. They represent the basic building blocks of each chapter and often point the way to your reading by providing clues as to which forms of core material to look for. **Boldface** and *italicized* words cause various forms of core material such as key concepts or principles to stand out from the rest of the text. Boldface terms tend to be first-priority core material; italicized terms usually are second-priority. Both tend to be followed by a brief definition that is essential in understanding what each emphasized word means.

Aids at the End of Each Chapter   Here you may find chapter summaries, glossaries of important terms, review questions, and suggested readings. *Chapter summaries* state in condensed form the essential content of the chapter. *Glossaries* list and briefly define most of the chapter's important concepts. In addition, some survey texts include several *review questions* (or study questions) at the end of each chapter to test acquisition of key material. *Suggested readings* reinforce and expand on the content of the text.

Task 3 (Optional): Use the Student Study Guide   As an optional task, you may wish to use the **Student Study Guide** that is available with many first- and second-year college texts. The primary purpose of such a guide is to help the student identify and learn core material. It is frequently a separate small book designed to go along with the text, available at extra cost at your college book store.

A few texts contain their own study guides, placed at the back of the book as a supplement.

A study guide may be very helpful to a beginning student the first semester or two at college. It often contains such learning aids as detailed *learning objectives* on which to focus study, detailed *chapter outlines, exercises* to facilitate learning, and *learning assessment tests* with sample questions not unlike those that could appear on a real exam. While study guides can be very helpful at first, mastering the task of Reading Preview will ultimately make their use unnecessary.

How to Use Study Aids: A Few Words of Caution The various study aids designed into texts and separate study guides can be very helpful to high school and first- and second-year college students; use and benefit from them.

Nonetheless, heed these words of caution. Learning aids should be used just as the name implies—as aids to check your ability to identify and understand core material on your own as a result of careful reading.

Unfortunately, some students, particularly those with negative first experiences with textbooks, fall into the habit of using such devices as crutches in an attempt to take shortcuts. Therefore they often don't read their text assignments thoroughly. Not only do these students tend to perform at a mediocre level at best during their first two years at college, if they survive that long, but they experience a rude awakening if and when they become juniors.

During the junior and senior years at college, most learning aids tend to disappear from required text material. At this level, the student is expected to have developed good study habits and to be able to perform as an autonomous learner. Learning becomes more complex and specialized.

It also becomes extremely impractical and expensive to produce textbooks for advanced courses with the production values contained in survey texts for courses that enroll hundreds of thousands of students nationwide. Color photographs, illustrations, and learning aids so common in survey courses thus tend to be the exception rather than the rule in textbooks written for advanced courses.

In addition, professors teaching advanced courses place increased emphasis on original (primary) sources. For example, in a freshman survey course in psychology you are typically told about the basic contributions of such theorists as Watson, Freud, and Skinner. At the junior and senior levels it is more likely that your psychology professor will assign you long excerpts or books written by selected theorists in the field.

While it is true that, at the junior and senior levels, most course work will be in your major and minor fields (in which you have the greatest interest), you nevertheless will be exposed to much reading material written by scholars for other scholars. Such material is usually devoid of the learning aids that characterize first- and second-year survey texts.

If you have plans to complete a four-year degree or perhaps pursue your studies further, be advised that it will be you versus the print on the page. Consequently, now is the time to develop your study skills to a mastery level. If you do, particularly if you master and use ESS—THE ADVANCED COURSE, there should be no limit to what you can accomplish in your future studies.

SKILL 3: Topical Mapping

Once you are able to separate core material from elaboration material successfully and to identify the core concepts, principles and theories, important men and women, and other essentials, it is time to clearly and visibly separate core material from elaboration. The essence (the meat) in your reading assignments is what you mainly will be tested on. So now is the time to separate the meat (core material) from the fat (elaboration material) for the purposes of maximum learning and effective exam preparation. To accomplish this, you must acquire and master the skill of Topical Mapping.

Have you ever taken a long trip by car several hundred miles to another part of the country? If so, you may have benefited from a technique some experienced travelers use. Many people find it helpful to take out a road atlas, get a highlighter pen, and mark the route they will be traveling for easy reference while they are driving. This way they have an easy visual way of knowing exactly how to reach their destination. Upon arrival they also know where they've been so that, by following the same route in reverse, they can easily get back home.

This same principle also applies to academic studies. By developing a skill called Topical Mapping you can visually chart your progress as you travel through your reading assignments. Then, once you've finished them and reached your reading destination, you'll have a visible record of where you've been and how you got there. This will be indispensable when you wish to return to study for the exam.

Topical Mapping refers to the visible separation of core material from elaboration material in reading assignments so that both can be identified easily and reduced to the most concise form possible. This is an active, task-oriented way to approach the material contained in a textbook so that maximum learning can take place. Topical Mapping thus points the way through, or maps, the chapter for future study.

> **Skill 3: Topical Mapping**
>> **Task 1: Use Strategic Highlighting (of core material)**
>> **Task 2: Complete Analytical Summary (of elaboration material)**
>> **The Benefits of Topical Mapping**
>> **Special Applications for High School Students**

Task 1: Use Strategic Highlighting (of core material)   The first task you must complete to master the skill of topical mapping is called **strategic highlighting**. It involves the use of a colored pen or marker to highlight precisely the core material contained in required reading. To avoid confusion and keep things simple, it is advisable in most cases to use only one color of highlighter pen. (If you are a high school student, read this entire section carefully to acquire an understanding of Topical Mapping as a textbook usage skill. Then see Special Applications for High School Students at the end of this section for specific instructions.)

College students today often use colored pens or markers to highlight what they consider important text material. However, many of them defeat their purpose by highlighting too much.

I have often observed beginning students who will take their text in one hand and their highlighter pen in the other and, like the swashbuckling movie swordsman Zorro, make bold strokes with the pen not unlike those made with a small sword. While this is certainly impressive to watch and makes for a very colorful textbook, it tends to be very ineffective. To highlight fully one-fourth to one-half of each page is to defeat your purpose.

How to Highlight Core Material Strategically   Although it is essential to separate the core material from the rest of the text visually, effective highlighting must be done with precision. In this regard, if you highlight more than 15 percent of the total text, you are highlighting too much. With practice, 10 percent will be sufficient in some cases.

Just as the Olympic target shooter uses a rifle to hit the target's 10-ring every time, you can use your highlighter pen. Your goal is to hit the bull's-eye every time, to make a perfect score in separating core material from the rest of the text. Unfortunately, many students wield the highlighter pen like a shotgun. In doing so they accomplish very little other than to splatter the page with vivid color.

Specifically, then, *all you should highlight is the precise core term or phrase and perhaps the one- or two-line definition or capsule explanation that usually accompanies it.* If the core material takes the form of a complex theory or event, it may be necessary to highlight the essential causes, elements, or propositions that follow. In most cases, however, anything else will most likely be elaboration material, which should be handled in a different way.

A Practical Exercise in Strategic Highlighting   As you probably have noticed, this book has been written like a college textbook in several respects—*on purpose.* For example, it makes use of numerous headings and subheadings, is written on a college level, and contains several learning aids—including key ESS concepts in boldface print.

As an exercise in practicing strategic highlighting, complete these two steps. First, reread the italicized sentence that appears two paragraphs back. Second, as you complete this section of the book, practice this technique by identifying concepts and other forms of core material according to the instructions we've just discussed. You may find it helpful to highlight the entire book this way. Nevertheless, use restraint and don't highlight more than 15 percent of the printed text.

Task 2: Complete Analytical Summary (of elaboration material)   In most cases, 85 to 90 percent of the material contained in high school and first- and second-year college textbooks is elaboration material, which is important in its own right. Without a firm grasp of the elaboration—examples and illustrations, anecdotes, in-depth explanations, and so on—the core material would have little or no meaning or significance. Therefore, for maximum learning to take place it too must be reduced to a more concise form that can be used later for exam preparation. An effective way to accomplish this is analytical summary.

Analytical summary consists of making brief marginal notes that summarize elaboration material. As such, it represents a continuation of Active Reading at a more sophisticated skill level. It too is task-oriented and is focused on developing and implementing analytical skills to reduce the bulk of text material to a form that can be more readily understood and retained by students.

How to Summarize Elaboration Material Analytically   As you move through your reading assignments and highlight core material, take time to carefully read the discussion that follows. This, in most cases, will be the elaboration. Read it in terms of how it supports and explains the concept or other core material you just highlighted. Then complete the following two-step exercise.

1. *Reflect on what you read.* First, take a moment to reflect on the elaboration. What does it say? How does it explain or expand on the core concept, principle, theory, or other form of core material? Does it tell you why the core material it refers to is important? If so, how does it accomplish this?

2. *Make a marginal record of your analysis.* Next, in just a word, phrase, or at most a sentence or two, summarize the elaboration and write your brief analysis in the margin of your book on the same page. If you find it useful, use a special pen to record such notes for yourself. If you find it necessary to keep track of which notes go with which highlighted material, draw a small arrow from your marginal comments to the highlighted core material it explains.

A Practical Exercise in Analytical Summary   You will get the most from this book and master ESS in the shortest time possible if you will begin right here to implement the task of analytical summary. In other words, use this book as a laboratory manual to master the Textbook Usage Skills in ESS STEP ONE.

To do so, follow these guidelines. First, deal with this part of the book in sections or chunks, as explained earlier. ESS—THE ADVANCED COURSE consists of several headings such as The Four Steps in the Study Cycle, STEP ONE: Textbook Usage Skills, and so forth. Second, as you read through each section (and as you complete the strategic highlighting exercise discussed above) pause periodically in your reading to write analytical summaries in the margins as needed. In this way, (1) you'll learn the material because of the active, task-oriented approach you apply to it and (2) you'll have a record of your understanding for future reference.

Begin by easing into it. Start with only a brief section of a few pages. Expand from there. If you use these Textbook Usage Skills on this entire book, you will already have a head start in mastering the entire ESS system.

The Benefits of Topical Mapping   The process of topical mapping will greatly assist you in understanding and retaining the material in your textbook, although it may seem a little awkward and difficult at first. However, the rewards will be evident enough when your grades begin to rise and you begin to pick up significant speed with time as you master the skills.

The primary benefit to highlighting core material is that you are able to pinpoint precisely the essential reading material from which exam questions tend to emerge. Also, because of the active, task-oriented manner in which you use this skill, your mind will much more readily grasp and retain the material.

This increased learning benefit will also become apparent when you engage in the analytical summary of elaboration material. By taking only a moment or two to pause, think about and reflect on what you read, and then summarize perhaps two or three paragraphs into a phrase or a sentence or two as a marginal note, you will engage in analysis and synthesis. This task-oriented concentration at a high mental level promotes effective learning. Consequently, the process of analytical summary furnishes a record of your understanding of core material that you can refer to later when you prepare for exams.

Special Applications for High School Students   In most public school settings, high school students are not allowed to mark their books because they don't purchase them: Textbooks are school property, purchased with public funds and then loaned to students each fall term for use during the school year. Therefore, if you are a high school student, you may have to use a special modified form of both Topical Mapping and the skill of Chapter Outlining that follows it. Here are three suggestions:

Arrange with School Authorities to Purchase Needed Textbooks This is the ideal solution. Some public school systems will allow students or their parents to purchase textbooks. Particularly if you plan to go to college, the skills you develop in high school along with the grades you earn are very important. Since ESS shows you how to use textbooks for maximum benefit and these same skills will be needed later to do well in college, any investment in high school textbooks is a wise one, an investment in your future. With your own books you can use the skill of Topical Mapping with no need for modification.

If Allowed, Conduct Topical Mapping in Pencil For a variety of reasons it may not be possible to purchase your own textbooks. In this case, show your teacher this book and ask if you may conduct Topical Mapping lightly in pencil. Then, at the end of the school year, you can use a good gum eraser to remove all traces of marks. Since (1) few students will demonstrate your dedication to excellence in striving for straight A's in the first place and (2) your teacher will tend to either be curious to see how well ESS works or will already know by experience or reputation that it does work, you may get the permission you seek.

If you are given a green light, simply underline in pencil the core material that normally would be highlighted with a colored marker pen. Then write your analytical summaries in the margins with your pencil. While your Topical Mapping in pencil won't be as visible and colorful as the more conventional approach, you'll find that it can be made to work just as well.

If Topical Mapping in Pencil Is Not Allowed, Use Separate Paper While this will be more cumbersome and inconvenient, it will still work. You will simply transfer the core material you identify in your text onto separate sheets of paper. In addition, you will also write down brief analytical summaries of elaboration material (examples, illustrations, explanations) contained in the reading assignments. These notes will result in an outline of each chapter. This outline will provide you with a much more concise tool to use later in preparing for exams.

SKILL 4: Chapter Outlining

The next Textbook Usage Skill in STEP ONE of ESS—THE ADVANCED COURSE is Chapter Outlining. So far you have seen how the effective use of text material begins first with Active Reading. This in turn leads to the Identification of Core Material and Topical Mapping. The fourth skill to be used, Chapter Outlining, acts to pull all text material together to provide an organizational framework for later study.

Briefly, **Chapter Outlining** is a process in which all essential reading content is organized into a logical framework within the text. This provides the mind of the student the logical structure it needs for more effective learning:

> **Skill 4: Chapter Outlining (in the book)**
> **Why Chapter Outlining Is Important**
> **Task 1: Use Outline Notation**
> **Task 2: Use Color Coding**

Why Chapter Outlining Is Important   The outlining of each chapter may seem an unnecessary chore to some students, since another more comprehensive outline will be constructed later. However, they are mistaken for several reasons.

First, use of this skill should take less than one minute per page once it is fully mastered. The fact that it will take more time in the beginning should tell students that they need to learn how to better organize material into a coherent framework.

Second, the ability to arrange content material into a coherent outline requires concentration and the complicated thought processes of analysis and synthesis. Use of these types of thought process facilitates learning. If you're thinking about it, you're learning it. You won't go to sleep, daydream, or wonder what you've read if you do this.

The time required to master the entire system is an additional consideration. Some repetition (reinforcement) in ESS—THE ADVANCED COURSE is necessary to master all its elements as a total learning system as soon as possible.

But the most important benefit to outlining is this: The mind looks for structure, for order, for category. It will grab onto material that is clearly and concisely organized. Consequently it is essential to get course reading material into a coherent form both for effective learning and for maximum performance on exams.

Many high school and beginning college students attempt to read and master course reading material in the same way they deal with other forms of reading. Such a passive approach usually meets with little success. This is because their texts bombard them with large numbers of abstract concepts, principles, theories, and so forth and they lack a structured way of organizing this information in an efficient and effective way.

The various forms of core material in reading assignments therefore register only briefly as sensory impressions. Without repetition, reflection, and meaningful classification, it never has a chance to be encoded first into short-term and then long-term memory (see ESS—THE BASIC COURSE, Action Principle 16). As a result some students fail to retain most of such material, which has a tendency to go over their heads.

The negative consequences of passive, unorganized study are compounded when students continue this process by cramming the day or two before the exam. At best they may somehow manage to retain enough material to pass. What they do recall through memorization tends to imprint itself only on short-term memory, which is quickly lost. Therefore not only does their performance on exams tend to be mediocre, they also finish a course with little if any significant benefit in regard to long-term learning.

In contrast, students who utilize the Textbook Usage Skills in ESS are provided a means of not only passing exams but also obtaining straight A's if they are willing to work hard for them. These skills also help students retain more material in long-term memory. Then they have something of ultimate value to show for the time, money, and energy they invested in their education.

The human mind tends to grasp and retain more readily material that is structured, patterned, or ordered. Chapter outlining acts as a capstone to effective textbook usage in that it provides students a coherent and logical synthesis of all material contained in a given textbook chapter. Students armed with such chapter outlines for all reading assignments on which they will be tested have a distinct advantage over those who don't.

Task 1: Use Outline Notation   To simplify this process as much as possible, complete the chapter outline in the book. This may be somewhat difficult if the author is disorganized and the book poorly written. If you do occasionally have to deal with such a book, all the more reason you should use outline notation. You will need to search through the material in the text to uncover the salient points, first highlight and analytically summarize them, and then use outline notation to place them into some form of meaningful organization.

However, given the high standards required by today's major publishers, this difficulty rarely occurs with high school or first- and second-year college textbooks. You therefore shouldn't have a problem in this regard. You will need only to use **outline notation** by adding Roman numerals, capital letters, and so on to the material already in the text to give it more structure and coherent organization.

How to Use Outline Notation   Let's say you are taking a course in the first half of American history, which covers the period from its inception to 1877. Your reading assignment for this week is the chapter that covers the Civil War. So far you have implemented the Textbook Usage Skills of Active Reading, Identification of Core Material, and Topical Mapping. You now wish to complete the process by outlining the chapter in the book.

To do so, go to the first chunk or section of the chapter and start your outline there. Then look at the first major heading in that section. Often such headings give clues as to the core material to follow and how to organize it. In this case, the major heading is *The Major Causes of the Civil War*. This you make Roman numeral I.

As you proceed through the next few pages devoted to this section, you come across the key elements of core material. The first one you have highlighted is The Dred Scott Decision. This becomes capital A. If the author discusses three major aspects of this first cause, they can be distinguished by 1, 2, 3.

In this way you can outline the material in as much detail as you feel is necessary. Therefore you proceed on through this first chunk or heading of the chapter adding capital letters, numerals, and so on until this first section of the chapter is outlined. Repeat this process for the entire chapter.

Task 2: Use Color Coding   For the sake of efficiency and easy identification, use **color coding**. This involves the use of a colored pen to apply outline notation in order to make the chapter outline in the text stand out from the rest of the material. For instance, you might use a red pen or pencil and write the Roman numerals, capital letters, numbers, lowercase letters, and so on either right in with the text or in the margin to the left of the core material you have highlighted.

> NOTE: To illustrate both the skills of Topical Mapping and Chapter Outlining, I have included here two pages from my own text in introductory sociology (*Sociology: A Core Text*. Fort Worth: Holt, Rinehart and Winston, 1990). It is fairly typical of the manner in which college textbook authors organize chapters into headings and subheadings and include additional learning aids such as boldface and italics to emphasize core material. Observe closely how this student has used the ESS skills to identify and capture the essence of the discussion and establish a record of his reading for later study.

SKILL 5: Time Management

As you use your Textbook Usage Skills, it is important to pace yourself carefully to get everything accomplished. Effective management of your study time is a crucial skill. Without it you will not be able to prepare effectively for the exams you must take in each of your courses. Time is a valuable resource and, like money, property, or other important things, it can be lost easily if not managed properly. To manage study time effectively, complete these tasks:

Skill 5: Time Management

Task 1: Complete Text Assignments Weekly

Figure 11-2 Argots: Examples from Two Deviant Subcultures

The Drug Subculture	Los Angeles Street Gangs
Black russian: black, potent hashish	*Benzo:* Mercedes Benz
Bag: a quantity of diluted heroin	*Breakdown:* shotgun (also *gauge*)
Blow: to inhale a drug (also *sniff*)	*Bustin':* to go out shooting
Bluebirds: amytal sodium capsules	*Dead presidents:* money
Change: a short jail or prison sentence	*Deuce-deuce:* .22 caliber gun
Clean: not carrying or using narcotics	*Do a ghost:* leave (also *Do a train*)
Chinese white: potent white heroin	*Fooled out:* made a mistake
Connect: to find source of drugs (also *score*)	*Four-five:* .45 caliber gun
Crystal palace: a place to take speed	*Glass house:* police headquarters
Flashing: glue sniffing	*Hook:* a phony person
Gorilla pills: barbituates/other sedatives	*Hoopy:* car
Juice head: a person who drinks liquor	*Jack:* hijack
Luding out: using methaqualone	*Kite:* letter from prison
Mainline: to inject drug intravenously	*Mark:* someone wanting to join gang
Narc: any narcotics officer (all levels)	*Mud duck:* an ugly girl
Off: high on a drug (also to get rid of or kill)	*Ride on:* a drive-by shooting
Peter: chloral hydrate (a sedative)	*Squab:* fight
Rifle range: withdrawal ward in hospital	*Take out of the box:* kill someone
Roach: a marijuana cigarette butt	*Talking head:* arguing
Rock: granulated heroin, cocaine, etc.	*You got four feet?:* Want to fight?

Sources: Adapted with permission from Lingeman, R. R. (1974). *Drugs from A to Z: A dictionary*, 2nd ed. New York: McGraw-Hill; The *Los Angeles Times* (1988).

LEVELS AND TYPES OF DEVIANCE

Levels of Deviance in Society

Behavior that violates the standards of social acceptability occurs at both the micro- and macrolevels of social organization. ██ ████ ████ involves ████ ████ ████ ████ ████ ████ ████ ████ ████ ████ ████. Examples include most suicides, behavior resulting from mental disorders, and many crimes of murder, rape, armed robbery, and burglary. Factors contributing to individual deviance may include faulty socialization and unequal opportunity, which produce frustration and alienation.

2. ████████████ refers to ██████ ████████████████. Group deviance is often reinforced by a deviant subculture that furnishes its members with a set of socially unacceptable norms to follow. When this occurs, individuals belonging to these groups often internalize their deviant norms and values rather than those of the dominant society, especially in large urban areas of the United States. Drug addicts and juvenile gangs, connected together in such groups, contribute significantly to the incidences of burglary and violent crime. In similar fashion, prostitutes have their own social networks and emotional support groups, usually at the community level.

[Handwritten annotations: "Examples: Most Suicide crimes."; "Contrib. Factors: a. Faulty Socialization → Frustration b. Unequal Opportunity → Alienation."; "Reinforced by Deviant Subculture: a. Drug Addicts. b. Gangs. c. Prost."]

Task 2: Use a Weekly Calendar to Budget Time
Task 3: Set Priorities to Make Time for Study

Task 1: Complete Text Assignments Weekly   It is perhaps best to plan the completion of text assignments on a weekly basis. This seems to work particularly well for first-year college students because (although there are exceptions) many survey courses cover about a chapter a week.

You now have knowledge of four overlapping Textbook Usage Skills which, if you develop as explained, will enable you to integrate and master your text as-

Sometimes, however, the distinction between group deviance and collective deviance becomes blurred. Such activities as those of organized crime, price fixing by executives in some corporations, and various types of corruption in government occur not only locally but at the macrolevel of society as well. Collective level deviance involves socially unacceptable behavior by large numbers of people at various levels of society. Take organized crime for instance. In the United States, there are an estimated twenty-four Mafia families spread across the country with "a formal, oath-taking national membership of some 1700" (Magnuson, 1986). Of these, about one-half are concentrated in five nationally powerful families headquartered in New York City. If we include drug trafficking as part of its activities, organized crime is even international in scope. Other examples of collective level deviance include acts of civil disobedience carried out by members of some social movements and civil wars that occasionally occur in some societies.

Examples:
a. Organized Crime.
b. Riots.
c. Civil War.

B. Sociological Types

Sociologists have categorized deviance in a variety of ways. However, a review of the literature reveals that five types in particular are useful in illustrating the diversity of deviant behavior, as well as the motivations of those who participate. In this regard, we will briefly examine the following sociological types: aberrant deviance, nonconforming deviance, socially acceptable deviance, deviance resulting from an inability to conform, and deviance by attributes.

1. *Aberrant Deviance.* According to sociologist Robert Merton (1966), aberrant deviance is deviant behavior in which a person violates a norm for selfish reasons and attempts to escape detection and punishment. The criminal is one obvious example. The aberrant deviant

Example: Criminals.

acknowledges the validity of the norms being violated, but finds it advantageous to violate them for personal gain or satisfaction. Most criminals are aberrant deviants in that they commit such acts for selfish gain, attempting at the same time to avoid detection, capture, and punishment. Those who feign illness to stay home from work and those who engage in extramarital sex might also be placed in this category.

2. *Nonconforming Deviance.* In contrast to aberrant deviance, Merton has identified nonconforming deviance as socially disapproved behavior in which the participant challenges the legitimacy of certain norms by violating them openly, regardless of the negative sanctions that might be imposed. This person acts out of conscience and often violates norms for unselfish reasons based on moral principles. In some cases, the nonconforming deviant is appealing to a higher moral good, an ultimate value that transcends particular norms of society. Although abortion (as of this writing) is a legal right for women that most Americans tend to support, "pro-life" demonstrators in recent years have picketed abortion clinics and many have been arrested for civil disobedience and criminal offenses. Many colonial citizens during the American Revolution were nonconforming deviants committed to certain social ideals. The same might be said for Confederate soldiers during the Civil War and the antiwar protesters and civil rights demonstrators during the 1960s and early 1970s.

Examples:
a. Activists Against Abortion.
b. Colonial "Patriots".
c. Anti-war Demons.
d. Civil Rights Activists.

3. *Socially Acceptable Deviance.* A third classification is socially acceptable deviance, a type of deviant behavior considered acceptable by significant portions of society (Sutherland, 1967). This sometimes occurs when laws or public policies are established because of pressure from interest groups instead of broad-based public support. Prominent twentieth-century examples in the United States include

signments. These skills will keep you task-oriented and focused on your goal of academic excellence if you will use your time wisely.

Task 2: Use a Weekly Calendar to Budget Time

To manage time effectively, use a weekly calendar with two hours set aside to study for every hour spent in class. This means that, if you are taking courses totaling fifteen credit hours, you need to spend thirty hours each week in study. Mastery of the entire ESS system will take this much time with such a course load, perhaps even more in the beginning.

As you plan your calendar, assess the time you need to spend with your family, at an outside job if you must work, in recreation and a social life, and so on. The mature student realizes that school is a serious commitment. Since there are only so many hours in the day and week, every effort should be made to use them wisely.

A weekly calendar is an integral part of the ESS Time Management System provided with Action Principle 15 in ESS—THE BASIC COURSE (see Figure 9–1). By taking a few minutes each week to plan the calendar included on this one-page form you will be able to use time much more productively. The results will translate into better grades.

Task 3: Set Priorities to Make Time for Study   If you work at an outside job, have family responsibilities, and are carrying a heavy course load at school, you probably will experience what sociologists call **role conflict**. This is stress caused when conflicting role demands are built into separate social positions we occupy in society: employee, student, or family member. Adjustments will have to be made.

If you have heavy responsibilities in all these areas, perhaps you should consider taking a smaller class load next term or think about cutting back on the hours at your job if you can. You also may need to impress on your family and friends the importance of your schoolwork. Just as you are not available at certain times because of your job, you should also be unavailable at designated times because of your need to study. Ultimately, of course, how you spend your time and energy is up to you. You must weigh these issues yourself and resolve them in a manner that best meets your priorities and needs.

However, if you truly expect to achieve academic excellence and go as far as your abilities will allow, school must be near or at the top of your priority list. In the final analysis, only for those students who are able to do this will ESS—THE ADVANCED COURSE provide significant benefit.

13 STEP TWO: CONTENT ORGANIZATION SKILLS

In the next section of ESS—THE ADVANCED COURSE you will learn how to build on your Textbook Usage Skills to effectively organize course content that comes from different sources. These include textbooks, class lectures, and collateral readings.

Content organization skills involve the development of a comprehensive written outline from all sources of course content. This comprehensive outline becomes the source document you study from as you prepare for an upcoming exam in a particular course.

As you master the skills of pulling everything together and constructing a final outline, such things as textbooks, lecture notes, and collateral readings can be put aside. You will not need them once your comprehensive outline is complete. Your final written outline thus becomes your blueprint for success. It will allow you to excel on each and every exam.

Some high school and beginning college students find themselves in a somewhat frustrating predicament as each exam approaches. Even if they have tried to study as they went along, they often find themselves sifting and sorting among several different sources of course content in a frantic attempt to pull everything together. For the student who crams, this can be a frustrating experience of using too little too late. The result, in many cases, is an F grade on the exam.

Just as the goldminer uses a long trough—a sluice—to separate an ounce or two of gold from tons of rich but muddy soil or silt, you can use the comprehensive written outline to capture all the valuable information that will appear on an exam. To accomplish this, it is important to acquire and make use of these skills:

STEP TWO: Content Organization Skills

The Benefits of a Comprehensive Written Outline

Skill 1: The Weekly Consolidation of Preliminary Outlines

Skill 2: Construction of the Final Comprehensive Outline

Skill 3: Time Management

Summary: STEP ONE and STEP TWO

The Benefits of a Comprehensive Written Outline

Even in the best of circumstances, the lack of a comprehensive written outline can represent a very inefficient way to prepare for an exam. Indeed, many students find themselves somewhat overwhelmed the day before the exam. They can be observed thumbing through a hundred or two hundred or more pages of text, sifting through dozens of pages of lecture notes, and, in some cases, needing to know all pertinent information contained in assigned articles or other forms of collateral reading assignments.

With the development of a final written outline, you will have a much more effective tool with which to prepare for exams for these reasons:

Writing Is an Active Learning Process   Writing things down facilitates learning. You will benefit from the effort you expend each week to consolidate the core material from the text, class notes, and all collateral readings into a comprehensive written outline (in your own words). Not only will this process reinforce your learning, but you will also be freed from the more bulky reading assignments and class notes. Everything you will need to know for the exam will be stated one time in one place.

No More Sifting and Sorting   Through the use of ESS—THE ADVANCED COURSE you will be spared the frustrations of the sifting and sorting routine so many students experience with their reading assignments and class notes. You will also be spared the anxiety many students feel as time ticks away and the appointed hour of the exam draws near.

Only Eight to Ten Sheets for Major Exams   You will have a plan of action and will be equipped with a final comprehensive outline which, once you learn how to develop and use it, will consist at most of only eight or ten sheets of paper for each major exam.

Only Thirty to Forty Sheets for Comprehensive Finals   When you prepare for final exams, you will again have it much easier than many students because you will have prepared in a focused, task-oriented manner as you went along. All you will have to do for a comprehensive final exam is pull out the written outlines you saved from each of the previous exams (study cycles) and use them along with the one you developed for the last part of the semester.

Therefore, while nonusers of ESS will for each final exam no doubt be sifting and sorting through several hundred pages of required semester reading or more and perhaps a hundred or more pages of lecture notes, you will have distilled and condensed everything down to thirty to forty sheets of paper, or less. In addition, because of the effort you expend condensing the course material and developing these outlines as you go along, you will already know the material fairly well and will find it much easier to study for the exam.

SKILL 1: The Weekly Consolidation of Preliminary Outlines

In STEP ONE: Textbook Usage Skills you were shown how to identify and organize different types of course content for effective learning. This involves the skills of Active Reading, Identification of Core Material, Topical Mapping, Chapter Outlining, and Time Management. Assuming that you use STEP ONE, not only will you be able to capture the essence of a given textbook chapter and learn it well, you will also pace yourself effectively through proper time management.

In STEP TWO you will learn how to consolidate weekly preliminary outlines (from text assignments, class notes, and collateral readings) into a comprehensive written outline for use in exam preparation near the end of each study cycle.

Let's assume that you are a first- or second-year college student or you plan to be one soon. Each of the courses you are taking probably requires a chapter or two of reading a week. If you begin on Monday, by the middle or near the end of the week you should have completed the text assignments for that week in each of your courses, using STEP ONE.

Then, for the purposes of STEP TWO, each weekly reading assignment for each course you have completed and outlined (in the text) becomes a **preliminary outline**. You will use this preliminary outline during STEP TWO along with other weekly preliminary outlines (from class notes and perhaps outside readings) to construct your comprehensive outline on a week-by-week basis (see Figure 13–1). To use such preliminary outlines properly, you will need to carry out the following tasks.

> Skill 1: The Weekly Consolidation of Preliminary Outlines
>
> > Task 1: Convert Textbook Assignments
> >
> > Task 2: Convert Class Notes
> >
> > Task 3: Convert Collateral Readings

Task 1: Convert Textbook Assignments   Suppose that you begin the semester with a course in which the first major exam over four textbook chapters will be in one month's time. To be successful in preparing for such an exam and others like it, you will need to carry out the task of converting **textbook assignments** into a final written outline.

To do this, use the following procedure: Each week for each course, the student should complete the reading assignments for that period using STEP ONE: Textbook Usage Skills. Then, at the end of the week, he or she should incorporate this material into the document that ultimately will become the final comprehensive outline.

THE WEEKLY CONSOLIDATION
OF PRELIMINARY OUTLINES

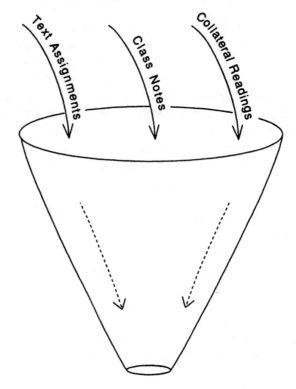

FINAL COMPREHENSIVE OUTLINE
(Constructed in Weekly Increments)

Figure 13-1

Task 2: Convert Class Notes   In addition to the preliminary outlines you develop weekly from text assignments, you will also have weekly outlines from one and possibly two other basic sources of course content, class lectures and collateral readings. Although some college instructors lecture almost exclusively from the text, many include in their lectures or class discussions a significant amount of additional material not found in the textbook.

For maximum success you will therefore need to read all appropriate reading assignments before coming to class and take comprehensive class notes (see ESS—THE BASIC COURSE, Principles 5 and 6). At the end of each week you should have several pages of class notes from each of the courses you take. **Class notes** for each course should be consolidated at the end of each week into the comprehensive outline.

Task 3: Convert Collateral Readings   In some of the courses you take, you also will have **collateral readings,** assignments in addition to those in the textbook. These assignments, sometimes called outside readings, will come in various forms: material placed on library reserve, a book of readings you buy as an additional text, material the instructor hands out in class, and so on.

Collateral readings, if required for any course, should be handled in exactly the same manner as textbook assignments. They should first be read and outlined, using all of the Textbook Usage Skills contained in STEP ONE. Then, they should be consolidated on a weekly basis into the comprehensive outline for a particular exam.

SKILL 2: Constructing the Final Comprehensive Outline

As you implement STEP TWO, you will develop a comprehensive written outline for each exam you take in each course. Consequently, in a given semester with a fifteen-hour course load, you might go through this process fifteen to twenty times or more, depending on the number of exams you have in each course.

This portion of STEP TWO focuses on the procedures you should use to construct this outline in the fastest and easiest way possible. For greatest success, you will need to carry out these tasks:

> **Skill 2: Constructing the Final Comprehensive Outline**
> **Task 1: Decide on an Outline Model**
> > **Textbook**
> > **Class Notes**
> > **Collateral Readings**
> > **The Benefit of Having an Outline Model**
> **Task 2: Decide on an Outline Format**
> > **The T Method**
> > **The Cornell Method**
> > **Mastering the Skill of Outlining**

As you progress through the several weeks of course content in the study cycle leading up to each exam you will be integrating the preliminary material you have gleaned from the text, the class notes, and any collateral readings into your final comprehensive outline. This outline will become the source document from which you will prepare for the exam. (How most effectively to use this outline in exam preparation will be explained fully in STEP THREE.)

Task 1: Decide on an Outline Model   To construct your comprehensive outline most effectively you must first choose the particular source of course content—textbook, class notes, or collateral reading—on which it should be based. To best make this decision, ask yourself this question with each exam you take in every course: "Which source of course content do I think the largest number of exam questions will come from?"

Your answer will decide the issue. If you feel most questions will come from the **textbook,** use the material you identified and outlined in the text as the model for your comprehensive outline. Then examine your class notes and applicable collateral readings for any core material that does not appear in the text and incorporate it into the outline as well. This way you will have all your bases covered and, if you have prepared well, little if any important material will be left out. However, if you feel the largest number of test questions will come from the **class notes** or **collateral readings,** use one of these sources of content for your outline model and make adjustments accordingly.

The Benefit of Having an Outline Model   Through use of this strategy you will increase your chances of being properly tuned in to the way each of your instructors structures the exams in his or her course. If at all possible, don't leave this valuable piece of information to chance. Some instructors state on the first day of class or on the class syllabus the source or sources from which most exam questions will come. If such information is not provided by the instructor, ask. Many instructors will be happy to tell you. If your instructor has a policy of not providing such information, look for other clues in the content or structure of class presentations.

Task 2: Decide on an Outline Format   Your next task with regard to the final comprehensive outline is to decide which type of outline format to use. This is basically a matter of personal preference. In a moment we'll examine two popular approaches: The T Method and the Cornell Method (see Figure 13–2).

Regardless of the preferred format, use letter-size paper until your skill for outlining is fully developed. (When you can successfully convert all the core material for a major exam from all sources of course content (along with analytical summaries as needed) onto one side of eight or ten sheets of paper in a legible form, you may want to go to index cards).

The T Method   With this approach, you obtain several sheets of paper and draw a horizontal line like the top of a T across the page near the top of each sheet. On top of this line you might want to write the name of the course, the title of the chapter or class topic, the exam number, and so on. Then draw a vertical line down the center of each page from top to bottom that divides it into two equal

THE FINAL COMPREHENSIVE OUTLINE: TWO RECOMMENDED FORMATS

"T" Method   Cornell Method

```
I.                    III.                    I.
   A.                    A.                       A.
     1.                    1.                        1.
     2.                    2.                        2.
   B.                    B.                       B.
     1.                    1.                        1.
     2.                    2.                        2.
   C.                 IV.                        C.
     1.                    A.                        1.
     2.                      1.                       2.
     3.                      2.                       3.
II.                        B.
   A.                      C.                   II.
   B.                      D.
   C.                                              A.
                                                   B.
                                                   C.
                                               III.

                                                   A.
                                                     1.
                                                     2.
```

Figure 13-2

sides. The purpose of this line is to help you learn to be as concise as possible and to write small.

To begin the process of writing your comprehensive outline you will need several sheets of letter-size paper. On one, which will become page 1 of the outline, start writing at the top of the left side of the line and progress downward until you reach the bottom. In other words, treat the left side of the T as if it is a separate sheet of paper.

Then start again at the top of the page on the right side of the line and move toward the bottom again. This way you will find that each sheet of paper becomes like two. You can get two to three times as much material on one side of a letter-size sheet than you could have otherwise.

Follow the same procedure with each sheet of paper until your final outline of the material for an upcoming exam is complete. If you decide to switch to index cards at a later time, the line down the middle will not be necessary, given both your mastery of outlining skills and the relatively small size of the cards.

The Cornell Method Devised several years ago at Cornell University as a note-taking technique, this method also may be used in constructing a final written outline for exam preparation.

Like the T method, the Cornell approach involves the use of a vertical line to divide each sheet. With this technique, however, the line is drawn so that one-third of the space is available on the left side while two-thirds is on the right. The left side is designed strictly for general headings or major ideas while the right side is used to list specific points of detail.

Suppose for your outline you need to name a theory along with its five basic propositions. Using the Cornell method, you might list the name of the theory by Roman numeral heading on the left of the vertical line. Then on the right-hand side, parallel with the title heading, you could list the theory's propositions as A, B, C, D, and E.

Mastering the Skill of Outlining The first time or two students put together a comprehensive outline it is not uncommon for them to have twenty pages or more. If this happens to you, be patient. You will reach full mastery with dutiful application and a little time.

In the beginning you may write larger than necessary and will more than likely include things that are not essential. But this is to be expected as you develop your skills. Keep in mind that it is always better to have too much than not enough in the beginning. The key is to not leave out core material if you can help it. With time and practice, you will learn to get your outlines down to eight or ten pages or even less.

SKILL 3: Time Management

Successful time management for STEP TWO can be accomplished through the completion of the following tasks:

> **Skill 3: Time Management**
> > **Task 1: Follow the Two-Day Rule**
> > **Task 2: Use a Weekly Study Schedule**
> > **Task 3: Construct the Final Written Outline in Increments**

Task 1: Follow the Two-Day Rule To complete your final outline successfully each time, it is important that you pace yourself carefully and follow the **two-day rule**. For purposes of effective time management, this means that the comprehensive written outline must be completed no later than two days before the scheduled exam.

For final exams given at the end of each semester, all comprehensive outlines in each course must be completed by two days before the final exam week or period begins. Following this rule is necessary to ensure that enough time (the day before each exam) will be available to implement STEP THREE (yet to be explained).

Task 2: Use a Weekly Study Schedule   To finish each of your comprehensive outlines on time, you will need to divide the time you have before each major exam into segments, such as weeks. In fact, you use a weekly study schedule if possible. A weekly study schedule is the basis for the ESS Time Management System discussed in ESS—THE BASIC COURSE (see Action Principle 15 and Figure 9–1 A and B).

At the end of each week, consolidate your reading assignments, class notes, and any outside readings into the final comprehensive outline.

Task 3: Construct the Final Written Outline in Increments   By continuing the use of weekly study schedules you will be able to organize content material and construct the comprehensive outline in increments or stages as you move toward the day of the exam. This is the most prudent way to study for maximum results. The benefits to you will be increased learning and higher grades.

SUMMARY: STEP ONE and STEP TWO

Success in any field of endeavor comes to the person who works hard and works smart. This statement will already apply to you as a student once each and every step, skill, and task explained so far in ESS—THE ADVANCED COURSE has been fully implemented. In other words, once you establish the habit of using STEP ONE and STEP TWO, you will have demonstrated that you have the maturity, commitment, and discipline to become an exceptional student if you continue in your efforts.

You therefore represent the most important ingredient in the formula for academic excellence. ESS furnishes only the basic tools needed for maximum success.

If the preceding paragraph describes you and these steps have already been completed, let's examine what you have accomplished so far. First, you have put into practice the twenty principles for student success contained in ESS—THE BASIC COURSE.

Next, you have put into practice STEP ONE of ESS—THE ADVANCED COURSE by implementing all the Textbook Usage Skills: Active Reading, Identification of Core Material, Topical Mapping, Chapter Outlining, and Time Management.

Finally, you have started to use the Content Organization Skills contained in STEP TWO: Consolidation of Preliminary Outlines, Construction of a Comprehensive Written Outline, and Time Management.

These are all valuable components of a study strategy that will make you a winner. What you will need is patience and perseverance for the next few weeks and months as you fully master all the skills. After you spend a school term or two in conscientious application, these skills can become internalized as competencies and habits. Then you'll find it much easier to perform successfully in school.

14 STEP THREE: EXAM PREPARATION SKILLS

Now it's time to discuss the skills you will need the day before the exam and during the exam itself to ensure maximum performance and an A grade. But first, a few words about attitude.

Sociologists who study attitude formation and how it affects performance have found that the reference groups people set for themselves play a crucial role in how they approach tasks. A **reference group** is a group a person refers to consciously or unconsciously as a basis for evaluating life goals and performance. Our reference groups are the yardsticks by which we judge our own successes and failures.

Suppose, for example, a group of students at your high school or college takes a major exam. Then, at the next class meeting, the instructor gives back the grades. The first student to receive a grade looks at it, sees the B−, and with a slight smile thinks "This means I can make a D next time and still get by." The

NANCY Reprinted by permission of UFS, INC.

second student looks at his grade, sees a B, and feels very disappointed because it is so low.

Both students received essentially the same grade but had different attitudes about it because of the reference groups with which they identified. If you identify with A students, see yourself in your mind's eye as an A student, and make every attempt to seek out and associate with A students, you will increase your chances of becoming one.

Exam Preparation Skills form the basis for STEP THREE. Taken as a whole, they will furnish you an efficient means of integrating everything you have learned previously for maximum performance. In addition, they will assist you in developing an effective strategy for use in the actual test situation and furnish techniques for overcoming common test-related problems. To acquire these benefits, you will need to learn how to use the following skills:

> **STEP THREE: Exam Preparation Skills**
> **Skill 1: The Final Study Session**
> **Skill 2: How to Take a Test**
> **Skill 3: How to Overcome Test Anxiety**

SKILL 1: The Final Study Session

By the time you get to STEP THREE in ESS—THE ADVANCED COURSE, your final comprehensive outline has been completed two days before each scheduled exam. All the core content you will be expected to know should be contained in this single, concise document. Consequently you have no more need for the textbooks, class notes, or collateral readings that are so often spread across dining-room tables and bedroom floors throughout America on that notorious night before the major exam next day.

For you, these images will soon be faint memories of the way things used to be before ESS. Now, after all the hard work and preparation, you will begin to realize and perhaps say to others "Hey! This is really great. Eight to ten sheets of paper for a major exam. Thirty to thirty-five or forty sheets for a comprehensive final. How could things be much better?"

Well, in truth, things couldn't be much better for you at this point. You have done your homework, prepared diligently, and learned the material responsibly in increments as you went along. Now you're ready for the final push to victory, the final study session that should result in content mastery and an A on the exam once ESS is fully mastered.

The **Final Study Session** refers to a concentrated study session with the comprehensive outline the day before the scheduled exam. Based on norms established by the reports of more than two thousand first-year college students used in the testing of ESS, the final study session should require about one to two hours for a major exam (when there are three or more exams per semester), two to three hours for a midterm exam, and three to four hours for a comprehensive final exam. (These times may need to be expanded for certain courses.)

During this final brief period of study, for maximum success you will need to follow these procedures:

> **Skill 1: The Final Study Session**
> **Task 1: Use Drill and Practice**
> > **One-Page Review Tests**
> > **Three-Page Review Tests**
> > **The Final Review Test**
> **Task 2: Use the Checking-Off Method**
> > **The Checkmark**
> > **The Circle Around the Checkmark**
> > **The X Through the Circle**
> **The Benefits of the Final Study Session**

Task 1: Use Drill and Practice   Here are the step-by-step instructions you will need to follow for this final study session. First, get your comprehensive outline, one or more blank sheets of paper, and something with which to write. Then go to a quiet place where you will not be disturbed.

Once there, you will carry out **drill and practice,** an intense process in which questions are asked repeatedly and answers given until complete mastery of all material on which you will be tested is demonstrated. This technique, properly used, is invaluable because it provides an effective way to anticipate practically any question that could be asked on an exam.

To use drill and practice effectively, you will need to restate the material contained in the comprehensive outline in the form of questions. This is what educators do when they design test questions for their students. They take essential content that they have organized and formulate it into various types of questions for exams.

When you take the same essential material and ask yourself questions about it, you are engaged in an approximate simulation of what will be experienced in the exam. Therefore, to borrow an expression from the theater world, it's like dress rehearsal before opening night.

This is what you need to do: Take a blank sheet of paper and, using it as a cover sheet, proceed to the first heading on the first page of your outline. Take care to keep everything else covered.

Now look at the statement, phrase, or word you see there and make a question out of it. If, for example, you are studying for an American History exam and the first heading on your outline says "The Major Causes of the Civil War," form a mental question such as "What were the main causes of the Civil War?" You may find it useful to write down such questions on a separate sheet of paper for quick reference later.

Try to answer each question without looking at the material hidden by the cover sheet. If necessary, peek at the answer, study it carefully, and then ask the same question again. When you feel confident about this first part of the outline and can answer the question each time, move down the page to the next key heading. Handle it in the same manner. Continue this process until you feel you have mastered all the core material contained on the first page.

One-Page Review Tests   After you have completed the drill-and-practice procedure with this first part of the outline, go back and perform a review test of the material on the first page. You do this by asking and answering all the pertinent questions you developed with the cover sheet placed over the answers. Once you can answer all such questions, go to the next page of the outline and repeat the procedure. Each succeeding page in the outline should (1) be handled in exactly the same manner and (2) be followed by a successful one-page review test before drill and practice with an additional page is attempted.

Three-Page Review Tests   Then, every three pages, perform a review test of the material you have covered to that point. Go forward with the drill-and-practice process, but only after all questions posed by the three-page review test are answered successfully.

The Final Review Test   When you have completed the drill-and-practice procedure for the entire outline, perform a final review test of all material on the outline. When you can answer all questions pertaining to the material on the comprehensive outline, you will be ready for the exam scheduled for the next day.

Task 2: Use the Checking-Off Method   As you progress through the final study session with drill and practice, you will need to engage simultaneously in another task called the **checking-off** method. This is a technique used in the final study session for identifying when content material has been mastered completely for an exam. It will help you keep track of what content you know well and what content requires more study as you move through the process.

The Three Steps of Checking Off   First, as you conduct each one-page review test, place a **checkmark** in the margin of the outline at the appropriate place whenever you answer a question correctly and feel confident that you understand it clearly. If you don't answer a question correctly, leave this section blank or unchecked until you can. The checkmarks will therefore tell you what you know well and the blank spaces will identify areas that need more study.

Next, place a **circle around each checkmark** in the outline when you successfully answer a question on each three-page review test. However, if you can't answer one or more questions, engage in additional drill and practice until you feel sure that you know it well. Then—and *only then*—apply the circle. When all material for a three-page review test has been checked and circled, you are then ready to move on to the next page.

Finally, place an **X in each circle** surrounding a checkmark when you answer a question correctly on the final review test. This should represent a final run-through of all the material for the exam the next day. Nonetheless, if you miss even a few of the questions you are not quite finished and should continue the study session until you can answer them all.

The Benefits of the Final Study Session   Your ESS skills prepare you to deal successfully with either rote recall or critical thought questions on exams. The ESS process leading to STEP THREE forces you to concentrate on the material, analyze it carefully, and then synthesize it into a clear and concise final outline. Therefore not only do you clearly understand discrete bits of core material such as concepts, you also understand the relationships between them. You are able to see the big picture as you progress on to the final study session.

Cramming, in contrast, involves little more than memorization for recognition and recall. The student who uses this study approach is cheated not only in terms of earning poorer grades but, more important, is also denied a good education although much time and money has gone into an attempt to acquire it.

With the final study session you deal in a concentrated way with content material that already has been thoroughly studied and organized. As a result, course content is more likely to become encoded into long-term memory. This contributes to your development as an educated person. Although you will forget much if not most of the particulars asked for on exams, you will tend to remember and understand more of the key ideas and concepts for years to come because of the way in which you prepared.

The most immediate benefit, however, is that the drill and practice component contained in STEP THREE thoroughly encodes everything you will need to know for the next day's test into short-term to midrange memory. This in turn leads to maximum performance on exams.

Once you are able go through the entire final outline without missing a single question, you will be ready and well prepared for the exam. In fact, assuming you used the ESS Steps and Skills correctly to this point, you should earn a B+ to A− grade at the least. Once you have implemented and mastered ESS—THE ADVANCED COURSE in its entirety, you may even score 99 or 100 percent on each exam. However, to perform this well consistently you will also need to know how to take different types of tests and how to deal effectively with test anxiety.

SKILL 2: How to Take a Test

Taking a test is an acquired skill, like most other forms of complex behavior. Effective test-taking can be learned and improved upon with the right information and a little effort. Likewise, deficiencies in test-taking techniques sometimes are at least partially responsible for mediocre or poor performance on exams. In a few cases, beginning college students may even fail an exam in part because they don't possess some of the essential skills involved in effective test-taking.

What you know and your ability to communicate or demonstrate what you know are two separate things. The possession of one shouldn't assume the other.

Exam Preparation Skills must include not only how to identify and master likely test material but also how to effectively communicate and demonstrate that knowledge. The tangible results of this twofold process are called *grades*. They tend to follow you as permanent records of your academic achievement for the rest of your life.

To improve your ability to transfer what you know on to a document called a test—which, together with other tests, will be recorded as grades—it is important to understand the basic methods of test-giving and test-taking:

> **Skill 2: How To Take a Test**
>> **Task 1: Take Objective Exams the ESS Way**
>>> **Know the Types of Objective Questions**
>>> **Avoid the Formula Fallacy**
>>> **Read Questions Properly**
>>> **Use the Deduction Strategy**

MISS PEACH By permission of Mell Lazarus and Creators Syndicate.

Task 2: Take Essay Exams the ESS Way
>   **Know the Types of Essay Questions**
>   **Follow the Cardinal Rule of Essay Writing**
>   **Practice Essay-Writing Etiquette**
>   **Use the Four Steps in Completing an Essay Exam**
>   **Include the Essential Elements of an Essay**
>   **Be Prepared for Special Cases:**
>   **Open-Book and Take-Home Exams**

Task 1: Take Objective Exams the ESS Way   Forms of evaluation that offer the student a predetermined number of possible answers or choices with which to demonstrate knowledge are **objective exams.** Many instructors prefer this form of test because, although they can be very time-consuming to develop, they are easy and quick to grade.

Know the Types of Objective Questions   Some of the more common forms of such tests make use of multiple-choice, true-false, matching, and fill-in-the-blank (completion) items or questions. Of these, **multiple-choice** and **true-false** questions tend to be the most popular among high school and college instructors.

Multiple-choice tests, for example, typically employ four or five possible responses that usually are arranged into choices of a, b, c, d, or e. The task for the student is to provide the correct or best answer from among a preset number of alternatives.

Some multiple-choice items measure only memorization and the rote recall of course content. Here the student need only correctly recognize or identify the material.

Others, however, may measure the student's understanding of the material and the ability to think critically with it. For instance, a multiple-choice question may first formulate a problem in a sentence or two or even a brief paragraph. Then the student is asked to analyze it and choose the best solution from among several alternatives. Choices like "All of the above," "None of the above," and "Both a and c above" are clues that the instructor is testing for understanding and critical thinking ability. While students unfamiliar with such approaches may regard them as tricky, you must prepare yourself for them, particularly if you are a college student or plan to be one.

Ineffective test-taking techniques can result in poor grades and a significant amount of discouragement. Some students may know and understand the material better than they demonstrate on exams. This problem is often easily corrected by learning and applying an effective strategy for taking tests. A significant part of any such strategy consists of avoiding some of the pitfalls that beset some beginning students.

Avoid the Formula Fallacy A common mistake many students make is to fall victim to the **formula fallacy**. This is the erroneous belief by some students that instructors use a set number of choices for multiple-choice or true-false items in a particular order. The instructor supposedly uses a formula of some sort in choosing the correct responses to items on a test.

Such mythical formulas take a variety of different forms, but only in the minds of some students. For example, a student may put down a "d" answer on a multiple-choice test for little reason other than that "it's time for a *d*." Since there hasn't been a "d" answer for eight questions (and the student takes precious test time to go back and count them—the answer must be "d." Likewise, a student who has made four "True" responses in a row might feel that it's time for a "False" or perhaps even go back and change one of the other "True" answers for more balance.

While instructors do see the need to have a variety of different choices as test answers, they rarely use a formula as such, if ever. Their primary concern is with choosing test items that are representative of the material on which you will be tested, not in how many of each type of correct response there are or the order in which they appear. Consequently, it is not uncommon to see several "a's" or "b's" or "Trues" or "Falses" in a row on objective tests.

There is an effective "best" strategy you can use for taking objective tests. It involves accepting this principle: *There is no substitute for knowing the material well.* This more than anything else will give you the self-confidence to ignore the formula fallacy.

Read Questions Properly One important aspect of taking objective tests is to **read questions properly**. *It is important to not go back and second-guess yourself by changing the answer once a selection has been made.* Many beginning students make the mistake of doing this, which can result in lower text scores.

NOTE: Some research has suggested that students who change answers get them right as often or more often by changing them. What such research really shows, when one studies the methodology of the researchers very closely, is that such students (1) don't know the material that well in the first place (which is one reason for the need to change answers) and/or (2) don't read the questions carefully the first time.

In essence, *it is sloppy scholarship and careless reading that results in the felt need by some students to change answers.* If you use ESS properly it will be totally unnecessary to engage in such a poor test-taking practice. Like the mastery of most any other skill, it is important to learn how to choose the correct answer on a test the first time.

1. *Two common traps in true-false items.* With true-false questions, watch for two things in particular:
   a. *Look for absolute statements.* Questions containing such words as *all, always, invariably, none,* or *never* should be examined closely. Few things are absolutely one way or another. Therefore, statements stated as absolutes are often false.
   b. *Be wary of true-false statements with two or more independent clauses.* One may be true while the other is false, which makes the entire statement false. Consider the following true-false item from an economics exam: Karl Marx had a class conflict view of history in which the bourgeoisie consisted of the industrial workers or "have-nots" while the proletariat was represented by the capitalist owners of industry or "haves." The first part of the statement (Karl Marx had a class conflict view of history) is true. However, the terms *bourgeoisie* (in reality, "the haves") and the *proletariat* (the true "have-nots") have been switched around. Be careful. Such test questions can be deceptive if you don't read them closely.

2. *Two common mistakes made with multiple-choice items.*
   a. *Underreading.* Many students underread questions on multiple-choice tests. They read a question until the choice containing the "correct answer" appears, which is then marked as the final response. However, the choices that appear after the "right answer" are not read. So, the student who marks "c" as the correct response without having read "d" and "e" may be in for a surprise when the tests are returned. In some instances, the correct answer to such a question might be "e," which was "both c and d above." Since the student never read "d," which was also correct, the question was missed.
   b. *Overreading.* Likewise, some students overread test questions. They read and reread them and all possible choices over and over again. When overreading occurs, it is easy to pay undue attention to individual words in each choice and take them out of context. This leads to a tendency to misperceive individual words or choices and read things into them that simply are not there. Questions dealt with in this manner are often missed because their original intent has been misinterpreted.

3. *The best reading strategy.* The best strategy in dealing with questions on ob-

jective tests, particularly multiple-choice tests, is to read each question once very carefully and then record your first firm impression as the final response.

4. *What if I don't know the answer?* If you don't know the answer to a question on an objective test, do the following:

a. *Skip it and go on.* Don't dwell on it and worry over it but skip it and move on. You can come back to it later. It might be that other questions that follow will give you clues to how to answer one that was skipped or, in some cases, trigger a complete response. If suddenly you realize the answer to a skipped question, you can go back and complete it.

b. *Complete the exam and then go back to it.* Unless the answer to a skipped question suddenly comes to you in a flash, it is best to wait until the rest of the exam has been completed. Then you can go back and deal with any questions that were skipped.

Use the Deduction Strategy   When you don't know the answer to a question on an objective exam and all else fails, use the **deduction strategy**. This is a process in which incorrect choices on some types of objective exams are carefully eliminated so that, if guessing becomes necessary, it involves the fewest alternatives. This is a particularly useful technique with matching and multiple-choice questions.

Let's say, for example, you are taking a political science course. On your midterm exam you are asked to match up a list of ten key U.S. Supreme Court cases on one side with the nature of what issues were involved and how they were decided on the other. You answer the six that you know but are unclear about the remaining four. So you take the first case left blank and try to eliminate the explanations that couldn't possibly fit. If you still have to guess from among two, your chances of a correct answer will now be one out of two instead of one out of four. Then do the same with the three remaining cases.

Once all your ESS skills are fully mastered, this situation will be rare. By then, you will find that you know all the material on exams.

Task 2: Take Essay Exams the ESS Way   In addition to objective exams, there are **essay exams**. These are forms of evaluation that require the student to demonstrate knowledge of the subject through one or more forms of expository writing. Here the student is required to give more open-ended answers than the more close-ended responses that characterize objective tests. Many instructors prefer this evaluation approach. In addition to taking little time to prepare, essay exams provide an effective way of assessing writing and critical thinking skills.

Know the Types of Essay Questions   There are several different types of essay questions which you may see on exams. Generally, however, they tend to fit into two general categories, questions that require little more than recall and description and those that necessitate some analysis and critical thinking. Descriptive essay questions tend to begin with or use headings like *List, Discuss,* and *Review.* Analytical essay questions tend to begin with terms like *Explain, Argue, Justify,* and *Compare and contrast.*

Descriptive questions typically are the easiest to answer. They require a description of some aspect of course content. With questions that begin with *List, Describe, State,* and *Review,* you are required to recall little more than all the parts that make up a whole rather than give an explanation of why each piece came to be or how the various parts fit together.

The different forms of descriptive questions have their own special characteristics. *List* questions tend to differ from *Describe* and *State* questions mainly in the sense that they are more specific such as "List the parts of a business letter" in an English class. By contrast, a *Review* question may be either specific (Review the causes of the Mexican-American War) or general (Review the nineteenth-century). However, regardless of whether the question asks you to list, describe, state, or review, be careful not to engage in a detailed explanation or analysis of the elements. This is not what the question is asking for.

Trace questions are also descriptive. They call for a sequence or chronological order of things or events in a step-by-step fashion. In courses like history and political science, they also may involve a time frame, so the student may need to structure the answer from one point in time to another, as in "Trace the prohibition movement from its beginning to its demise."

Identify questions ask for a specific type of description in terms of one or more elements of Who?, What?, When?, Where?, and Why? The nature of the subject matter to be identified tells you which or how many of these elements to use and in what order to use them.

So if you were asked to identify Sri Lanka in geography, the focus would tend to be on What? and Where? as you identified it as an island in the Indian Ocean, formally named Ceylon, which lies off the southeastern tip of India. If you were asked to identify Sigmund Freud in psychology, you would first tell Who?, then When?, and finally What? he did to make him such a prominent figure in behavioral science. *Identify* questions call for brief answers, varying from one or two sentences to about a page or so.

Discuss questions tend to be somewhat more difficult than some because they are so general. Unlike questions that usually give you some specifics to work with, such as "List the causes of the Great Depression" in American history or

"Describe the parts of a cell" in biology, *Discuss* questions tend to be somewhat more challenging. You have to make the decision regarding what is to be described and even explained to some degree.

If, for example, you get a question in biology that says "Discuss the cell," you have to decide to tell a story in the manner you feel is best. Do you discuss the parts of the cell, what a cell looks like, how it functions and divides, or all three or none of these aspects? The choice is yours. The instructor is testing not only what you know but also how well you organize and prioritize information.

Analytical questions tend to be more complex and lengthy than descriptive questions and address the ability of the student to think critically about the course material. The most straightforward and often the simplest form of analytical questions begin with such terms as *Explain, Cite the reasons for,* or *What were the causes of . . . ?* Explanation questions ask for the causes or reasons that account for something.

If, for example, the question asked in an American history course was "Explain the causes of World War I," the student could satisfy the question in most instances by listing each of the major causes and elaborating on each one in some detail. However, if the question began with *Analyze the causes of,* the message would be clear that a more highly sophisticated response was being called for. However, if you have any doubt as to what your instructor means by the term *Explain,* ask for some clarification.

If you get an essay question that begins with *Analyze,* you are being asked to do two things in the following sequence: (1) identify the important parts of something and (2) show how they are interrelated in forming the whole. With the first task, it is essential that you prioritize the parts and place the most important element at the top of the list. This shows the instructor you have thought the question through and understand the big picture.

Suppose your sociology instructor asked you: "Analyze the development of twentieth-century sociology." You would first describe, in rank order of prominence, the different schools of sociological thought that emerged in this century and then explain how they developed and interfaced with one another to develop the state of sociological knowledge as it is today.

Your ESS skills are essential here because, if you have used the system as explained, you have already prioritized elements of several types of anticipated questions before entering the test situation. All that is left to do when you take the test is to take your outline, which is firmly impressed on your mind, and convert it to paragraph form. Consequently, rather than having to use a great deal of exam time thinking such issues through, you will have already done most of this as you prepared for the test.

Argue questions are those in which students are asked to choose a side or position on an issue and support it with good evidence and logic. Usually, the position to be taken is left to the student. The instructor is interested not in which side you take but in how well you marshal your facts and present them in an organized, persuasive, and logical manner as you plead your case to its conclusion.

For these questions, simply memorizing facts through cramming won't help you much. The instructor, when grading such a response, will be just as interested in *how* the facts are organized and argued as in what pieces of information are used.

You can anticipate such questions in the way you use your ESS skills to construct your comprehensive outline. If, for instance, you are taking an economics, English composition, history, or political science course, which are notorious for both essay exams and *Argue* questions, you can focus on key issues and be prepared to argue them from any point of view before you take the test.

This is often prudent, because some instructors don't offer students the luxury of choosing which side of an issue or argument to take. Instead, they sometimes may have one or more questions on an essay exam that begin with *Justify*, *Defend*, *Prove*, or *Show that*.

These are questions in which the instructor has predetermined the side of an argument the student is to take and then support with good evidence and logic. As an illustration, you might take a course in history in which the instructor asks you on an exam "Justify the bombing of Pearl Harbor from the Japanese point of view." Again, this would measure not only your command of the facts and issues surrounding a question but also your ability to develop a particular line of argumentation to plead a case.

Another form of exam question is that which begins with *Compare and contrast*. This is a question that instructs students to establish the extent to which two or more things are similar to and different from one another. This is a popular type of question among instructors who make use of essay tests because it is an excellent measure of how much students know about two different issues or topics and their ability to compare them in an organized way.

SHOE   Reprinted with permission: Tribune Media Services

Sometimes two things will have a fair balance of similarities and differences. However, the two may be almost completely alike or different. Students who know the material well will be able to structure their answers to reflect how the situation really is between the two or more things being compared.

Follow the Cardinal Rule of Essay Writing   The cardinal rule of essay writing is: Always assume that the reader (the instructor) knows absolutely nothing about the topic to be written on and you, therefore, will teach this person everything he or she will ever know on the subject.

In placing yourself in the role of teacher and, through your essay, developing a lesson for the reader, you will be sensitive to the concerns of the reader. Too many times, students assume that the instructor will "know what I mean" by a response. This too often leads to imprecise essay writing. But if you take the attitude that you will teach someone everything you know about something in a straightforward, organized, and clear manner, you are likely to do much better on these types of exam.

Of course, in structuring your essay you must always consider the nature and level of your audience. Here you are writing to an educated adult, not a seventh-grade child. The level and tone of your essay should reflect this.

Practice the Etiquette of Essay Writing   There are other rules to use that together comprise **the etiquette of essay writing.** Five of the more important are:

1. *Arrive on time for the exam.* Not only is it disruptive when someone is late, but students generally need every minute afforded them to complete the exam.

2. *Come prepared with two pens (in case one runs out of ink) and plenty of writing paper.* In some classes your instructor will require you to write your responses in a "blue-book," usually available at any college book store. Writing an essay exam in pencil is not acceptable to most instructors.

3. *Write in a neat and legible fashion.* Your instructor will be reading anywhere from dozens to a couple of hundred such exams or more. If your paper looks like Egyptian hieroglyphics, many instructors will not take the time to carefully decipher it. So be sensitive to this and show some consideration. The A grade you might save will be your own.

4. *Avoid using inappropriate language and tone.* Slang and colloquial expressions are to be avoided (except for emphasis, enclosed in quotation marks), and profanity or "cute" attempts at humor must never be used. Essay writing is formal writing and should be handled with decorum.

5. *Write in complete sentences and in paragraph form.* Such things as phrases, outlines, and diagrams usually are inappropriate on essay exams unless specified by the instructor. If in doubt, be sure to ask.

Use the Four Steps in Completing an Essay Exam   In preparing for an essay test, it is important to know the four steps in completing an essay exam. Once in the exam situation, using them will help you in managing your time effectively. These steps are:

Step 1: *Read the entire exam.* If your instructor allows you to make choices among the questions to answer, do so at this time. This entire process, in most cases, should take only about five minutes.

Step 2: *Construct an outline for answering each major question.* This will help organize your thoughts and provide you a structure for writing. In most instances, it should take no more than five to ten minutes to outline the entire exam. As a guide, spend no more than ten percent of the total time allowed for the exam on outlining. Through the use of ESS, this will be simplified tremendously because you will have a complete outline of the material in your head as you go into the exam.

Step 3: *Write the answers and complete the exam.* As you do this, keep track of the time and allocate the necessary amount of time to each question. Be sure to prioritize the questions so that the largest amount of time is spent on those that will count the most.

Step 4: *Review the exam.* If time remains when you finish, review what you wrote. Check for complete sentences, proper spelling, and correct punctuation. Making minor corrections like these will improve the looks of your exam and the way it reads.

Include the Essential Elements of an Essay   A proper essay-exam response consists of three **essential essay elements:** the introduction, the thesis, and the conclusion. An essay response on an exam thus contains the same elements as an essay written in an English composition class or almost anywhere else. These elements, expressed as procedures the essay writer must perform, are:

1. *Write the introduction.* In brief, this is accomplished in the first sentence or paragraph or two by identifying for the reader the subject of the essay, its basic parts, and how its content will be handled. In a sense, an essay is like a story. In the introduction, you tell the reader what it is about and how it will be told.

2. *Write the thesis.* The thesis contains the main part or body of the essay. Here, the subject and its elements are discussed in detail according to the

instructions set forth in the exam question. You may be asked to List, Show that, Describe, Review, Discuss, Analyze, Justify, or otherwise deal with the subject in a particular way.

3. *Write the conclusion.* This is a brief summary of the points mentioned in the thesis and concluding remarks about the subject of the essay. Some essays, because of what the instructor asks for, may require one or more formal conclusions about the subject. Conclusions may therefore become reasons why or explanations of something, based upon the evidence set forth in the thesis.

Be Prepared for Special Cases: Open-Book and Take-Home Exams Essay exams usually are given in the classroom with all books closed and no notes allowed. However, some instructors make use of **open-book** or **take-home** exams in which students are tested on their ability to organize and analyze known information and engage in critical interpretation with it.

Beginning college students often seem attracted to the prospect of open-book or take-home exams. However, they ultimately come to realize that these are among the most difficult and challenging of all exam types. For this reason many college instructors use such exams only with third- and fourth-year students and graduate students working on advanced degrees.

Since such exams tend to be the exception rather than the rule, our discussion here has focused on the more typical form of essay exams, those taken in class with no prepared notes. Nonetheless, these techniques also apply to both open-book and take-home exams.

The key to successfully completing either of these special types of exams lies in carefully reading the instructions. What, specifically, is being asked for in each question? After you understand that, it's a matter of using the components of ESS—THE ADVANCED COURSE.

For example, with an open-book exam to be taken in class, the Textbook Usage Skills in STEP ONE are especially useful. In fact, the student who doesn't use ESS is at a decided disadvantage. By having completed the Identification of Core Material, Topical Mapping, and Chapter Outlining, you will be able to find and use information you need from the text in the shortest time possible. You will already understand the text material and will be able to apply it in an analytical way to each exam question.

SKILL 3: How to Overcome Test Anxiety

Many students, particularly beginning college students and those who have been out of school for several years, experience high levels of anxiety related to taking tests. In addition to causing a significant amount of distress, such anxiety can also inhibit test performance.

Test anxiety occurs when negative thoughts and feelings interfere with test-taking by distracting the student from being able to concentrate on the task at hand.

The consequence of this condition is what psychologists call **cognitive interference,** the inability to concentrate on a mental task. When this occurs, affected students tend to perform poorly on a test because, much like a radio that buzzes with static when the signal is weak, their minds can't seem to "tune in" to the exam. This is unfortunate because, in many cases, these students have a good grasp of the material. The difficulty lies in being able to perform successfully in a test situation.

If this problem is affecting you (or someone you know) even slightly, this brief discussion may be of some benefit.

> **Skill 3: How to Overcome Test Anxiety**
> **Task 1: Understand the Causes**
>> **Cognitive Causes**
>> **Emotional Causes**
> **Task 2: Recognize the Symptoms**
>> **Cognitive Symptoms**
>> **Emotional Symptoms**
>> **Physical Symptoms**
> **Task 3: Implement Effective Treatment Strategies**
>> **Achieve Cognitive Control**
>> **Achieve Emotional Control**

Task 1: Understand the Causes   According to most available research, test anxiety stems from **cognitive causes** (negative thoughts) and **emotional causes** (negative feelings). These factors appear to have an adverse effect on students in the form of test anxiety because these individuals become focused on a negative view of themselves ("I will fail") rather than the task at hand (the exam). This negative self-preoccupation takes the form of self-doubt, insecurity, and worry, which in turn can incapacitate a person's ability to concentrate on the task at hand, the test. The result is often cognitive interference, the inability to concentrate.

This can lead to poor performance or even failure on an exam. In extreme cases, failure can increase self-deprecation and worry ("I knew I would fail") and a vicious cycle is created. If nothing is done to break this cycle, the anxiety and negative feelings may reach such a point that the student may try to escape the situation by leaving school. When this occurs, it is often a real tragedy in terms of lost potential because, in many cases, such students have the ability to succeed. They just don't believe in themselves.

Task 2: Recognize the Symptoms   The **cognitive symptoms** of test anxiety tend to occur as worry and thoughts irrelevant to the test. *Worry* takes such forms as preoccupation with failure, thoughts during a test about how others are doing, and a pronounced state of uncertainty during the period immediately preceding a test. *Irrelevant thoughts* may include thinking about things that occurred in the recent past and various forms of daydreaming during the test. It's not unusual for a test-anxious person to have various irrelevant pieces of information come and go in his or her mind while the test is being taken.

The **emotional symptoms** of test anxiety tend to occur as tension. This tension may take such forms as feelings of distress, uneasiness, the "jitters," and general anxiety. During the exam, feelings of inadequacy, fear approaching panic, and nervousness tend to be typical reactions. A symptom that probably has both cognitive and emotional dimensions is "freezing up" or having one's mind go blank either before or during the test.

The final category of symptoms related to this problem are **physical symptoms**. These occur as various forms of physical discomfort or distress. Before the test, those plagued by test anxiety may experience such things as upset stomach, headaches, and cold hands. While taking the exam, some students may also have their mouths go dry, exhibit nervousness to the point of trembling, and experience such physical reactions as increased heart rate, perspiration, nausea, and intestinal distress. Immediately after an exam, some students may continue to exhibit some of these symptoms as well as dizziness.

An effective strategy for combating and overcoming test anxiety involves learning to better focus attention on taking the test rather than on oneself. Those who experience various forms of high anxiety often feel that they are caught in a state of inertia. They feel "in limbo" and they can't seem to accomplish much or get things done. This is because they direct their energies inward toward themselves rather than outward toward setting and then attaining a goal.

Those suffering from test anxiety worry and experience tension because they lack self-confidence. So they get depressed. Once depressed, they don't feel like doing much of anything. By not doing much of anything, nothing gets done. When nothing gets done, they either get nowhere or fail by default. When this happens, they feel inadequate, trapped, and depressed. Feelings of self-doubt and inadequacy are then reinforced and the whole cycle repeats itself over and over again.

Task 3: Implement Effective Treatment Strategies   To break this self-defeating cycle, students with test anxiety must exert and gain cognitive and emotional control over the situation rather than continue to allow the situation to dominate them. If this applies to you, these strategies should help you if you will use them:

How to Achieve Cognitive Control   To gain **cognitive control,** you will need to shift your thoughts off yourself and onto the task of preparing for your exams. Simply stated, you must become task-oriented rather than ego-oriented in behavior. If you have *a plan of action,* implement it, and remain focused on it. Then everything else will tend to take care of itself. You won't have time to worry or dwell on yourself because you will be too busy.

The plan of action you should implement for academic success is ESS. If you use it and all of it, you should succeed.

Many students entering college for the first time don't know what to expect and where to turn. Since nobody has taken the time to show many of them how to study, they don't know where to start. Consequently, the newness and the challenge of the college experience can be intimidating. With ESS as a tool, much of the uncertainty can be neutralized because with it, students have a plan, a blueprint for success.

How to Achieve Emotional Control: Two Approaches   The emotional dimension of test anxiety must be dealt with as well. To achieve **emotional control,** you must make use of cognitive techniques to change feelings about yourself and the test situation from negative to positive, from feelings of inadequacy to those of self-confidence which will impact positively on behavior. This involves using both your social relationships and your thought processes to send different messages to yourself than those sent before, positive messages instead of negative ones. This in turn will tend to have a positive impact on behavior.

Each of us is influenced greatly in how we see ourselves by our social relationships with others. Positive people tend to encourage us. Negative people often act in ways that can discourage us. As a consequence of our relations with others, we learn social scripts for carrying out our lives. Some of these scripts can lead us to success. Others can doom us to failure.

In addition, most of us engage in an inner talk with ourselves in the form of mental images or actual verbal messages. Behavioral scientists refer to these mental images we develop about ourselves as visualization and inner talk as self-talk. The repeated use of these inner cues tends to reinforce our self-image as well as what we think we are capable of achieving.

Visualization and self-talk are often used by Olympic athletes, actors, and others who need to attain peak performances. You too can use them as tools to harness your ability to overcome negatives such as text anxiety. With practice, you can learn to use them as tools for achieving your goals, not only in school but in other endeavors as well. If I hadn't used these techniques myself, none of my published books, including this one, would ever have been written.

1. *Use positive social scripting.* Sociologists have found that much of our behavior results from the social scripts we learn while growing up. We act to a significant degree on the social cues and habits given to us by others. So it is beneficial to use **positive social scripting** to surround ourselves with others such as family, instructors, and fellow students who will encourage us to succeed in school.

   As children, we have few choices in our social relations—particularly with family members—because of the accidents of birth and other circumstances beyond our control. However, as adults we each have within us the power to make such choices. All that is required is that we have the desire and courage to do so.

   This can often be very difficult. Yet each of us ultimately is left with this most fundamental of all choices. Either we as adults take responsibility for scripting our own behavior—and with it our life destiny—or allow negative people to do it for us. If we choose the latter, we usually lose.

   The most effective way to get the positive encouragement you need for academic success is to associate with successful students and others who possess a positive mental attitude. You will find that they will encourage you in addition to acting as positive role models. If you watch them carefully, you'll notice that they tend to be very task-oriented and time-conscious, especially straight-A students.

   You'll also discover that A students and those who want to become A students seek the company of successful students. Positive energy tends to rub off on others. Try it and find out for yourself.

   Negative students who consistently do poorly in school also tend to gather in groups. If you choose to surround yourself with such students, you will find that some of them tend to sit around saying "Woe is me" about practically everything related to school. Negativism as well as positivism tends to rub off on other people.

   As far as you're concerned, which group is it going to be? Are you going to socially script your own behavior for success or failure? The choice is yours.

2. *Use positive inner scripting.* Behavioral scientists have discovered that, in addition to social scripting, we can encourage ourselves through **positive inner scripting**. This is where both visualization and self-talk become

valuable means of rescripting both our attitudes about ourselves and our ability to transfer these new feelings into positive behavior. In this sense, social scripting and inner scripting mutually reinforce one another.

a. *Visualization.* **Visualization** allows individuals to see themselves in their mind's eye actually engaged in action or inaction, success or failure. It represents a form of mental rehearsal for what we think we may accomplish or not accomplish in the future. If we visualize negative images of what we are likely to do or not to do, this tends to reinforce our self-image negatively. This, in turn, discourages us from setting positive goals and mustering the ability to act on them.

Conversely, positive visualization furnishes us with a positive mental image of ourselves engaged in the world of action. We thus visualize ourselves setting and achieving positive, significant goals. These positive thought images then tend to influence positive behavior.

Here are some examples of negative visualization used by people to set themselves up for failure:

> *The exams are returned and I make the lowest grade.*
> *I receive my grades in the mail and flunk everything.*
> *In my mind's eye, the other students see me as stupid.*
> *I see myself being placed on academic suspension.*
> *My adviser suggests that I drop school and learn a trade.*
> *I see myself next year no better off than I am today.*

In contrast, these are examples of positive visualization you can use to propel you toward success:

> *My grades come in the mail and I make the Dean's List.*
> *In three more years I am a college graduate.*
> *Next semester I receive all A's on my grade report.*
> *By the time I graduate I am invited to join some honor societies.*
> *I take my political science exam next Friday and ace it.*
> *By next year I fully master ESS and get A's in all my courses.*

b. *Self-talk.* **Self-talk,** which works in a similar manner, is a process by which individuals send to themselves inner messages that help shape their behavior. If these inner messages are negative, which tends to be the case with those suffering from test anxiety, behavior tends to be self-defeating. But if you inner-speak to yourself in a positive, encouraging manner, you will be more likely to learn to script your behavior for success than for failure.

Here are some illustrations of negative self-talk messages that can cause and reinforce test anxiety:

I'm getting nervous.
Nothing will work with this test.
What if I make the lowest grade in the class?
My head is beginning to hurt.
I'm going to flunk this test.
The instructor will know I'm stupid when I get an F on the test.

In contrast, there are many positive messages you can send to yourself to help reduce test anxiety. If you will begin to believe in yourself and combine this technique of positive self-talk with a task orientation regarding exam preparation, this problem should be significantly reduced if not resolved altogether.

Here are a few examples of positive inner-talk messages you can use to help achieve success:

Positive thinking leads to positive results.
I am going to do well on this test.
He who keeps cool never sweats.
All I have to do is use ESS and I will make it.
I'm going to make it; all I have to do is stay calm.
By preparing well I'll make an A.

15 STEP FOUR: DIAGNOSTIC FOLLOW-UP

STEP FOUR, the last step, is designed to show you how to monitor your progress with the ESS Principles, Steps, Skills, and Tasks so that, after each exam, you can accurately assess why you missed each question. In doing so, you will learn how to retrace your steps to find out what skills need additional work.

Diagnostic Follow-up is a method of retracing steps taken in exam preparation to pinpoint precisely why any test questions were missed, which ESS Steps and Skills were involved, and what actions are required to further sharpen skills and improve performance. Through this diagnostic component you will be able to learn from the test itself how to study more effectively next time.

Employ this process for maximum results: Use the first three steps of ESS to prepare for each exam. Then use this fourth step to test your level of skill usage for future improvement. This way, both mastery of the ESS system and academic success should be assured.

STEP FOUR involves the use of three skills in sequence:

> **STEP FOUR: Diagnostic Follow-up**
>
> **Skill 1: Going over the Exam**
>
> **Skill 2: Diagnosing Your Performance**
>
> **Skill 3: Implementing the Action Plan for Improvement**

The first few times you implement ESS—THE ADVANCED COURSE, it will be necessary to use this diagnostic follow-up component. You should use it in all courses for at least the first half of the semester in which you begin implementing the ESS system. Some students may find it useful in all courses throughout the first year or two of college. However, once it is clear that your study skills are developing and performance on exams shows significant improvement, ESS STEP FOUR can be abandoned. So, as mastery of the skills is demonstrated, diagnostic follow-up becomes an optional step.

SKILL 1: Going over the Exam

Some instructors take the time to go over the exam afterward with the class. However, until ESS came along, few high school and college students knew precisely how to diagnose their performance after each exam. Therefore, even if they knew what questions they missed, they often didn't know precisely why they missed them. In many cases, neither did their teachers.

This diagnostic component is beneficial to both students and teachers. It provides them both with an effective mechanism for pinpointing areas that need improvement. When going over an exam, this is the process to follow:

> **Skill 1: Going over the Exam**
>> **Task 1: Schedule an Appointment to Go over the Exam**
>> **Task 2: Prepare the Action Plan Sheet**

Task 1: Schedule an Appointment to Go over the Exam   Shortly after the exam is taken, contact your instructor and schedule an appointment to go over the test. If you are attending an auditorium class at a major university, you may need to make this appointment with a teaching assistant. You will find that most instructors will oblige this request and will be pleased to assist you. They will be impressed that you are using a system like ESS and are conscientious about your studies.

However, a few words of caution are necessary. It is important to explain your purpose to the instructor. *Make sure that your instructor understands what you are doing and why you are doing it.* If you don't, it might be easy for your instructor to assume that you are writing down the test questions and their answers. This is not your intent, nor is this what you need to do. Instead, you want to record only content missed, not test questions or their numbers. Your only purpose is to find out what areas of content were missed and why you missed them in order to develop your study skills and improve performance next time.

If for some reason you still meet some resistance (maybe because the instructor is unfamiliar with ESS), show your instructor this passage in the book. In most cases, this should resolve the matter. Your instructors want you to succeed. However, tests are often difficult and time-consuming to develop. So teachers must ensure that they not be allowed to get out and circulate among those students who might be tempted to cheat.

Task 2: Prepare the Action Plan Sheet   When you begin to examine the test, you must prepare the **action plan sheet**. This is a written document that pinpoints (1) areas of content missed on an exam along with (2) areas of deficient skill usage so that such skills can be developed more fully for the next exam.

To begin, get a blank sheet of paper and write *Action Plan* across the top (see Figure 15–1). Then, near the top of the sheet on the left side, write the heading Content Missed. Finally, write another heading called ESS STEP Involved near the top of the right side of the sheet. Now your **action plan** document has been formatted and you're ready to begin.

THE ACTION PLAN SHEET

ACTION PLAN

Content Missed	ESS STEP Involved
1.	
2.	
3.	
4.	
5.	

Figure 15-1

Next, go over your exam and identify the specific form of core content contained in each question that was answered incorrectly. As you do, record the content you missed with each question under the heading Content Missed. If the exam was essay in form, you may need to ask your instructor what areas of specific content or writing form you need to reexamine. When you have finished looking over your exam, the left column of your **action plan sheet** should be complete.

SKILL 2: Diagnosing Your Performance

After finding out *what* you missed on the exam, it is next important to learn *why* you answered portions of the exam incorrectly. This way, each time you make an incorrect response you can learn to pinpoint what skill elements were involved so that study skills can be improved. The skill of diagnosing your performance is as follows:

Skill 2: Diagnosing Your Performance.

> **Task 1: Prepare Your Academic Tool Kit (to be used with the Action Plan Sheet)**
>
> **Task 2: Use the Reverse-Order Diagnostic Strategy: Part A**
>
> **Task 3: Use the Reverse-Order Diagnostic Strategy: Part B**

Task 1: Prepare Your Academic Tool Kit (to be used with the Action Plan Sheet)   After you have examined your performance on the test and recorded the content you missed, be sure to go to the place where you regularly study—such as your home or the library. It is here that you will complete this diagnostic process.

Once there, prepare your **academic tool kit.** To do this, bring together all sources of course content used to prepare for the exam (see Table 15–1). This tool kit consists of all the components used to prepare for the exam from the first day of the study cycle: (1) the textbook, (2) all class notes, (3) all collateral reading assignments, (4) the final comprehensive outline, and (5) a complete written copy of ESS (for detailed instructions).

These tools will now be used to assess exam performance. With such a tool kit, you will be able to ascertain two very important things: (1) why each question was missed (in terms of inadequate skill usage) and (2) what needs to be done next time to increase skills and improve performance.

Task 2: Use the Reverse-Order Diagnostic Strategy: Part A   Since your **action plan** document is now formatted and ready to be used, let's complete the diagnostic process. When you prepared for the exam, the first three steps of ESS were used in ascending order; STEP ONE (Textbook Usage Skills), STEP TWO (Content Organization Skills), STEP THREE (Exam Preparation Skills). Throughout this process the content for the exam was constantly condensed, refined, and reinforced until the day of the test arrived and you took it.

With Diagnostic Follow-up, the process is reversed. Consequently, with each area of content you missed on the exam, you will trace back through what you did in descending or reverse order: STEP THREE, STEP TWO, STEP ONE. You will be operating in a troubleshooting or diagnostic capacity.

This troubleshooting approach is called the **Reverse-Order Diagnostic Strategy.** It involves retracing steps used in exam preparation in reverse order (3, 2, 1) so that the whys involved in missing certain questions can be clearly identified. Once this is done, you will know what study skills are being used correctly

---

**Table 15–1—The Academic Tool Kit
(For Use in Diagnosing Exam Performance)**

1. The textbook
2. All class notes
3. All collateral reading assignments
4. The final comprehensive outline
5. A complete copy of ESS (for reference)

---

and, likewise, which ones need more work. Part A of this process is outlined here:

Reverse-Order Diagnostic Strategy: Part A

(Starting with ESS STEP THREE: Procedures to use in sequence with the content contained in each question missed)

1. Question missed is identified and the content noted on the **action plan sheet** under the heading Content Missed.
2. Final *comprehensive outline* is examined. (This is the tool you used during STEP THREE to prepare for the exam.)
3. If the content material in the question missed is in the comprehensive outline, there are *two reasons* why the question may have been missed:
   a. Inadequate use of Exam Preparation Skills contained in STEP THREE
   b. Inadequate use of Content Organization Skills contained in STEP TWO
4. A notation of the reason that question was missed is placed on the **action plan sheet** under the heading ESS STEP Involved.

Let us now consider an example. Suppose that when you made the appointment to go over your test, you found that the first question missed was question No. 8. So, at that time, you recorded the content contained in the correct answer under Content Missed on the left side of your **action plan sheet** as No. 1. You then completed this process with all the items of content missed on the exam and numbered them 2, 3, 4, 5, and so on.

Now, you will complete the ESS STEP Involved portion of the **action plan sheet** located on the right side of that document. To do so, you consult the tool from your academic tool kit used in completing STEP THREE (Exam Preparation). This will be your comprehensive written outline.

Is the content you missed on question no. 8 contained in the outline? If it is, this will tell you one of two things. First, you may have been overconfident and didn't properly use the STEP THREE tasks of Drill and Practice and Checking Off. If this was what happened, you didn't follow through and something called question 8 slipped through the cracks. So you write STEP THREE under the heading on the right side of your **action plan sheet** called ESS STEP Involved. Next time you'll know you have to work more diligently on the Exam Preparation Skills contained in STEP THREE.

The only other explanation, if the content missed in question 8 is on the outline, would be that inadequate information was placed on the final outline. For example, if the question missed dealt with a concept and it was on the outline but the definition and examples relating to it weren't included, you might not have had enough information with which to answer the question. So you would write STEP TWO (Content Organization Skills) under the heading ESS STEP Involved.

This will tell you that next time you will need to work more diligently on your outlining skills and include more specific material in the comprehensive outline. When you construct your outline next time, take care to perhaps include some of your marginal summaries of elaboration material (examples, illustrations, explanations) from your text. This way you will have more elaboration from which to better understand the core material contained in the final outline.

Task 3: Use the Reverse-Order Diagnostic Strategy: Part B Let's now move on to the second phase of the reverse-order diagnostic strategy, Part B. Suppose, for example, the content contained in question 8 (No. 1 on the **action plan sheet**) can't be found in your final outline. It simply isn't there. Then you consult one or more elements in the academic tool kit that were used at STEP TWO (Content Organization Skills). These tools—which you used to construct your comprehensive outline—consist of your textbook, class notes, and possibly outside readings. They are to be used during Part B of this step-by-step troubleshooting process:

Reverse-Order Diagnostic Strategy: Part B

(Moving on to ESS STEPS TWO and ONE: Procedures to use in sequence)

1. The content in the question missed on the test is not found in the comprehensive outline used to prepare for exam in STEP THREE. Therefore you must look elsewhere.
2. The *textbook* (your first source of course content) is examined.
3. If the content material contained in the question missed is in the textbook, there are *two reasons* why the question may have been missed:
   a. Inadequate use of Content Organization Skills contained in STEP TWO
   b. Inadequate use of Textbook Usage Skills contained in STEP ONE
4. Notation of the reason the question was missed is placed on the **action plan sheet** under the heading ESS STEP Involved.
5. If the reason the question was missed can't be determined through an examination of the text, turn next to the *class notes* (another source of course content) and repeat Procedures 2 through 4 in sequence.
6. If the reason the question was missed can't be determined through an examination of the class notes, turn finally to any assigned *collateral readings* (a final source of course content) and repeat Procedures 2 through 4 in sequence.

Let's now continue the illustration we were using for Part A of this diagnosis. Begin with your textbook. If the material you answered incorrectly in question 8, the first question missed, is in your text and you did identify it as core material through strategic highlighting, then you have a STEP TWO problem, Content Organization Skills (outlining). You used your STEP ONE skills correctly and identified the core material pertaining to the question missed. But you didn't transfer this material (STEP TWO) from the preliminary outline in the text to the final written outline. So you make the appropriate STEP TWO notation on the **action plan sheet** under the heading ESS STEP Involved.

If, when you consult the textbook, the material missed on question 8 is there but you didn't identify it as core material through strategic highlighting, then you missed the question for another reason. In this case, you have a STEP ONE problem because inadequate use was made of Textbook Usage Skills. Specifically, you will need to work on the STEP ONE skills of Active Reading and Identification of Core Material along with the Topical Mapping task of strategic highlighting.

What if the content material contained in question 8 is not found in the textbook? Then you need to consult your class notes. If you find what you are looking for in these notes but this material was not transferred to the final outline, you made inadequate use of the STEP TWO skills. You will need to make the appropriate notation on your **action plan sheet** and work more diligently next time on your Content Organization Skills related to the development of the final outline.

If the material in the question missed was not found in either the text or the class notes, then you will need to troubleshoot further. It might be that you were absent the day those notes were given, your attention lapsed for a few minutes that day, or you just need to work on active listening in class.

Another possibility might be a collateral reading assignment. The question might have been based on this source of course content. If that's the case, you can trace this back by using the same procedure already mentioned with regard to the textbook. The same ESS steps and skills apply in this case as well.

By conducting this two-part diagnosis of your exam performances until mastery of all skills in the ESS system is acquired, academic excellence will be yours and A grades should take care of themselves. The only other element you will need to implement for total success is explained below.

SKILL 3: Implementing the Action Plan for Improvement

Once the Diagnostic Follow-up is completed, you will have completed a document called the Action Plan. This sheet now will allow you to begin **implementing the Action Plan for Improvement**.

This document will now become your guide as you work further on developing all the ESS skills to a mastery level. As you examine the Action Plan, you will notice that each item of content missed has been identified along with the category of skills representing the reason it was missed on the test. In other words, the reason you missed a given test item will be listed under the heading of ESS STEP Involved on the plan. It will be listed as STEP ONE (Textbook Usage Skills), STEP TWO (Content Organization Skills), or STEP THREE (Exam Preparation Skills).

With this Action Plan at your disposal, *you should be able to pinpoint exactly the specific skill or skills involved in each item of content you missed.* With care and concentration on your part, you can even identify which specific tasks under each skill were not carried out properly. You will know precisely which areas of skill usage you are performing well and which areas require additional work. With a little time and diligent application, you should be able to achieve mastery of all the ESS skills. By using the ESS system, you should be able to obtain success in any academic endeavor.

MASTERING ESS:
How Skill-Based Learning Works

In many respects, learning academic skills takes place in much the same way as the acquisition of other important skills. The key ingredients are commitment, regular practice, and hard work. Few if any professional athletes, corporate executives, great inventors and scholars, or leaders in any field obtain their level of success through native talent alone. They all work hard to achieve excellence and recognition. It is not handed to them. In fact, it was Thomas Alva Edison who said "Genius is one percent inspiration and ninety-nine percent perspiration."

Learning the skills to accomplish almost anything also requires a plan, a course of action. Louis Pasteur once said "Chance favors the prepared mind." With regard to academic skills, your plan will be ESS. It requires only dedicated implementation to work. As you use ESS, you will progress through several stages of learning until you ultimately reach mastery with all the principles (Basic Course), Steps, Skills, and Tasks (Advanced Course). This process is summarized in the outline below:

MASTERING ESS: How Skill-Based Learning Works
The Four Stages of Skill-Based Learning
    Stage 1: Unconscious Lack of Skill
    Stage 2: Conscious Lack of Skill
    Stage 3: Conscious Skill
    Stage 4: Unconscious Skill
    The ESS Learning Curve
The 90-Day ESS Assessment
ESS: Advanced Applications

16 THE FOUR STAGES OF SKILL-BASED LEARNING

As you put ESS into practice, it may be helpful to know how skill-based learning works. In essence, we progress through *four stages of skill-based learning* in order to achieve mastery of almost anything. These same four levels tend to apply whether skills to be learned are cognitive (intellectual), affective (emotional), psychomotor (physical), or a combination.

The learning of a new skill begins at what some learning theorists call the unconscious lack of skill level. Then we progress through conscious lack of skill and, with the benefit of some learning experiences, reach the conscious skill level. Finally, after a period of practical application, we may reach the level of unconscious skill or mastery learning.

STAGE 1: Unconscious Lack of Skill

The **unconscious lack of skill** is where we all tend to begin in life's many pursuits. It exists when (1) a person doesn't know that a certain skill is required to perform a task and (2) doesn't possess it. This is very common among small children as they first begin to acquire the skills of walking and running. A two-year-old, not knowing that the psychomotor skill for running is not present, will try anyway and often fall in the process. A four-year-old may jump into a pool of water, not knowing about the need for swimming skills. As adults, however, we usually know when we don't know how to do something.

Nonetheless, some entering college students are not aware of the many skills that will be required of them in order to succeed and excel in school. Indeed, such an unconscious lack of ability can have a somewhat shocking impact when such students realize that college is not a continuation of high school. This realization usually begins to occur with these students when the grades from their first college exams are made available. Shortly after midterm grades are reported, the realization is fully dawning.

STAGE 2: Conscious Lack of Skill

Most adults begin at the **conscious lack of skill** level. This involves realization by the individual that deficiencies exist in certain skill areas or new skills need to be learned. This occurs with many entering college students with regard to study skills. Many entering freshmen have the background and maturity to know that college is not simply the thirteenth grade and that much more will be required of them in higher education. Indeed, it's fairly common for many students to enter college with some uncertainty and anxiety about the challenges that lay ahead.

However, like people who seek out learning experiences needed to master skills in other areas of life, you will have ESS to use in mastering necessary study skills. If you implement it and continue to use it until mastery level is reached, you should do extremely well in school.

Do you swim? If so, do you remember what learning how to swim was like? Keeping your nose above water at least in the beginning made for some anxious moments. Those of us who operate at the conscious lack of skill level often seek out learning experiences to overcome skill deficiencies in certain areas or learn new skills in order to enrich our lives. People who have the desire and commitment to learn how to swim typically will enroll in swimming classes or otherwise get someone to teach them the swimming skills they will need. Then they practice stroking and kicking and more stroking and kicking until proficiency in swimming is reached.

If you are a swimmer, you will remember this. You probably will remember stroking when you were supposed to be kicking or kicking when you were supposed to be stroking. You got water up your nose a few times and probably more than once wondered if you would make it to the other side of the pool. You made mistakes, got frustrated at times, and struggled to master the skills. But you made it. You learned how to swim. This you did because it was important to you. You were willing to overcome the obstacles necessary in order to reach the goal.

STAGE 3: Conscious Skill

When a person in a skill-based learning situation first tries to implement new skills, this is conscious skill usage. **Conscious skill** refers to the process in which, as a new skill is acquired, the learner must consciously think about how the skill is to be used as it is being practiced. Do you remember learning how to drive a car and how awkward that was? If you learned on a standard shift with a clutch, you probably gave the person teaching you some anxious moments when you jerked the car forward those first few times. Those who learn to drive with a clutch also tend to avoid hills for several weeks until they get more comfortable with their driving skills.

As you apply ESS to your courses at school you will go through a similar learning experience. You will be progressing through the conscious skill level of learning for the first few months. This will require careful thought on your part as you implement and get comfortable with all the Steps, Skills, and Tasks you will need to perform. Mistakes will be made. Frustrations will occur. In the beginning, progress may seem slow and tedious.

In fact, don't be surprised if, the first time you take a test after having used ESS, you do little or no better than before. Just as you had to struggle with learning to swim or drive a car, you will have to "pay your dues" in learning to be an excellent student. Learning how to be successful at almost anything worthwhile in life requires time and effort. If you are really serious in your goal to succeed and excel as a student, the time spent in mastering ESS will be well worth it.

STAGE 4: Unconscious Skill

The final level of skill-based learning is **unconscious skill**. This is mastery-level learning in which the skill or skills learned have become internalized and are used habitually without the need for conscious thought. For example, anyone who has learned how to swim can get in a pool and swim across without having to think about it. The skills to be used come automatically. When you drive a car, the skills used are implemented with little conscious thought on your part. Such skills involve a learning curve that requires a certain amount of time and effort for full proficiency to be reached.

The ESS Learning Curve

Like most endeavors, study skills also involve a learning curve. For most students, the ESS system will take several months to a year to fully master. Although this is certainly longer than the time required to master basic swimming or drive a car, study skills are much more complex and certainly more valuable.

Also like swimming, driving, and other simpler skills, you can get a little rusty with study skills if, once mastery is attained, they fall into disuse for a time. This can happen, to some extent, over a summer vacation. Assuming not too long a period has transpired, renewed use will bring them back to full potency within a short period.

However, when ESS is first used, you will not need several months to see results. Improvements in study skills will be apparent in a few short weeks. It is fairly common to see, during the first semester of use, an increase in grade performance for most students of about a letter grade or more over what might have been experienced otherwise. Nonetheless, ESS must be implemented as a total system to be fully effective. Use of certain parts of it, while beneficial to a limited degree, will significantly reduce the potential benefits.

It should also be noted that ESS—THE ADVANCED COURSE shouldn't be implemented in the middle of a study cycle. If you first find out about this system two or three weeks away from a major exam, don't try to play catch-up by using it for that test. Do the best you can using the techniques you have implemented before. Then use ESS for the next exam and begin as soon as the study cycle for that exam starts.

17 THE NINETY-DAY ESS ASSESSMENT

To test your progress with both the Basic and Advanced courses of ESS, conduct **the Ninety-Day ESS Assessment.** This involves giving the entire ESS system a full trial for ninety days and then testing the results. A correct and valid assessment will require a three-step process.

STEP 1: Take the ESS PRETEST and Record Baseline Grades

Prior to implementing ESS as a total system, take the ESS PRETEST. If you took this test as it appeared earlier in the book, record your score along with the date on which it was taken. If you haven't taken the pretest, do it now. Then establish baseline grades for all courses in which you are now enrolled.

For a fair trial, ESS shouldn't be implemented as a total system until you already have taken an exam in each of your courses before you begin using it. These grades will be your baseline grades. If this is not possible or practical because you wish to use ESS immediately, use your current grade-point average as a baseline assessment of grade performance.

STEP 2: Use Both ESS—THE BASIC COURSE and ESS— THE ADVANCED COURSE as a Total System for Ninety Days

This means putting into regular practice all twenty Principles of student effectiveness in ESS—THE BASIC COURSE and all four Steps of ESS—THE ADVANCED COURSE in their proper sequence.

To ensure that you do this, pretend that you have been chosen at random to participate in a validation study of ESS to be conducted by a team of researchers. Since a valid test might require proof that you have been using ESS conscientiously, you must document your use of these principles and skills. For example, the researchers would want to know whether you dropped any courses during the ninety-day trial period (Principle 3), your class attendance records (Principle 5), and where you sat in each class (Principle 7). Likewise, they would want to see if the class notes you prepared for each course were constructed according to the techniques explained in ESS—THE BASIC COURSE (Principle 8).

Moving on to ESS—THE ADVANCED COURSE, you would need to provide documentation that you used the ESS Steps, Skills, and Tasks properly and in their right sequence. For instance, an examination of your textbooks would tell the researchers whether you were attempting to use the various Textbook Usage Skills contained in ESS STEP ONE. Likewise, your comprehensive written outline would provide proof of whether you were using the Content Organization Skills and Exam Preparation Skills contained in ESS STEP TWO and ESS STEP THREE. Finally, the researchers would want to see your Action Plan sheet as documentation that you carried out the Diagnostic Follow-up contained in ESS STEP FOUR.

STEP 3: Take the ESS POSTTEST and Record Your Current Grades

Since the study cycle for most major college exams takes at least three or four weeks, complete the following ESS POSTTEST about 120 days after having taken the ESS PRETEST. This way you will complete the posttest about ninety days after the first exam you took since using the entire ESS system. Then you can compare your score on the ESS PRETEST and the grades you had earned three months ago with the score on the ESS POSTTEST and your current grades. For the purposes of completing the Ninety-Day ESS Assessment, the ESS POSTTEST is reproduced here:

ESS POSTTEST

TODAY'S DATE _____
CURRENT GRADE IN EACH COURSE BEING TAKEN (IF UNAVAILABLE OR NOT APPLICABLE, USE MOST RECENT OVERALL GRADE POINT AVERAGE):

Course 1 _____; Current Grade _____

Course 2 _____; Current Grade _____

Course 3 _____; Current Grade _____

Course 4 _____; Current Grade _____

Course 5 _____; Current Grade _____

Course 6 _____; Current Grade _____

Current Grade Point Average (GPA) _____

COMPUTE AFTER TEST:
RAW SCORE _____ X2 = _____ Pretest Score

(continued)

Please respond to the following statements about student behavior. If you do engage in the behavior described in each item, circle Y for yes. If not, circle N for no.

Y   N   1. I use a dictionary regularly to look up unfamiliar words.

Y   N   2. I miss more than one or two days from school each semester.

Y   N   3. I am tardy for a class more than one or two times per semester.

Y   N   4. I regard my success as a student to be mainly the responsibility of my teachers.

Y   N   5. I regularly participate in class discussions (make comments/ask questions).

Y   N   6. I rarely sit in the front row in class.

Y   N   7. I almost always complete reading assignments before class.

Y   N   8. I sometimes daydream in class.

Y   N   9. I sometimes find it difficult to stay awake in class.

Y   N   10. I write my class notes in outline form as a regular practice.

Y   N   11. I sometimes use a tape recorder in class.

Y   N   12. I spend at least two hours of study for each hour spent in class (Example: 15-hour course load X 2 hrs. = 30 hrs. per week).

Y   N   13. I find it difficult to have enough time for study.

Y   N   14. I attended the first meeting of each class this semester (or the last school term for which I was registered).

Y   N   15. I sometimes miss deadlines for class papers/projects.

Y   N   16. I sometimes ask teachers I plan to take in the future for a copy of their class syllabus.

Y   N   17. I rarely if ever visit the class of a teacher I plan to take for a course next term.

(continued)

Y	N	18. I regularly consult a teacher I respect as an adviser.
Y	N	19. I take five to ten minutes to systematically preview each reading assignment before I begin reading it.
Y	N	20. I usually can tell specifically which text material is likely to appear on an exam.
Y	N	21. Reading text material for class sometimes puts me to sleep.
Y	N	22. My mind often wanders when I read textbooks.
Y	N	23. I find it difficult to tell which paragraphs in textbooks contain the most important material.
Y	N	24. I sometimes read textbook assignments two or three times in order to better learn the material.
Y	N	25. Using a highlighter pen to mark portions of the required reading material is not very helpful to me.
Y	N	26. I write notes to myself in the margins of my textbooks about the material I have read.
Y	N	27. I find it difficult to identify the study aids authors design into their textbooks.
Y	N	28. I regularly use Study Guides when they are available with my textbooks.
Y	N	29. I rarely if ever outline my reading assignments in the book.
Y	N	30. I make regular use of a weekly written calendar to budget study time.
Y	N	31. I rewrite my notes taken in class in order to prepare for exams.
Y	N	32. Compared with my other activities, I place study at the top of my priority list.
Y	N	33. I prepare for exams by condensing my reading assignments and class notes into a final, comprehensive written outline.
Y	N	34. I effectively use "drill and practice" techniques to master all the specific material likely to appear on exams.

(continued)

Y   N   35. I often put off studying until a day or two before a scheduled exam.

Y   N   36. I am confident with my note-taking skills.

Y   N   37. I usually get at least seven or eight hours of sleep the night before a major exam.

Y   N   38. I perform as well on essay exams as with other types of tests.

Y   N   39. I sometimes experience test anxiety to such a degree that it prevents me from doing my best on exams.

Y   N   40. I seldom make an appointment with my instructor to go over my test.

Y   N   41. I don't know how to use the library effectively to complete research assignments.

Y   N   42. I have an effective step-by-step method for completing term papers that enables me to get good grades.

Y   N   43. I usually take advantage of extra-credit opportunities.

Y   N   44. I don't have a clear understanding of plagiarism and what it involves.

Y   N   45. I have an effective method for writing a résumé to use in applying for jobs.

Y   N   46. I submit written papers to my instructors with few if any errors in grammar or spelling.

Y   N   47. I have a clear understanding of the key parts of an essay.

Y   N   48. I can name at least five memory techniques that I use regularly for effective study.

Y   N   49. I usually write two or three drafts in preparing term papers.

Y   N   50. I don't know how to write an effective cover letter to a prospective employer for use in applying for a job.

TO COMPUTE YOUR SCORE, TURN TO THE KEY PROVIDED IN THE APPENDIX.

18 | ESS: ADVANCED APPLICATIONS

As a system for academic success, ESS works so well that after several months of application, you may be able to use all skills as a total system in a streamlined form for advanced students. This should not be attempted, however, until you are sure all skills in the entire system have been completely mastered. A good rule of thumb here might be grade-point average. Once you are consistently performing at the level necessary for inclusion on the dean's list, you may then wish to go on to ESS: Advanced Applications.

How to Use ESS: Advanced Applications

After several months to one year of diligent application, the entire ESS system should be mastered. By this time, each Principle, Step, Skill, and Task should be internalized as habit. Then the ultimate benefits of ESS will be truly realized. You probably will discover that it now takes only half as much time and effort to deal with a similar amount of course content as it did before. This will enable you to effectively handle much more lengthy and challenging course content in the future if you have the desire.

Those who become master students and then go on to get the scholarships and complete the MBA's, MD's, PhD's, law degrees, and other advanced degrees have learned through experience and application much if not all of what is contained in ESS. All I have done is to put it together for you in a systematic framework that is usable as a total learning system.

There is one main difference between these students and you. Many if not most of them had to learn these principles and study elements through trial and error, the "school of hard knocks." In doing so, they sought out many sources: separate books on success, study skills, memory techniques, critical thinking, preparing term papers, writing résumés, and so on. With ESS all the critical principles and skills have been designed into a single volume as a total learning system.

Once you master this system you will be able to move on to what I call ESS: Advanced Applications. This allows for a streamlined use of the steps and skills that combines and integrates many of the tasks. It involves the following basic components:

Use of Your Index Finger as a Skimming Device   Once you have reached mastery with the ESS system, you may want to use your index finger or a six-inch ruler as a skimming device as you read text assignments. Since the Textbook Usage Skills contained in ESS STEP ONE should be fully mastered by this time, the distinction between core material and elaboration will be automatic. If you are typical of many students, core material will almost leap out at you as you read.

Use of Text Material (Reading Assignments) as the Model for the Final Comprehensive Outline in All Courses   As you progress to the junior and senior levels at college, it will become necessary to use text material as the model for the final comprehensive outline in all courses. Since more and more reading material will be required as you move into more advanced courses, this will tend to be a natural transition and a very logical one to make. Particularly at the graduate-school level, courses tend to consist mainly of discussion seminars based on reading assignments.

Instructors in the more advanced courses at junior, senior, and graduate levels tend to lecture less and less. The emphasis increasingly is placed on reading assignments. Typically, the three hundred to five hundred pages assigned per course to first- and second-year college students becomes five hundred to eight hundred or more pages for juniors and seniors. First-year graduate and professional students often are required to read a thousand pages or more for each course and doctoral students, depending on the field, are expected to read much more.

Construction of the Comprehensive Written Outline Simultaneously with Your Reading   Your outlining skills should be well developed by this time, so separate in-text outlining will become unnecessary. The same could be said of tasks such as Strategic Highlighting and Analytical Summary. You'll still use all the skills, but in a more advanced and efficient application. Analytical summaries of elaboration material will still be made, but written only once in the comprehensive outline as necessary. You can then have a notepad or index cards handy to literally construct a final comprehensive outline of the text material as you read along.

The ESS system will prove invaluable should you decide to complete a baccalaureate or higher degree. Once mastered, ESS can take you as far as you desire to go in higher education.

I wish you every success as you pursue your studies in the months and years ahead. By reading this far, you have been exposed to a resource that I and thousands of others wish we had had when we first entered the portals of higher education years ago. Many of us never had anyone tell us in a concise, step-by-step manner how to study. We had to fly by the seat of our pants and learn by trial and error. You, fortunately, can be different. Consequently, ESS represents a key to a very large and important door. Use it. On the other side lies what could be your future, a bright one.

A P P E N D I X : Scoring the ESS PRETEST and POSTTEST

SCORING:

The ESS PRETEST and POSTTEST both contain exactly the same items. They both represent an inventory of the same behaviors, with two assessments taken a few months apart.

Award one point for each of the following items on either the PRETEST or POSTTEST that were answered with a YES: 1, 5, 7, 10, 12, 14, 16, 18, 19, 20, 26, 28, 30, 31, 32, 33, 34, 36, 37, 38, 42, 43, 45, 46, 47, 48, 49.

YES RESPONSES = _____ POINTS.

Award one point for each of the following items on either the PRETEST or POSTTEST that were answered with a NO: 2, 3, 4, 6, 8, 9, 11, 13, 15, 17, 21, 22, 23, 24, 25, 27, 29, 35, 39, 40, 41, 44, 50.

NO RESPONSES = _____ POINTS

CUMULATIVE SCORE

YES RESPONSES = _____ POINTS

NO RESPONSES = _____ POINTS

TOTAL = _____ POINTS (RAW SCORE)

NOTE TO EDUCATORS: You may wish to give the ESS PRETEST on the first day of the school term in either a regular or orientation course as an assessment of your students' study habits. The POSTTEST then can be given on the last day of the school term. The score on this test may be useful as a counseling or tracking tool.

REFERENCES

Adams, M. J. and Collins, A. 1977. *A schema-theoretic view of reading.* Champaign: University of Illinois, Center for the Study of Reading (Technical Report No. 32.).

Adler, M. and Van Doren, C. 1972. *How to read a book.* New York: Simon & Schuster.

Alexander, S. 1981. *Advanced rhinocerology.* Laguna Hills, CA: The Rhino's Press.

The American heritage dictionary, second college edition. 1985. Boston: Houghton Mifflin.

Anderson, J. R. 1983. A spreading activation theory of memory. *Journal of Verbal Learning and Verbal Behavior,* 22, 261–265.

———. 1987. Skill acquisition: Compilation of weak-method problem solutions. *Psychological Review,* 94, 192–210.

Anderson, R. C. 1984. Role of the reader's schema in comprehension, learning and memory. In R. C. Anderson, J. Osborn, and R. J. Tierney (eds.), *Learning to read in American schools: Basal readers and content texts* (pp. 243–258). Hillsdale, NJ: Erlbaum.

Anderson, T. H. 1978. *Another look at the self-questioning study technique.* (Technical Educational Report No. 6). Champaign: University of Illinois, Center for the Study of Reading.

Applebee, A. N. 1984. Writing and reasoning. *Review of Educational Research,* 54, 577–596.

Apps, J. W. 1982. *Study skills for adults returning to school.* New York: McGraw-Hill.

Baddeley, A. 1982. *Your memory: A user's guide.* New York: Macmillan.

Bailey, R. and Hankins, N. 1984. *Psychology of effective living* (2nd ed.). Prospect Heights, IL.: Waveland Press.

Ballantine, J. H. 1983. *The sociology of education; A systematic analysis.* Englewood Cliffs, NJ: Prentice Hall.

Baker, L. 1985. Differences in the standards used by college students to evaluate their comprehension of expository prose. *Reading Research Quarterly,* 20, 297–313.

Bazerman, C. and Wiener, H. S. 1988. *Writing skills handbook* (2nd ed.). Boston: Houghton Mifflin.

Beck, A. 1984. Cognitive approaches to stress. In R. L. Woolfolk and P. M. Lehrer (eds.), *Principles and practice of stress management.* New York: Guilford Press.

Bloom, B. S. (ed.). 1985. *Developing talent in young people.* New York: Ballantine.

Bloom, D. S. (ed.). 1956. *Taxonomy of educational objectives: Handbook I, Cognitive domain.* New York: McKay.

Boltwood, C. R. and Blick, K. A. 1978. The delineation and application of three mnemonic techniques. *Psychonomic Science,* 20, 339–341.

Boocock, S. S. 1972. *An introduction to the sociology of learning.* Boston: Houghton Mifflin.

Bousfield, W. A. 1953. The occurrence of clustering in the free recall of randomly arranged associates. *Journal of General Psychology,* 49, 229–240.

Bower, G. H. 1970. Organizational factors in memory. *Cognitive Psychology,* 1, 18–46.

Bower, H. D. 1982. *The state of the nation and the agenda for higher education.* San Francisco: Jossey-Bass.

———. 1981. Mood and memory. *American Psychologist,* 36, 129–148.

Bower, G. H. and Clark, M. C. 1969. Narrative stories as mediators for serial learning. *Psychonomic Science,* 14, 181–182.

Bower, G. H. and Cohen, P. R. 1982. Emotional influences in memory and thinking: Data and theory. In M. S. Clark and S. T. Fiske (eds.), *Affect and cognition.* Hillsdale, NJ.: Erlbaum.

Brewer, W. F. and Pani, J. R. 1984. The structure of human memory. In G. H. Bower (ed.), *The psychology of learning and motivation,* vol. 17. New York: Academic Press.

Brown, A., Campione, J. C., and Barclay, C. R. 1979. Training self-checking routines for estimating test readiness: Generalizations from list learning to prose recall. *Child Development,* 50, 501–512.

Bruner, J. S., Goodnow, J. J., and Austin, G. A. 1956. *A study of thinking.* New York: Wiley.

Burka, J. B. and Yuen, L. 1983. *Procrastination.* Reading, MA.: Addison-Wesley.

Calfee, R. C. 1987. The structural features of large texts. *Educational Psychologist,* 22, 357–375.

Calfee, R. C. and Henry, M. K. 1986. Project READ: An inservice model for training classroom teachers in effective reading instruction. In J. V. Hoffman (ed.), *Effective teaching of reading: Research and practice* (pp. 199–299). Newark, DE: International Reading Association.

Carlisle, K. P. 1985. Learning how to learn. *Teaching and Development Journal,* 39, 75–80.

Carver, R. P. 1972, August. Speed readers don't read; they skim. *Psychology Today,* 23–30.

Chase, W. G. 1987. Visual information processing. In K. R. Boff, L. Kaufman, and J. P. Thomas (eds.), *Handbook of perception and human performance. Vol. 2: Information processing* (pp. 28–1 to 28–60). New York: Wiley.

Chase, W. G. and Ericsson, K. A. 1981. Skilled memory. In J. R. Anderson (ed.), *Cognitive skills and their acquisition.* Hillsdale, NJ: Erlbaum.

Commitment to excellence. 1984. Lombard, IL.: Great Quotations.

Cox, S. D. and Wollen, K. A. 1981. Bizarreness and recall. *Bulletin of the Psychonomic Society,* 18, 244–245.

Craik, F. I. M. and Lockhart, R. S. 1972. Levels of processing: A framework for memory research. *Journal of Verbal Learning and Verbal Behavior,* 11, 671–684.

Craik, F. I. M. and Talving, E. 1975. Depth of processing and the retention of words in episodic memory. *Journal of Experimental Psychology: General,* 104, 268–294.

Craik, F. I. M. and Watkins, M. J. 1973. The role of rehearsal in short-term memory. *Journal of Verbal Learning and Verbal Behavior,* 12, 599–607.

Cross, P. K. 1976. *Accent on learning.* San Francisco: Jossey Bass.

Current, R. N., Williams, T. H., Freidel, F., and Brinkley, A. 1987. *American history: A survey* (7th ed.). New York: Knopf.

Daehler, M. W. and Bukatko, D. 1985. *Cognitive development.* New York: Knopf.

Davis, R. 1986. Knowledge-systems. *Science,* 231, 957–963.

Davis, R. A. and Moore, C. C. 1935. Methods of measuring retention. *Journal of General Psychology,* 12, 144–155.

Deffenbacker, J. L. 1978. Worry, emotionality and task generated interference in test anxiety: An empirical test of attentional theory. *Journal of Educational Psychology,* 70, 253–263.

Dellarosa, D. 1988. A history of thinking. In R. J. Sternberg and E. F. Smith (eds.), *The psychology of human thought* (pp. 1–18). New York; Cambridge University Press.

Eddy, J., Martin, B., and Semones, J. 1983. *Adult learning and program development: From psychosocial theory to social policy.* Minneapolis: Burgess/Alpha Editions.

———. 1984. *Adult education: Theory and practice.* Minneapolis: Burgess/Alpha Editions.

Egan, D. and Schwartz, B. 1979. Chunking in recall of symbolic drawings. *Memory and Cognition,* 7, 145–158.

Ennis, R. H. 1985. Critical thinking and the curriculum. *National Forum,* 65, 28–30.

Entwistle, D. R. 1960. Evaluations of study skills courses: A review. *Journal of Educational Research,* 53, 243–251.

Epstein, H. 1981. Learning to Learn: Matching instruction to cognitive levels. *Principal,* 60, 25–30.

Ericsson, K. A. and Chase, W. G. 1982. Exceptional memory. *American Scientist,* 70, 607–615.

Feder, B. 1979. *The complete guide to taking tests.* Englewood Cliffs, NJ.: Prentice-Hall.

Flavell, J. H. 1985. *Cognitive development* (2nd ed.). Englewood Cliffs, NJ.: Prentice-Hall.

Flavell, J. H. and Wellman, H. M. 1977. Metamemory. In R. V. Kail and J. W. Hagen (eds.), *Perspectives on the development of memory and cognition.* Hillsdale, NJ.: Erlbaum.

Flesch, R. 1955. *Why Johnny can't read.* New York: Harper.

Fowler, R. L. and Barker, A. S. 1974. Effectiveness of highlighting for retention of text material. *Journal of Applied Psychology,* 59, 358–364.

Frase, L. T. and Schwartz, B. J. 1975. Effect of question production and answering in prose recall. *Journal of Educational Psychology,* 67, 628–635.

Gagné, E. D. 1985. *The cognitive psychology of school learning.* Boston: Little, Brown.

Gladstone, G. A. 1960. Study behavior of gifted stereotype and non-stereotype children. *Personnel and Guidance Journal,* 38, 470–474.

Glover, J. A., Ronning, R. R., and Bruning, R. H. 1990. *Cognitive Psychology for Teachers.* New York: Macmillan.

Grassick, P. 1983. *Making the grade.* New York: Arco.

Great quotations. 1984. Lombard, IL.: Great Quotations.

Green, G. W. 1985. *Getting straight A's.* Secaucus, NJ.: Lyle Stuart.

Hay, J. E. and Lindsay, C. A. 1969. The working student: How does he achieve? *Journal of College Student Personnel,* 10, 109–114.

Hayes, J. R. 1988. *The complete problem solver* (2nd ed.). Hillsdale, NJ: Erlbaum.

Herbert, W. 1983. Remembrance of things partly. *Science News,* 124 (24), 378–381.

Hidi, S. and Anderson, V. 1986. Producing written summaries: Task demands, cognitive operations, and implications for instruction. *Review of Educational Research,* 56, 263–284.

Houston, J. P. 1981. *Fundamentals of learning and memory* (2nd ed.). New York: Academic Press.

Hull, G. 1987. The editing process in writing: A performance study of more skilled and less skilled college writers. *Research in the Teaching of English,* 21, 8–29.

Jenkinson, E. B. 1988. Learning to write/writing to learn. *Phi Delta Kappan,* 69, 712–717.

Johnson, M. P. and Walsh, E. J. 1978. Grade inflation or better comprehension. *Teaching Sociology,* 5, 363–378.

Jones, B. F., Palinscar, A. S., Ogle, D. S., and Carr, E. G. (eds.). 1986. *Strategic teaching and learning: Cognitive learning in the content areas.* Elmhurst, IL: North Central Regional Educational Laboratory.

Just, M. A. and Carpenter, P. A. 1987. *The psychology of reading and language comprehension.* Boston: Allyn & Bacon.

Kaplan, R. M., McCordick, S. M., and Twitchell, M. 1979. Is it the cognitive or the behavioral component which makes cognitive-modification effective in test anxiety? *Journal of Counseling Psychology,* 26, 371–377.

Katz, J. 1985. *Teaching as though students mattered: New directions for teaching and learning.* Vol. 21, San Francisco: Jossey Bass.

Katz, W. 1984. *Your library: A reference guide* (2nd ed.). New York: Holt, Rinehart and Winston.

King, J. R., Biggs, S., and Lipsky, S. 1984. Students' self-questioning and summarizing as reading study strategies. *Journal of Reading Behavior,* 16, 205–218.

Kintsch, W. 1986. Learning from text. *Cognition and instruction,* 3, 87–108.

Lavin, D. E. 1965. *The prediction of academic performance.* New York: Russell Sage Foundation.

Lester, J. D. 1990. *Writing research papers: A complete guide* (6th ed.). Glenview, IL: Scott, Foresman.

Liebert, R. M. and Morris, L. W. 1967. Cognitive and emotional components of test anxiety: A distinction and some initial data. *Psychological Reports,* 20, 975–978.

Loftus, E. F. 1984. The eyewitness on trial. In B. D. Sales and A. Alwork (eds.), *With liberty and justice for all*. Englewood Cliffs, NJ: Prentice-Hall.

Lorayne, H. and Lucas, J. 1986. *The Memory Book*. New York: Ballantine Books.

Marks, M. B. 1966. Improve reading through better format. *Journal of Educational Research*, 60, 147–151.

Marschark, M., Richman, C. L., Yuille, J. C., and Hunt, R. R. 1987. The role of imagery in memory: On shared and distinctive information. *Psychological Bulletin*, 102, 28–41.

Martindale, C. 1981. *Cognition and consciousness*. Homewood, IL: Dorsey.

Mayer, R. E. 1984. Twenty-five years of research on advance organizers. *Instructional Science*, 8, 133–169.

McClelland, D. C. 1985. How motives, skills, and values determine what people do. *American Psychologist*, 40, 812–825.

McCloskey, M., Wible, C. G., and Cohen, N. J. 1988. Is there a special flash-bulb memory mechanism? *Journal of Experimental Psychology: General*, 117, 171–181.

McCloskey, M. and Zaragoza, M. 1985. Misleading postevent information and memory for events: Arguments and evidence against memory impairment hypotheses. *Journal of Experimental Psychology: General*, 114, 1–16.

McDaniel, M. A. and Einstein, G. O. 1986. Bizarre imagery as an effective memory aid: The importance of distinctiveness. *Journal of Experimental Psychology: Learning, Memory, and Cognition*, 12, 54–65.

Meyer, B. J. F. 1975. *The organization of prose and its effects on memory*. Amsterdam: North-Holland.

Miller, G. A. 1988. The challenge of universal literacy. *Science*, 241, 1293–1299.

Miller, G. A., Galanter, E., and Pribram, K. H. 1960. *Plans and the structure of behavior*. New York: Holt, Rinehart and Winston.

Millman, J. and Pauk, W. 1969. *How to take tests*. New York: McGraw-Hill.

Milton, O. et al. 1986. *Making sense of college grades*. San Francisco, Jossey Bass.

Mishkin, M. and Appenzeller, T. 1987. The anatomy of memory. *Scientific American*, 256, 80–89.

Morris, L. W., Davis, M. A., and Hutchings, C. H. 1981. Cognitive and emotional components of anxiety: Literature review and a revised Worry-Emotionality Scale. *Journal of Educational Psychology*, 73, 541–555.

Morris, W. (ed.). 1976. *The American heritage dictionary of the English language*. Boston: Houghton Mifflin.

National Commission on Excellence in Education. 1983. *A Nation at risk: The imperative for educational reform*. Washington, DC: U. S. Government Printing Office.

Neisser, U. 1981. John Dean's memory: A case study. *Cognition*, 9, 1–22.

Newby, R. W. 1987. Contextual areas in item recognition following verbal discrimination learning. *Journal of General Psychology*, 114, 281–287.

Nickerson, R. S., Perkins, D. N., and Smith, E. E. 1986. *The teaching of thinking.* Hillsdale, NJ: Erlbaum.

Niple, M. L. 1968. *The relationship of different study methods to immediate and delayed comprehension.* Unpublished Doctoral Dissertation, Ohio State University.

Norris, J. A. and Bruning, R. H. 1988. Cohesion in the narratives of good and poor readers. *Journal of Speech and Hearing Disorders,* 53, 416–424.

Osborne, R. and Freyberg, P. 1985. *Learning in science.* Portsmouth, NH: Heinemann.

Palmer, S. E. 1975. The effects of contextual scenes on the identification of objects. *Memory and Cognition,* 3, 519–526.

Pauk, W. 1965. Study skills and scholastic achievement. *Reading Teacher,* 19, 180–182.

Pavalko, R. M. 1968. *Sociology of education.* Itasca, IL.: F. E. Peacock.

Pearson, P. D. and Tierney, R. J. 1984. On becoming a thoughtful reader: Learning to read like a writer. Urbana-Champaign: University of Illinois, Center for the Study of Reading (Reading Education Report No. 50).

Peters, T. and Austin, N. 1986. *A passion for excellence: The leadership difference.* New York: Warner.

Phifer, S. J., McNickle, B., Ronning, R. R., and Glover, J. A. 1983. The effect of details on the recall of major ideas in text. *Journal of Reading Behavior,* 15, 19–29.

Powell, W. J., and Jourard, S. M. 1963. Some objective evidence of immaturity in under-achieving college students. *Journal of Counseling Psychology,* 10, 276–282.

Pressey, L. C., and Pressey, S. L. 1932. *Essential preparation for college.* New York: Holt, Rinehart and Winston.

Preston, R. C. 1948. The reading habits of superior college students. *Journal of Experimental Education,* 16, 196–202.

Puff, C. R. 1970. Role of clustering in free recall. *Journal of Experimental Psychology,* 86, 384–386.

Raaijmakers, J. G. W., and Shiffrin, R. M. 1981. Search of associative memory. *Psychological Review,* 88, 93–134.

The Random House college dictionary, revised edition. 1988. New York: Random House.

The Random House thesaurus, college edition. 1984. New York: Random House.

Ratcliff, R. and McKoon, G. 1986. More on the distinction between episodic and semantic memories. *Journal of Experimental Psychology: Learning, Memory, and Cognition,* 12, 312–313.

Reed, S. K. 1982. *Cognition.* Monterey, CA: Brooks/Cole.

Reynolds, J. H. and Glaser, R. 1964. Effects of repetition and spaced review upon retention of a complex learning task. *Journal of Educational Psychology,* 55, 297–308.

Robinson, F. P. 1970. *Effective study* (4th ed.). New York: Harper.

Rogers, C. R. 1961. *On becoming a person.* Boston: Houghton Mifflin.

Roget's II: The new thesaurus. 1988. Boston: Houghton Mifflin.

Rosch, E. and Lloyd, B. B. (eds.). 1978. *Cognition and categorization.* Hillsdale, NJ: Erlbaum.

Rowe, D. W. and Rayford, L. 1987. Activating background knowledge in reading comprehension. *Reading Research Quarterly,* 22, 160–176.

Rivin, H. N., Fraser, D. M., and Stern, M. R. 1965. *The first years in college: Preparing students for a successful college career.* Boston: Little, Brown.

Rogers, G. W. 1959. *Lecture listening skills: Their nature and relation to achievement.* Unpublished Doctoral Dissertation, Ohio State University.

Samuels, S. J. 1988. Decoding and automaticity: Helping poor readers become automatic at word recognition. *The Reading Teacher,* 41, 756–760.

Sanford, A. J. 1985. *Cognition and cognitive psychology.* New York: Basic Books.

Sarason, I. G. 1984. Stress, anxiety and cognitive interference: Reactions to tests. *Journal of Personality and Social Psychology,* 46, 929–938.

Sarason, I. G., Sarason, B. R., Keefe, D. E., Hayes, B. E., and Shearin, E. N. 1986. Cognitive interference: Situational determinants and traitlike characteristics. *Journal of Personality and Social Psychology,* 51, 215–226.

Selig, M. E. P. 1970. On the generality of the laws of learning. *Psychological Review,* 77, 406–418.

Semones, J. K. 1990. *Sociology: A core text.* Fort Worth: Holt, Rinehart and Winston.

Shaw, P. 1961. Teaching reading skills at college. *School and Society,* 89, 121–123.

Skinner, B. F. 1968. *The technology of teaching.* New York: Macmillan.

Smith, S. 1979. Remembering in and out of context. *Journal of Experimental Psychology: Human Learning and Memory,* 5, 460–471.

Smith, S. M., Glenberg, A. M., and Bjork, R. A. 1978. Environmental context and human memory. *Memory and Cognition,* 6, 342–355.

Solso, R. L. 1988. *Cognitive psychology* (2nd ed.). Boston: Allyn & Bacon.

Spiro, R. J., Bruce, B. C., and Brewer, W. F. (eds.). 1980. Theoretical issues in reading comprehension. Hillsdale, NJ: Erlbaum.

Squire, L. R. 1986. Mechanisms of memory. *Science,* 232, 1612–1619.

Strunk, W., Jr. and White, E. B. 1979. The elements of style (3rd ed.). New York: Macmillan.

Summer, R. 1968. The social psychology of cramming. *Personnel and Guidance Journal,* 47, 104–109.

Thomas, E. L. and Robinson, H. A. 1972. *Improving reading in every class: A sourcebook for teachers.* Boston: Allyn & Bacon.

Thompson, D. M. and Tulving, E. 1970. Associative encoding and retrieval: Weak and strong cues. *Journal of Experimental Psychology,* 86, 255–262.

Thompson, R. F. 1986. The neurobiology of learning and memory. *Science,* 233, 941–947.

Thorndike, E. L. 1932. The fundamentals of learning. New York: Teachers College, Columbia University.

Tresselt, M. E. 1966. A preliminary study of factors in learning in a how-to-study course. *Journal of Psychology,* 64, 91–93.

Trabasso, T. and Bower, G. H. 1968. *Attention in learning.* New York: Wiley.

Troyka, L. Q. 1985. *Simon & Schuster handbook for writers.* Englewood Cliffs, NJ: Prentice-Hall.

Tryon, G. S. 1980. The measurement and treatment of test anxiety. *Review of Educational Research,* 50, 343–372.

Tulving, E. 1962. Subjective organization in free recall of "unrelated" words. *Psychological Review,* 69, 344–354.

———. 1985. How many memory systems are there? *American Psychologist,* 40 (4), 385–398.

———. 1986. What kind of hypothesis is the distinction between episodic and semantic memory? *Journal of Experimental Psychology: Learning, Memory, and Cognition,* 12, 307–311.

Turabian, K. L. 1976. *Student's guide for writing research papers* (3rd ed.). Chicago: University of Chicago Press.

Turk, T. G. ed. 1982. *Methods of evaluating student performance.* Washington, D. C.: ASA Teaching Resources Center.

Underwood, B. J. 1957. Interference and forgetting. *Psychological Review,* 64, 49–60.

Van Zoost, B. L. and Jackson, B. T. 1974. Effects of self-monitoring and self-administered reinforcement on study behaviors. *Journal of Educational Research,* 67, 216–218.

Vernon, P. E. 1962. The determinants of reading comprehension. *Educational and Psychological Measurements,* 22, 269–286.

Wallach, M. A. and Wing, C. W., Jr. 1969. *The talented student.* New York: Holt, Rinehart and Winston.

Waller, T. C. 1987. *Reading research: Advances in theory and practice,* vol. 5. New York: Academic Press.

Webster's collegiate thesaurus. 1988. New York: Random House.

Webster's ninth new collegiate dictionary. 1988. Springfield, MA: Merriam-Webster.

Winograd, T. 1984. Strategic difficulties in summarizing texts. *Reading Research Quarterly,* 14, 404–424.

Yates, F. A. 1966. *The art of memory.* Chicago: University of Chicago Press.

Yuill, N. and Joscelyne, T. 1988. Effect of organizational cues and strategies on good and poor comprehenders' story understanding. *Journal of Educational Psychology,* 80, 152–158.

Zinsser, W. 1985. *On writing well: An informal guide to writing nonfiction* (3rd. ed.). New York: Harper.

Zivian, M., and Darjes, R. 1983. Free recall by in-school and out-of-school adults: Performance and metamemory. *Developmental Psychology, 19,* 513–520.

INDEX

Academic toolkit, preparing the, 212
ACT scores, 36
Active listening (in class), 79–80
Active reading (a textbook usage skill)
 chunking by chapter section and,
  159–160
 an overview of, 155–156
 paragraph classification and, 160–162
 reading preview and, 156–159
Acronyms, *see* Memory techniques
Action plan sheet, preparing the, 210–211
Alexander, Scott, 28
Appeal to authority, *see* Critical thinking
  (faulty arguments)
Appeal to emotion, *see* Critical thinking
  (faulty arguments)
Appeal to the person, *see* Critical thinking
  (faulty arguments)
Appeal to pity, *see* Critical thinking (faulty
  arguments)
Aptitude tests, 36
Assessment, 90-Day ESS, 3
Attendance in classes, 76
Aural learners, 81

Bazerman, Charles, 69
Beethoven, 19
Boldface words (an in-chapter study aid),
  164
Brinkley, Alan, 157
Burns, Robert, 24

Campbell, Joseph, 19
Career decisions, 35–36
Causes of test anxiety
 cognitive, 203–204
 emotional, 203
Chapter headings and subheadings (an in-
  chapter study aid), 164
Chapter outlining (a textbook usage skill)
 an overview of, 170–171

importance of using, 171–172
 use of color coding, 173
 use of outline notation, 172
Chapter outlines
 as in-chapter study aid, 164
 reading preview and, 156–159
Chapter summaries (an end-of-chapter
  study aid), 164
Checking off method (a final study session
  task), 190–191
Chunking by chapter section (an active
  reading task), 159–160
Churchill, Winston, 26
Circular reasoning, 9, 135
Class
 asking questions in, 78
 attendance in, 76
 notetaking in, 78–81
 participation in, 77–78
 punctuality, 77
 schedules, 62, 64–68
 where to sit in, 77
Color coding (a topical mapping task), 173
Composites, *see* Success (People . . .)
Concepts (a form of core material), 161
Confucius, 4
Constructing the final comprehensive outline (a content organization skill),
  181–184
 determining outline format in, 182–184
 determining outline model, 182
Content organization skills (a step in
  ESS—The Advanced Course),
  177–186
 benefits of a comprehensive written
  outline and, 177–178
 constructing the final comprehensive
  outline and, 181–184
 overview of, 177
 time management and, 184–185
 weekly consolidation of preliminary outlines and, 179–181
Core material, identification of in class
  notes, 79

ESS TIME MANAGEMENT SYSTEM
Weekly Study Schedule

Fall/Spr./Sum. Semester, 19___			Week Ending Saturday _____							
Courses This Term Listed by Code Number		**Month** -----------	**Day of Week**							**Notes:** Things To Do This Week
		Date →								
Course	Code No.	Hour	Sunday	Monday	Tuesday	Wednesday	Thursday	Friday	Saturday	
	1	8-9								
	2	9-10								
	3	10-11								
	4	11-12								
	5	12-1								
	6	1-2								
	7	2-3								
	8	3-4								
Other Activities Listed by Code Letter		4-5								
		5-6								
		6-7								
Activity	Code Letter	7-8								
		8-9								
In Class	C	9-10								
Work Obligations	W	10-11								
Extracurricular Activities	E	11-12								
Tests Scheduled This Week			**Papers or Projects Due**							

ESS TIME MANAGEMENT SYSTEM
Weekly Study Schedule

Fall/Spr./Sum. Semester, 19____			Week Ending Saturday _____							
Courses This Term Listed by Code Number		**Month** - - - - - - - -	**Day of Week**							**Notes:** Things To Do This Week
		Date →								
Course	**Code No.**	**Hour**	Sunday	Monday	Tuesday	Wednesday	Thursday	Friday	Saturday	
	1	8-9								
	2	9-10								
	3	10-11								
	4	11-12								
	5	12-1								
	6	1-2								
	7	2-3								
	8	3-4								
Other Activities Listed by Code Letter		4-5								
		5-6								
		6-7								
Activity	**Code Letter**	7-8								
		8-9								
In Class	C	9-10								
Work Obligations	W	10-11								
Extracurricular Activities	E	11-12								

Tests Scheduled This Week	Papers or Projects Due

248